Managing for
Responsibility

Managing for Responsibility

A Sourcebook for an Alternative Paradigm

Editors

Radha R. Sharma, Merrill Csuri, and
Kemi Ogunyemi

BEP BUSINESS EXPERT PRESS

Managing for Responsibility: A Sourcebook for an Alternative Paradigm

First published in 2017 by
Business Expert Press, LLC
222 East 46th Street, New York, NY 10017
www.businessexpertpress.com

ISBN-13: 978-1-63157-288-3 (paperback)
ISBN-13: 978-1-63157-289-0 (e-book)

Business Expert Press Principles for Responsible Management Education Collection

Collection ISSN: 2331-0014 (print)
Collection ISSN: 2331-0022 (electronic)

Cover and interior design by Exeter Premedia Services Private Ltd., Chennai, India

First edition: 2017

10 9 8 7 6 5 4 3 2 1

Printed in the United States of America.

Abstract

The cascading effects of globalization in the form of changing business environment, economic uncertainties and economic meltdown have brought about a plethora of unprecedented challenges for industry and organizations across the globe in recent years. Management education, which prepares human capital for industry, is expected to address these challenges along with others such as intensifying competition, advancing technology, increasing workforce diversity and accelerating complexity. Yet, current management education is largely based on traditional capitalism where the focus tends toward profits and competitiveness rather than toward a balance among profitability, responsibility, social accountability and sustainability. Consequently, management education in general, and MBA education in particular, need to adopt a paradigm shift in order to be more responsible and sustainable.

This book has been prepared keeping in view the Principles for Responsible Management Education (PRME). The PRME initiative is the largest organized relationship between the United Nations and business schools. The book unfolds an alternative paradigm in management based on a competency framework labeled as CAMB (Sharma 2015) for Principles for Responsible Management Education. This model has found validation with many PRME schools. The book contains a brief interview with the Professor R. Edward Freeman, the pioneer of Stakeholder Theory.

The book contains contributions on the core management topics covered in general management, organizational behavior, ethics and social responsibility, with a focus on responsible management. Its chapters come from many authors in PRME schools from eight countries. Hence, it is expected to be useful to all the B-schools, across geographies, that are interested in embedding responsibility in their management curriculum and teaching methodology.

Keywords

Context of Management Education, Corporate Governance, CSR, CSR Tools for Financial Institutions/SMEs, Ethics for Sustainable Organizations, Ethics in Business, Goal Setting and Decision making,

HR Policy for Responsibility, Management Education for Responsibility, Managing Conflicts Responsibly, Morality in Brand Management, Negotiation with Cultural Sensitivity, New Paradigm in Management Education, Redefining Manager's functions, Responsible Organizational Change in the Information Age, Social Entrepreneurship for Value Creation

Contents

Preface

"Managing for Responsibility: A Sourcebook for an Alternative Paradigm" was conceptualized by me in 2013–2014 during my tenure at HHL Graduate School of Management, Germany. This was the result of my continued interest in the field of social responsibility since 2002 when, with the support from British Council India, I had launched a three-tier initiative on "Business and Social Responsibility" to introduce and popularize CSR in management education curriculum. I had included "CSR in India" as a topic in my OB textbook co-authored with Steven McShane and Mary Ann Von Glinow (McGraw-Hill 2011, 2008, pp. 22–29) but realized its inadequacy in bringing about mindset change among management students. The value crisis leading to economic meltdown reinforced the need for a paradigm shift in management education, which required responsibility to be embedded in the management curriculum across geographies for sustainability.

I interacted with Professor R. Edward Freeman whose seminal work on "stakeholder theory" (included as his interview later), inspired me. Further, my interactions with Mr. Jonas Haertle, Head, PRME Secretariat, who had been passionately promoting PRME (Principles for Responsible Management Education) among B-schools across the globe, intensified my urge for search for an alternative paradigm. Later, my presentations and deliberations during international conferences in the United States, Europe, and Asia with scholars and academics, striving to develop curriculum, andragogy, teaching-learning material, stirred my mind and enabled me to evolve an alternative paradigm based on competency framework labeled as CAMB (Sharma 2015) for PRME, described in Chapter 1. This model found validation with PRME schools who participated in 6th PRME Asia Forum in November, 2015.

I approached like-minded academics and practitioners from across countries to collaborate in this project and was able to get support from eminent academics and scholars from Germany, Austria, France, India Italy, Mexico, Nigeria, and United States. I am grateful to each of them for sharing their knowledge, research, and practice in the chapter contributed by them and sparing their time for enriching peer review. I thank my coeditors, Ms. Merrill Csuri, former Manager, PRME Secretariat, New York and Dr. Kemi Ogunyemi, Director, Christopher Kolade Centre for Research in Leadership and Ethics, Lagos Business School, Nigeria, for their support in this endeavor. I express sincere thanks to Oliver Laasch for his continued support at critical stages of the book publication. I am grateful to Charlene Kronstedt, Director, Production and Rob Zwettler, Executive Acquisitions Editor, Business Expert Press, USA for pushing the publication of this volume. Exeter team have done intense work and I sincerely thank them.

I sincerely thank Professor Dr. Andreas Pinkwart, Dean and Rector; Dr. Axel Baisch, Chancellor, and Mr. Frank Hoffmann, Director, International Relations, HHL Graduate School of Management, Germany, and Management Development Institute (MDI), Gurgaon, India, its Board of Governors, Acting Director, C.P. Shrimali for providing conducive academic environment to work on this PRME project involving several countries across continents. My family has been my pillar: Chandresh, my husband and my children, Anu-Vishwa, Swati, and Abhinav; I cannot thank them enough for their love, encouragement, and support enduring my prolonged preoccupation with development of this research book.

Radha R. Sharma
January, 2017

Acknowledgments

- Mr. Jonas Haertle, Head PRME Secretariat at UN Global Compact, New York, USA
- Prof. Dr. Andreas Pinkwart, HHL Graduate School of Management, Germany
- Prof. Mary Gentile, GVV, University of Virginia, USA
- Prof. Agata Stachowicz-Stanusch, Silesian University of Technology, Poland
- Prof. June Qian, Tsinghua University, China
- Dr. Michael Pirson, Fordham University, USA
- Dr. Ben Teehankee, De Salles University, Philippines
- Mr. P.S. Narayan, Head, Sustainability, Wipro Ltd., India
- Prof. Wolfgang Amann, HEC Paris, Qatar
- Prof. Raghu Ram Tata, XLRI Jamshedpur, India
- Prof. Ranjini Swamy, Goa Institute of Management, India
- Dr. Mitsuhiro Umezu, Keio University, Japan
- Dr. Nirja Mattoo, SP Jain Institute of Management, India
- Prof. Ernst von Kimakowitz, Humanistic Management Network, Switzerland
- Prof. Shailesh Gandhi, Indian Institute of Management, Ahmadabad, India
- Prof. Claus Dierksmeier, Global Ethic Institute, Germany
- Prof. Subhashis Ray, XIM, Xavier University, India
- Prof. Rakesh Chaudhary, IILM, New Delhi, India
- Prof. Osmar E. Arandia Pérez, Universidad Cristóbal Colón, Mexico
- Prof. Shiban Khan, EBS University of Business, Germany

Interview with Professor R. Edward Freeman

It is a privilege seeing you receive another Lifetime Achievement Award at Berlin since this honor was conferred upon you at Philadelphia a year ago. I have a few questions which are pertinent in the present context of management education:

Question: From your rich experience how you would like to define the role of a manager in stakeholder assessment (stakeholder identification and stakeholder prioritization)? How could management students be prepared for this role?

Response: *"I don't divide up managing for stakeholders into these discrete roles. I especially dislike separating 'prioritization' out since it gives the impression that there are trade-offs to be made among stakeholders. I continue to think that the main insight of the stakeholder view is that stakeholder interests are joint. And, that great companies are built when managers recognize the jointness of stakeholder interests and stop making tradeoffs."*

Question: Good stakeholder management benefits both internal and external stakeholders, while caring for both, in your view, how can a company benefit adequately? What are the key factors to be kept in view for maintaining the balance?

Response: *"I used to talk about balancing stakeholder interests but I prefer the metaphor of 'harmonizing' their interests. In music harmony refers to different notes (stakeholder interests) that sound good when played together. Balance again is more of a trade-off metaphor."*

Question: There is talk about integration of stakeholder and business responsibility (Visser 2010) how do you visualize the role of stakeholders in the management of organizations in the future?

Response: "Well, frankly I don't know how to think about organizations in any other terms. Businesses always have and always will create (and sometimes destroy) value for customers, employees, communities, suppliers and financiers. What else could it do? My view of stakeholder theory is very far from 'corporate social responsibility'. I think that if an organization creates as much value as possible for all of its stakeholders, then the question of corporate social responsibility is moot."

Question: The 2013 CSR policy of Govt. of India mandates firms to earmark funds for CSR. Do you have any suggestions for the utilization of the funds for promoting stakeholder engagement and co-creation?

Response: "I am skeptical of the rule, but maybe it will have some good effects. I would encourage companies to figure out how they can be 'community builders' and put their efforts into that stakeholder."

Interviewer: Prof. Radha R. Sharma

About the Editors
and Authors

Radha R. Sharma is Dean, Centers of Excellence, Case Centre; Chair, Center for Positive Scholarship for Organizational Sustainability; Hero MotoCorp Chair Professor, and Professor, Organizational Behavior at Management Development Institute, Gurgaon, India. She is an executive alumnus, Harvard Business School and has completed CSR certifications from World Bank Institute, the British Council and New Academy of Business UK. She has completed research supported by the World Health Organization, McClelland Centre for Research and Innovation, IDRC, Academy of Management, Humanistic Management Network, among others. Her publications include 12 books, popular among them being Change Management and Organizational Transformation (McGraw-Hill Co. 2012), Reinventing Society: Search for a Paradigm Co-ed. (Macmillan 2013), Change Management: Concept & Applications (McGraw-Hill Co. 2007), 360 Degree Feedback, Competency Mapping & Assessment Centers (Tata McGraw-Hill 2002), Organizational Behavior (co-authored with Steven McShane and Mary Ann Von Glinow, (McGraw-Hill Co. 3 editions: 2011/08/06), Organizational Behavior: An Online Book, 2003, and Enhancing Academic Achievement: Role of Personality Factors (Concept 1985). She is Editor, Vision-Journal of Business Perspective: (SAGE), Associate Editor, Frontiers in Psychology and on the Editorial Board, and Reviewer for AIMS International Journal, Business Ethics: A European Review; International Journal of HRM, Journal of Management Spirituality & Religion, Journal of Management Development (Emerald), Cross cultural Management—An International Journal (Emerald) and Manpower Journal, among others. She is recipient of Best Paper Award, IJTD, 2013; Outstanding Cutting Edge Research Paper Award, 2005, AHRD, USA; AIMS International Outstanding Management Researcher Award (2008); Best Faculty Award: Excellence in Research, 2007 and 2006, MDI and Outstanding Editor Award 2007,

AIMS International Journal of Management (USA). She has successfully supervised several PhD dissertations and has been PhD examiner for several. She has been visiting Professor to premier institutes in Germany, Italy, and France. She is a member of UN PRME Working Group on the Sustainability Mindset.

Merrill Csuri, Former Manager, Principles for Responsible Management Education (PRME) Secretariat, United Nations Global Compact, USA.

Kemi Ogunyemi, PhD, is the Director of the Christopher Kolade Centre for Research in Leadership and Ethics at the Lagos Business School, Nigeria. She teaches Business Ethics, Managerial Anthropology, and Sustainability Management. Her consulting and research interests include personal ethos and organizational culture, responsible leadership and sustainability, and work-life ethic.

Uche Attoh is a Senior Fellow at Lagos Business School, Pan-Atlantic University, Nigeria. He was appointed by the Federal Government of Nigeria to the Industrial Arbitration Tribunal. He worked in a multinational as Human Resources Director West and Central Africa region. Uche was Chairman of the National Joint Negotiation Council of the Chemical and Pharmaceutical Industry.

Jyoti Bachani, PhD, is the Chevron Professor of Strategy and Innovation at Saint Mary's College of California, USA, a board member of the North American Case Research Association, a former Fulbright Senior Research Scholar, Editor-in-Chief of the Emerald Emerging Markets Case Study Collection, and Past President of Western Casewriters Association.

Gloria Camacho Ruelas Professor Gloria Camacho has a PhD in Management Sciences at EGADE Business School, Tecnológico de Monterrey, Mexico. She is a professor of Marketing in Marketing and International Business Department at Tecnológico de Monterrey. Her main research areas are Sustainable Marketing, Corporate Sustainability, Corporate Social Responsibility, and Humanistic Management.

Arjya Chakravarty, Program Chair, SOIL-School of Inspired Leadership, Gurugram, executive PhD Scholar at MDI, India. Arya has over 22 years of work experience, with 11 years in Human Resource Management and Strategic Initiatives in the automobile, manufacturing, FMCG, BPO industry. In the last 11 years, she has been teaching, researching, and consulting. She has published research papers and cases in international publications and has also participated in international conferences.

Roger Nion Conaway, Professor Emeritus of Management Director, Leadership Institute, College of Business & Technology, The University of Texas at Tyler, was Professor in the EGADE Business School, Tecnológico de Monterrey, Mexico and taught courses in Business Administration, International Business, and Entrepreneurship. He has lectured in the Master of Arts in Responsible Management program, Steinbeis University, Berlin, Germany and Florence University of the Arts. Dr. Conaway is coauthor of Principles of Responsibility Management: Glocal Sustainability, Responsibility, and Ethics (first official textbook for the United Nations, Principles of Responsibility Management Education (PRME) academic network).

Chantal Epie is a Professor of Human Resource Management at Pan-Atlantic University, Nigeria. She holds a Doctor of Business Administration degree from Business School Lausanne. Chantal has over 30 years of experience as a Management Trainer and Consultant. She teaches Management Communication, Organizational Behavior, and Negotiation.

Consuelo García-de-la-Torre is PhD in Management, HEC University of Montreal and she is currently full-time Professor at the EGADE Business School, Tecnológico de Monterrey, Mexico. She is a member of the Mexican National Research System (SNI 1). She is responsible for the regional chapter of PRME Latin America and the Caribbean. She is Member of the Academy of Management. She represents the Mexico chapter of the International Network of Humanistic and Management. She has published articles books, and chapter's books regarding Corporate Social Responsibility, Ethics for Higher Education, Humanistic and

Perspectives on International Business Management, Humanistic Management in Latin America, among others in prestigious scientific publications nationally and internationally.

Nakul Gupta is a Fellow (PhD) of Management from Management Development Institute, Gurugram, India. He has been a research fellow at MDI Gurugram in the area of Information Management. Before he joined MDI Gurugram as Assistant Professor, he was Assistant Professor and Chairperson, International Relations at Indian Institute of Management, Kashipur.

Christian Katholnigg graduated in business administration at Innsbruck University. In 1999 he founded his company for environmental consulting which grew to an international partner network in the field of CSR by 2016. Being a specialist in CSR, Environmental and Occupational Health management systems he consults and audits companies worldwide in this matter. Together with his business partner he developed academic courses and a Master program on CSR in cooperation with the University of applied sciences in Vienna where is also lectures in these courses.

Giovanni Lombardo, PhD in Economics, adjunct professor of Responsible Business Conduct at the University of Genova, Italy. He is Researcher of Finance and Business Engineering. He has extensively worked as CSR Consultant, Auditor for Risk Assessment and Anticorruption Systems, for public administration, private organizations, OECD Italian Contact Point, and Ministry of Economic Development.

Olutayo Otubanjo is a senior faculty of Marketing at Lagos Business School, Nigeria. He holds a PhD in Marketing with emphasis on Corporate Identity from Brunel University. He has published in various top tier peer review journals, some of which are: Academy of Marketing Science, Tourist Studies, and Management Decision. His research interest sits at the interface of Social Constructionism and Corporate Marketing.

Pramod Pathak, PhD, is a Professor of Management, currently heading the Department of Management Studies, Indian School of Mines,

Dhanbad. A student of Psychology for over four decades Prof. Pathak is a researcher, trainer, and consultant of a long experience. He is a regular columnist for several mainline dailies of the country and writes on behavior, spirituality, and related issues.

Andreas Pinkwart, PhD, Hbl, is Dean and Professor of Innovation Management and Entrepreneurship at HHL Leipzig Graduate School of Management, Germany. He earned his PhD at the University of Bonn and held a Full Professorship at the University of Siegen. He served as the Minister for Innovation, Science, Research and Technology of the state of North Rhine-Westphalia.

Roberto Quaglia is Professor of Strategy and Management at ESCP Europe, Paris campus, France. He teaches Strategy, Family Business, and Problem Solving and Decision Making at Masters, as well as Corporate Strategy, Organizational Behaviour, and Leadership at MBAs and custom programs. Roberto's research interests are in strategic renewal, corporate governance, and change management. He published many articles, books, case studies, and papers, and participated at various conferences.

In 2004, he founded the Italian campus of ESCP Europe, leading it until 2013 as Managing Director and Associate Professor. Roberto is also an entrepreneur investing in start-ups and working with private companies and institution.

Segun Shogbanmu is a doctoral student of Marketing, Pan Atlantic University, Nigeria. His research lies in the intersection of consumer psychology and branding. He is a member of Association of Consumer Research, American Marketing Association, and African Academy of Management. He is a reviewer for Academy of International Business, Sub-Saharan Africa and has published in The Marketing Review.

Saumya Singh, PhD, Associate Professor of Management, Department of Management Studies, Indian School of Mines, Dhanbad, is an academic, trainer, and researcher having over around one and half decades of experience. An MBA and PhD, Dr. Singh deals in the area of Consumer Behaviour and Strategic Management.

Christian Strenger, as former CEO of Deutsche Asset Management (DWS) (with retails assets under management of EUR 150 billion), Prof. Christian Strenger is currently multiple member of supervisory boards. He is also Academic Director of the Center for Corporate Governance at HHL Leipzig Graduate School of Management, Germany.

He is Deputy Chairman of the "Private Sector Advisory Group" (International Finance Corporation and World Bank) and member of the board of directors of the International Integrated Reporting Council.

Andreas Suchanek, PhD, Hbl, studied Economics at the universities of Kiel and Goettingen, Germany. He is Chairholder of the Dr. Werner Jackstaedt-Chair for Business and Economic Ethics at HHL Leipzig Graduate School of Management, and Chairman of the Board of the Wittenberg Center for Global Ethics, Germany. His main areas of research are Business and Economic Ethics, Corporate Responsibility, Management of Trust, and Leadership Ethics.

Federica Viganò, PhD, in Philosophy, appointed as researcher in Applied Economics at the University of Bolzano, Italy (2011). She has specialization in Capability, Poverty, and Wellbeing Measurement, by the Human Development and Capability Association. Since 2014, she is member of the CIRIEC Scientific Commission on Social and Cooperative Economy Working Group on Nonprofits and NGOs. Free University of Bolzano, Italy.

CHAPTER 1

The New Paradigm

A Competency Model for Management Education

Radha R. Sharma

The cascading effect of globalization in the form of changing business environment, economic uncertainties, and economic meltdown have brought about plethora of unprecedented challenges for industry and organizations across the globe in recent years. Management education which prepares human capital for the jobs in the industry and organizations is expected to address these challenges along with intensifying competition, advancing technology, increasing workforce diversity and accelerating complexity. But the current management education is largely based on traditional capitalism where the focus tends towards profits and competitiveness rather than on a balance among ethics, profitability, social accountability, and sustainability. The corporate scandals, scams, and global meltdown and their repercussions on people, organizations, and countries in this interconnected world have created a compelling case for rethinking of management education. Consequently, management education in general and MBA education, in particular, needs to adopt a paradigm shift in its knowledge-generating (research) system, knowledge-dissemination (teaching or training) system, and knowledge-utilization (learning, consulting, or industry projects) system to be responsible and sustainable.

Globalization has made the managerial role transnational where managers work, interact, or conduct business with people across geographies; therefore, every manager needs to have knowledge of internationally recognized responsible practices to be able to conduct business with them, besides pursuing business ethically and responsibly in the national context. There is need for providing an alternative paradigm for management education which integrates principles of managing self, people, and business and the various management functions with integrity and social responsibility. This paradigm will lead to development of appropriate values, attitudes, and behaviors toward society, economy, and stakeholders for responsible management and organizational sustainability.

Principles of Responsible Management Education

The UN-supported initiative "Principles for Responsible Management Education" (PRME) addresses the responsibilities of management education institutions in preparing current and future business professionals for the challenge of conducting more responsible and sustainable business. It expects fundamental changes in the conduct of business, on the premise that companies have wider responsibilities for the society and the environment than simply profit making and meeting shareholders' interest. The expectation that management education institutions should lead thought and action on issues related to social responsibility and sustainability, has been reinforced by failings of business leaders, increasing incidents of corporate corruption, global economic meltdown, ecological repercussions of global warming on various geographies, and system failings (Godemann et al. 2013, 2014).

The PRME initiative, launched by UN Secretary General Ban Ki-moon in 2007 at the Global Compact Leaders Summit, was developed by an international group of deans, university presidents, and representatives of 60 business schools in collaboration with several other institutions including the United Nations Global Compact (UNGC which hosts the PRME Secretariat), the Association to Advance Collegiate Schools of Business (AACSB), the European Foundation for Management Development (EFMD), the Aspen Institute's Business and Society Program, the Globally Responsible Leadership Initiative (GRLI), the European Academy of Business in Society (EABIS, now simply ABIS), and Net Impact, a student organization with more than 13,000 members. They all have remained partners of the initiative while the steering committee that guides the initiative has received further support from the Graduate Management Admission Council, the African Association of Business Schools (AABS), the Latin American Business School Council (CLADEA), CEE-MAN, representing management schools in transforming markets, and the Association of Asia-Pacific Business Schools (AAPBS). As such, the initiative represents a multilateral effort to embed social responsibility and sustainability into management education institutions and core areas of education, research, and organization or operations (www.unprme.org).

Similar to the UNGC, which expects signatory companies to commit to 10 principles of responsible business, the PRME initiative offers principles for business and management schools to follow, and provides an environment for information sharing and learning. The initiative stresses the importance of continuous improvement along six (plus one) principles of transparency in the form of regular Sharing Information on Progress (SIP) reports (www.unprme.org).

To embrace the increased demands of more sustainable future and societal expectations of managers, the first three principles focus on a shift in business education:

Purpose: "We will develop the capabilities of students to be future generators of sustainable value for business and society at large and to work for an inclusive and sustainable global economy." (Principle 1)

Values: "We will incorporate into our academic activities and curricula the values of global social responsibility as portrayed in international initiatives such as the United Nations Global Compact." (Principle 2)

Method: "We will create educational frameworks, materials, processes, and environments that enable effective learning experiences for responsible leadership." (Principle 3)

The fourth principle addresses the relationship of knowledge generation and the businesses' role in and interaction with society and the natural environment:

Research: "We will engage in conceptual and empirical research that advances our understanding about the role, dynamics, and impact of corporations in the creation of sustainable social, environmental, and economic value." (Principle 4)

With the mission of preparing responsible managers and enabling them to deal with complex global problems, Partnership and Dialog were added as additional principles. These two principles emphasize fostering a stakeholder-oriented ethic in management education. These also draw attention to the role of business schools in organizing deliberations and discussions about social responsibility, sustainability, and engagement with stakeholders to better understand and meet future challenges.

Partnership: "We will interact with managers of business corporations to extend our knowledge of their challenges in meeting social and environmental responsibilities and to explore jointly effective approaches to meeting these challenges." (Principle 5)

Dialogue: "We will facilitate and support dialogue and debate among educators, business, government, consumers, media, civil society organizations, and other interested groups and stakeholders on critical issues related to global social responsibility and sustainability." (Principle 6)

Finally, the initiative also underscores the need to transform organizational practices to reflect the business schools' overall commitment to responsibility and sustainability.

Operations: "We understand that our own organizational practices should serve as the example of the values and attitudes we convey to our students." (Additional Addendum Principle)

Another parallel to the UNGC is the PRME initiative's requirement, with effect from 2010, to regularly disclose information in progress by individual institutions. Reporting on progress to other business schools and stakeholders by signatory institutions is an essential part of the active commitment to the UN PRME initiative. The purpose of SIP reports is twofold (UN PRME 2012): a key learning opportunity through sharing experience and good practice among the PRME network, and the provision of a regular account of achievements made by the signatories to all the stakeholders (at least every 24 months; although yearly communication is encouraged).

Though management education, as a discipline, has established itself by providing knowledge for optimizing resources and maximizing economic returns through knowledge and skills of business management, it is still grappling with the challenge of developing appropriate curriculum and andragogy for imparting management education for responsibility and sustainability (Sharma and Mukherjee 2010). This is important as Amartya Sen said: "A business world without moral codes would not only be poor from a regulatory point of view but also very weak in terms of performance" (Sen 2001). There has been a lot of churning among academics across the globe as to how to develop responsible managers for the future. The consensus seems to emerge that it is through the curriculum and andragogy that the foundations of responsible management could be laid among business students.

This book aims to provide knowledge and skills with an alternative paradigm with inputs from specialists from across the globe.

The next question emerges is "How this curriculum is going to be different and what are the competencies that need to be developed." "A competency is an underlying characteristic of an individual that is causally related to criterion-referenced effective or superior performance in a job or situation" (McClelland 1973).

Based on her earlier work on competencies (Sharma 2002, 2008, 2010, 2011a, b, 2012, 2013, 2014, and 2015; Sharma and Boyatzis 2011; Sharma 2015)[1] has developed a competency framework and a competency model for PRME. As the framework is based on principles for responsible management education, it can be applied to all the management institutions across geographies irrespective of the school's membership of PRME network.

The competency model presented in Figure 1.2 comprises competencies which are visible or observable and others which are embedded in

---

[1] Sharma (2015) presented "Competency Framework & Competency Modelling for Principles of Responsible Management Education" at the 6th PRME Asia Forum on Towards Responsible Management Education in support of Sustainable Development Goals during November 27–28, 2015.

At the 75th Academy of Management (AOM) Conference, Sharma (2015) made a round table presentation on "emotional and social intelligence competencies" during professional development workshop on "Responsible Management Education in Action: A Competence-Based Approach" (AOM submission 11289) at Vancouver, Canada on August 8, 2015.

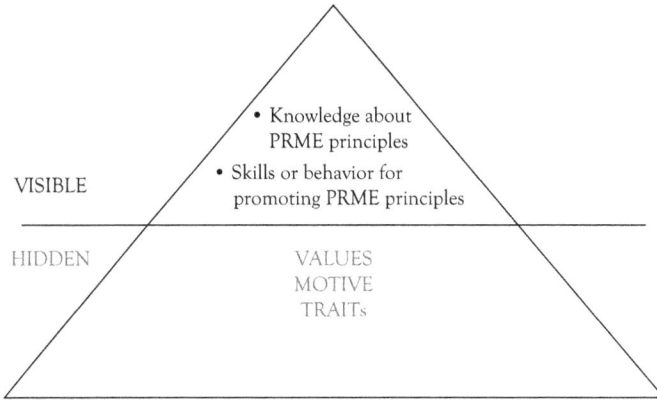

Figure 1.1 Nature of PRME competencies

the individual (Figure 1.1) and influence his or her behavior. These are described above.

Competencies Framework for PRME

The competency framework developed on the principles of PRME can be applied in the development of curriculum, pedagogy, teaching-learning material, co-curricular activities, internship training and faculty development, and administration of the institute. Competencies for PRME can be classified into four broad clusters as discussed below.

1. **Cluster of cognitive competencies**

   Cognitive competencies (C) comprise knowledge of responsible management, corporate social responsibility (CSR), and sustainability linked with domain knowledge (inspired by PRME Principles 1 and 2). Some of these are identified below:
   - Principles of responsible management
   - Knowledge about sustainability
   - Integration of responsibility and sustainability with domain knowledge
   - Corporate social responsibility
   - Embracing responsibility for society
   - Cognitive empathy

2. **Cluster of affective competencies**

   Affective competencies (A) involve emotional, social, or spiritual competencies such as empathy, relationship orientation, humaneness, compassion, generosity, service to community or society, not driven by job responsibility (inspired by PRME Principles 1, 2, 3, and 4)

   - Empathic concern
   - Emotional sensitivity
   - Idealized influence
   - Care and concern for others
   - Emotional maturity
   - Humanism
   - Transcendence
   - Open mindedness
   - Acknowledging diversity
   - Ability to let go of one's own mistakes
   - Ability to let go of others' mistakes

3. **Cluster of moral competencies**

   Moral competencies (M) consist of honesty, integrity, conscience, values, and virtues (inspired by PRME Principles 1, 5, and 6)

   - Integrity
   - Values and beliefs
   - Truthfulness
   - Righteousness
   - Acting consistently with principles
   - Keeping promises

4. **Cluster of behavioral competencies**

   Behavioral competencies (B) comprise skills and behavior for responsibility such as initiative for social, economic, and environmental sustainability, ethics, transparency, standing up for what is right and so on (inspired by PRME Principles 1, 5, and 6)

   - Taking responsibility for personal choices
   - Taking organizational or social responsibility
   - Admitting mistakes and failures
   - Standing for and providing justice
   - Fairness
   - Building relationship or team

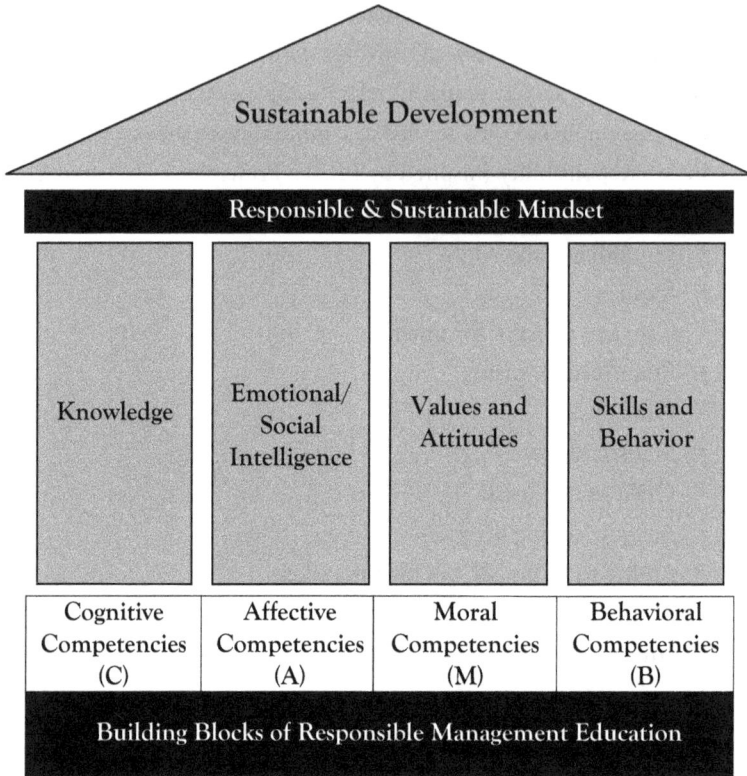

Figure 1.2 CAMB competency model for PRME
Source: Developed by Radha R. Sharma (2015).

- Developing others
- Conflict management
- Transparency
- Partnership and dialogue with stakeholders

Based on the competency framework presented above, CAMB model has been developed by Sharma (2015) for PRME but it can be applied to other management institutions and their stakeholders across geographies. The competencies identified under this framework are relevant not only for the students but also for faculty, educators, employers, and the self-employed. A common understanding of competencies for responsibility and sustainability will help create a conducive environment; therefore, academia and industry need to work in tandem to develop and strengthen these competencies to promote a responsible and sustainable society.

In order to develop these competencies, the book provides necessary inputs in the form of concept, theories, recent developments, national and international perspectives with illustrations from a variety of organizations from across geographies to prepare management students to develop responsible and sustainable mindset. The book would also sensitize educators and educational administrators to promote responsibility and sustainability in the teaching-learning processes and in the culture of the institution. The conceptual inputs have been supplemented with discussion questions, cases, simulation exercises, and project work. A standalone course on ethics, CSR, or social responsibility is not enough to develop integrity, empathic concern, and attitude for responsibility and sustainability. It needs to be supplemented with creating a "culture of integrity and responsibility" (McCabe, Ingram, and Dato-on 2006) and that is possible through responsible management education as management students come from and go back to corporate settings (Treviño, Butterfield, and McCabe 1998). They can explore it further with dialogue and project work and a core skill-oriented course on affective competencies for developing emotional and social intelligence competencies.

References

Godemann, G., J. Haertle, C. Herzig, and J. Moon. 2013. "United Nations Supported Principles for Responsible Management Education: Purpose, Programmes & Prospects." *Journal of Cleaner Production* 62, pp. 16–23.

Godemann, J., J. Bebbington, C. Herzig, and J. Moon. 2014. "Higher Education and Sustainable Development." *Accounting, Auditing & Accountability Journal* 27, no. 2, pp. 218–33.

McCabe, A.C., W.R. Ingram, and M.C. Dato-on. 2006. "The Business of Ethics and Gender." *Journal of Business Ethics* 64, no. 2, pp. 101–16.

McClelland, D.C. 1973. "Testing for Competence Rather Than for Intelligence." *American Psychologist* 28, no. 1, pp. 1–14.

PRME (Principles for Responsible Management Education). 2015. www.unprme.org/ (accessed September 2015).

Sen, A. 2001. "Amartya Sen on Justice, How to Do It Better." www.economist.com/node/14164449 (accessed September 10, 2015).

Sharma, R.R., and R.E. Boyatzis, eds. 2011. "Special Issue on Managerial Competencies." *Vision-The Journal of Business Perspective* 15, no. 2.

Sharma, R.R., and S. Mukherjee, S. 2010. "Can Business and Humanism Go Together? The Case of the Tata Group with a Focus on Nano Plant." In *Humanistic Management in Practice*, eds. E.V. Kimakowitz, M. Pirson, H. Spitzeck, C. Dierksmeier, and W. Amann, 247–265. Basingstoke: Palgrave Macmillan.

Sharma, R.R. 2015. "Competency Framework and Competency Modeling for Principles of Responsible Management Education (PRME)." *Presented at 6th PRME Asia Forum*, Goa, India, November 27–28.

Sharma, R.R. 2002. *360 Degrees Feedback and Competency Mapping and Assessment Centre*, 239. New York: Tata McGraw-Hill.

Sharma, R.R., ed. January–March 2008. "Special Issue on Emotional Intelligence." *Vision-The Journal of Business Perspective* 12, no. 1.

Sharma, R.R. 2011a. "Intertwining 360 Degree Feedback & Multi-method to Enhance Emotional Intelligence of Managers in India." *Academy of Taiwan Business Management Review* 7, no. 2, pp. 1–14.

Sharma, R.R. 2011b. "An Empirical Investigation into the Role of EQ/Emotional Intelligence Competencies in Mental Well-being." *Vision: The Journal of Business Perspective* 15, no. 2, pp. 177–92.

Sharma, R.R. April 2012. "Measuring Social and Emotional Intelligence Competencies in the Indian Context. *Cross Cultural Management: International Journal* 19, no. 1, pp. 30–47.

Sharma, R.R., and R. Pardasani. 2013. "Unshackling Management Education through a Trishul Approach." In *Reinventing the Society: The Search for a Paradigm*, eds. P. Pathak, R.R. Sharma, and S. Singh, 83–101. India: Macmillan Publishers.

Sharma, R.R. August 1–5, 2014. *PDW on Developing an Alternative Paradigm: Global Perspectives on Humanistic Management' at Academy of Management Conference*. Philadelphia, USA.

Sharma, R.R. August 8, 2015. *Round Table Presentation on Emotional & Social Competencies During PDW on "Responsible Management Education in Action: A Competence-Based Approach" at the 75th Academy of Management (AOM) Conference*. Vancouver, Canada.

Treviño, L.K., K.D. Butterfield, and D.L. McCabe. 1998. "The Ethical Context in Organizations: Influences on Employee Attitudes and Behaviors." *Business Ethics Quarterly* 8, pp. 447–76.

UN PRME SIP. 2012. www.unprme.org/reports/PRMEFINAL311012low.pdf (accessed in September 2015).

CHAPTER 2

The Contemporary Context of Management Education

Radha R. Sharma and Nakul Gupta

At present businesses and organizations are confronted with competition from within the industry as well as from unexpected quarters. The global meltdown has made the organizations cautious as the uncertainty has made the environment unpredictable and sometimes turbulent. The organization, to some extent, can sustain through adaptability as posited by *Tom Austin, Vice President and Gartner fellow.*[1]

"Work will become less routine, characterized by increased volatility, hyper-connectedness, 'swarming' and more."

Change in the nature of work has been fueled by globalization, economic and social uncertainties, unpredictable business environment, workforce diversity, constant technological up-gradation and competition, among others. There is increasing concern regarding change in demographics of generation X and generation Y at workplaces in certain geographies. While working population is aging in most of the countries in Europe and the United States, in India over 65 percent population is below the age of 35 which is often referred to as its demographic dividend.[2] An increased number of women employees has led organizations to introduce flexible hours and provision of support services like crèche and personal services (payment of bills and school fees etc.) to enable them to manage their dual roles at work and home effectively. Globalization has increased movement of people across countries; consequently religious,

---

[1] Gartner (2010).
[2] India's Population (2011).

ethnic, and cultural diversity are the order of the day where intercultural skills have gained importance as many expatriates are a part of the workforce. Therefore, honing skills of diversity management, emotional and cultural intelligence, cross-cultural communication, business and social etiquettes, new marketing techniques, and cultural adaptation skills have become a necessity in the present scenario for effective functioning. Employees are becoming techno nomads and are required to leverage technology such as iPhone, iPads, internet, video-conferencing, webinars, and con-calls to make optimum utilization of resources to produce the high quality output. While technology is facilitating efficiency and reach, its fall-out effects are cyber crimes, frauds, workplace bullying, and the like which call for a new look at the competency requirement of the present and future generation of the managerial staff.

Features of Changing Nature of Work

According to a study by Gartner (2010), the changes expected in nature of work over the next few years include de-routinization of work, work swarms, weak links, and working with the collective, work sketch-ups, spontaneous work, simulation and experimentation, pattern sensitivity, hyper connected, and individual workspace. These terms have been explained in the following paragraphs.

De-routinization of work means individuals would have their own uniqueness in analytical or interactive contribution that would result in discovery, innovation, selling, learning, teamwork, and leadership. This uniqueness that each individual would bring to the workplace cannot be automated. Importance would be given to collective work or team work.

Within team work there is emergence of "work swarms" wherein individuals known or unknown, from within or outside the organization come together to attack a problem or an opportunity and quickly disperse. In *swarms,* individuals, if they know each other, would work through a person who already knows the people with whom they would have to work; it is called *Weak Links.* Networking across professional, personal, and social spaces has become crucial in the present networked world of work. For working in swarms integrity would be an important behavioral competency. Organizations also need to *work collectively with informal groups* outside the organization, which can impact its performance.

The nonroutine process would be highly informal, the emphasis would be on *sketch-ups*. Though at present organizations adopt predetermined criteria in decision making, over the years standard patterns would not be followed. This means structured process of decision making or the pattern to follow frameworks would be replaced with simple sketch-ups. *Spontaneity* would increase involving proactiveness at work and seeking new opportunities, new models, and designs where trust would play an important role.

Encouraging *simulation and experimentation* at the workplace would be on the rise, in view of the ever-changing and increasing usage of technologies. This is leading to the convergence of cyber and physical worlds at the workplace.

Employees would be in 24×7 mode as they would be connected with people across geographies in different time zones. People would not need large physical space either at the workplace or at home and would be equipped with gadgets easy to handle, carry and operate, and work from the comforts of home. The lines between personal, professional, and family life would blur or slowly disappear along with the increasing work demands. Individuals would need to manage this complexity to maintain work-life balance. Individuals would be faced with increasing stress due to information overload and constant changes at work which, if not managed effectively that may impact their performance. Therefore, affective competencies would be needed to manage emotions of self and others as due to emotional contagion negative emotions are likely to cause toxicity, distress, and burnout.

Other Aspects of Changing Work

At present individuals have the option to work either as consultant, employee, agent or part-time employee. The following trends will increase depending on the talent of the individual, need of the firm, and opportunity and growth for future (Aggarwal 2006):

- *Face to screen interactions* would increase, saving time, money and being environmentally sustainable.
- *No more superannuation* as employees would continue to work till it suits them.

- *Socially oriented approaches* would be crucial in every aspect of the workplace.
- *Greater transparency* would be increasingly required regarding employees, and organizational decision making and business transactions.
- *Cultural adaptation* is becoming crucial with increase in workforce diversity and employees taking up foreign postings or assignments.
- *Change in role of human resource (HR):* The HR professionals are no longer limited to HR function but are supposed to be strategic business partners. They have knowledge about the business of the organization, and take up pivotal tasks relating to strategic sourcing, talent management, change management culture building, need-based training and development along with the traditional role they used to perform.
- *Ethics and social responsibility of* an organization are gaining importance among employees and other stakeholders. These aspects would be given significant weight for monetary incentives and benefits given to the employees.
- *Employee retention* is keeping organizations on the edge due to increasing competition and employment opportunities. Consequently, current and future employees are likely to hop jobs more frequently unless the organizations have robust talent management system.

Diversity in the Work Culture

Globalization and liberalization have, no doubt, enhanced opportunities but have brought about several challenges for the organizations. Organizations operate across countries, which lie in different time zones. According to a study (Olson and Olson 2000; Olson, Zimmerman, and Bos 2008) the following challenges and issues have emerged in the context of different time zones:

Readiness to collaborate: There is increasing readiness of individuals to collaborate and participate with others from different cultures within or across countries. Therefore, appreciation of individual and cultural differences and alignment with goals of collaboration and incentive schemes are crucial for the success of collaboration(s).

Promptness to adopt technologies: In this technologically advanced era, technology adoption and technology savvyiness of both the individuals and the organization are vital, especially in the context of geographically distributed work. Organizations need to be equipped with not only technical support systems but also with ability to train the individuals in handling new technologies with responsibility. Besides, technology etiquettes and values assume significance in the present and future contexts where management education can play a significant role.

Commonality: Working with multicultural, multidisciplinary, and dispersed workforce requires common understanding of the subject knowledge and vocabulary. This is most challenging when it comes to collaborative work spread across geographies. Therefore, training in language, culture, communication, business and work etiquettes, and so on is essential for the future employees. Working with responsibility needs to be ingrained in all the disciplines of management education, be it finance, marketing, operations, or HR management.

Characteristics of work: Characteristics of work need to be assessed to know its feasibility in long-distance and different time-zone work environments. This would require effective communication.

Management of the organization and decision-making process: Culture, leadership, and management style of an organization have an impact on distributed work environment. Leadership would require fair and transparent decision making process and clear communication.

Coordinating different time zones: Coordination is a challenge when individuals in collaboration are dispersed and located in different time zones. Employees would be in different points in their habitual rhythms.

Cultural issues: Cultural differences would be at three levels: organizational level differences, cultural differences within a country, and transnational cultural differences. Dealing with cultural issues at the three different levels is challenging for the organizations and due to sensitivities involved, it can have long-term impact on its performance and growth.

Building and sustaining trust: Building and sustaining trust in multicultural and multidisciplinary collaboration across geographies is an ongoing process. Organizations need to have support system to handle the aspect of trust building. The foundation for business management is laid in the management education.

The Context of Management: Mergers and Acquisitions

Mergers and acquisitions (M&A) have been worldwide phenomena during the past few decades. Some M&A have been fruitful while others have met with fallout where employees have been ignored for financial return. The initial concern for many organizations has been strategic, financial, or operational side of mergers; however, the human side of M&A has been gaining importance in the recent years as it needs to be understood from psychological, social, and cultural perspectives. The psychological perspective looks into the impact of M&A on an individual's stress level, coping mechanism, and commitment level (Amiot, Terry, and Terry 2007); the social perspective includes group dynamics, group membership, social comparison, and status (Terry, Callan, and Sartori 1996) and the cultural perspective considers the whole organization and cultural clashes that erupt during M&A processes (Angwin and Vaara 2005), which have been discussed in the following paragraphs.

Psychological perspective: Employees of an organization, whether from the acquired or the acquirer organization, assess an M&A scenario based on the available information and the context. They assess cultural similarity and their own position in the deal structure and its impact on their job. Whenever an M&A deal is proposed, employees of the organization undergo anxiety regarding their job and career path, and experience uncertainty and conflicts regarding the roles. If these employee issues are not addressed adequately, these cause low motivation, low productivity, job dissatisfaction, physical and mental health problems. Therefore, the knowledge of how organizations can take care of the psychological perspective of its people is important. It can be achieved through top-down communication, two-way communication, social support, encouraging participation in decision making, training managers to empathize with employees, constant and consistent communication, clarification regarding roles and responsibilities, and golden parachutes, thereby speeding up the M&A process (Seo and Hill 2005).

Social perspective: An individual is concerned about the impact of M&A on one's professional identity in one' work group, organization and the society. If social perspective is not handled properly it would cause loss of face, grief and anger, resistance to change, intergroup bias, conflicts, and noncompliant behavior. The social perspective can be handled by the organizations through disengagement efforts, to assess the strengths of existing identities and to frame attractive new identities and foster cross-organizational arrangements and activities (Seo and Hill 2005).

Higher levels of uncertainty have direct relation with higher anticipated conflict, intention to leave, low level of satisfaction and willingness to collaborate. When organizations plan M&A, they need to have tailor-made communication for each group of employees in accordance with the context of the deal and their position in the deal structure. The groups can be classified on parameters such as functional, hierarchical, unit-wise, and acquired-acquirer basis. The communication should clearly address the concerns of the respective groups in order to reduce the uncertainty. Moreover, improvement of power position of certain group of employees may reduce intention to leave; however, equal importance needs to be given to in-group power of groups as each of the groups may be equally important.

Cultural perspective: Culture is crucial for any M&A deal. Individual's perception about cultural match between the two organizations enables them make sense of the deal. *Cultural clash potentially* affects employees' perception regarding cultural similarity. There is an inverse relationship between cultural clash potential and cultural similarity. Aspects of cultural adjustment need due consideration otherwise it would lead to acculturative stress and resistance, interorganizational conflicts, tension, and cultural clash. This can be taken care through cultural due-diligence, developing multiculturalism, encouraging intercultural learning, and by creating awareness about behaviors and thoughts that fuel clashes. In the context of international M&A deals, national cultures also need to be given due consideration. Researches reveal that there is no relation between national cultural differences and employee resistance to M&A (Very et al. 1997; Larsson and Finkelstein 1999). This could be because organizations easily adjust to national cultures by making operational methods adaptable to the local environment. Organizations along with strategic and financial aspects should also concurrently take care of HR which is crucial to make an M&A deal successful. Uncertainty is more painful than bad news and poor communication creates uncertainty (Larkin and Larkin 1996, 97). Thus, engaging and reassuring employees through effective and consistent communication is essential.

Organizational cultural differences increase post-acquisition conflicts due to in-group and out-group categorization (Goulet and Schweiger 2006). Conflicts increase post-acquisition because acquisition partners are likely to be less accepting and more attentive to cultural differences and have low inclination toward building a new shared culture. There are acculturation factors which need to be considered, that is, partner's attractiveness, organizational culture preservation, and multiculturalism. When two organizations in an M&A deal have mutual attraction, it would have positive impact on post-acquisition, preservation of a new shared organization culture; and managing diversified workforce plays a key role in managing cultural aspects. Empathy and warmth given by the organization ensures emotional attachment and loyalty of key employees in turbulent times.

Sensitivity, empathy, and compassion can reduce potential cultural clash. Also, communicating cultural similarities may significantly reduce uncertainty and negative attitudes associated with M&A.

The Skills Developed Through the Management Education

Initiative taking ability, skills that enable solving of problems, communication adroitness, and creative thinking are some of the skills that business school students are expected to possess (Aiken, Martin, and Paolillo 1994). Table 2.1 summarizes various studies addressing the same.

Table 2.1 Literature highlighting objectives of management education

Research studies	The skill developed through management education
Aiken and Martin (1994)	• The ability to communicate • The ability to get along with others • Dependability • Initiative • Problem-solving ability • Creative thinking
Arensdorf (2009)	• Problem-solving skills • Communication skills • Teamwork skills • Change and innovation behaviors • Ability to manage self • Being civic-minded
Dumas (2002)	• Leadership • Critical thinking • Teamwork and cooperation • Active and lifelong learning abilities
Conrad and Newberry (2011)	• Organizational communication skills (such as using information technology, creating information network) • Leadership communication skills (such as creating group synergy, being a change catalyst) • Interpersonal communication skills (such as active listening, relating to people of diverse backgrounds)
Conrad and Newberry (2012)	• Outcome-based managerial and communication skills
Eberhardt, Moser, and McGee (1997)	• Oral and written communication • Interpersonal and leadership skills • Decision-making capability • Analytical skills • Previous work experience • Financial skills and technical skills
Robinson, Garton, and Vaughn (2007)	• Problem solving and analytical skills • Decisions making • Organization and time management • Risk-taking • Time management • Creativity, innovation, and change • Lifelong learning • Motivation
Levenburg (1996)	• Communication skills • Presentations skills • Teamwork

(Continued)

Table 2.1 Literature highlighting objectives of management education   (Continued)

Research studies	The skill developed through management education
	• Decision-making skills • Leadership • Project management • Multicultural appreciation
Verville (1995)	• Ability to use technology • A focus on client value • Ability to work in teams • Executing commitment • Building and applying competencies
Wardrope (2002)	• Writing skills to be more important to business communication courses than other communication skills, such as Speaking Technology-mediated communication Interpersonal communication Team or group communication Listening and cultural literacy skills

One observes that the skills to be developed in management education on a variety of skills but have not focused on values, ethics, responsibility, and sustainability.

The Shift in Competency Requirement and Teaching Methodology

While the traditional education focused on development of knowledge, skills, and attitudes, the future management education needs to focus on competencies (explained in Chapter 1). Management education needs to focus on enhancing value for the various stakeholders in the globally competitive and ever-changing environment. This would enable students to develop skills for the formulation and implementation of appropriate competitive strategies. This calls for continuous reinvention of business school education (Knight and de Wit 1999).

The objectives of management education are undergoing a shift from merely imparting knowledge and skills for maximum economic return to a blended approach where knowledge is to be fused with socially, economically, and responsible education for sustainable growth with a set of relevant competencies discussed in Chapter 1.

Andragogy today has become a function of ethical conduct, personal, and social responsibility and this relationship assumes pivotal importance when addressing the educational needs of the changing and fast evolving business or management education.

Thus the focus of the management education needs to include *principles of responsible management education so that augmentation of knowledge and skills can happen in an ethical and responsible manner.*

Teaching Methodology

Experiential Learning Theory (Fiedler 1964; Kolb 1984) is the pivotal theory that enables us to understand elements of experiential learning and transparency and accountability in the context of contemporary management education.

Experiential Learning

Mutual experiences, shared learning, and overlapping personal spaces together amalgamate to yield a learning environment that not only bestows experiential learning but learning with increased reach. Karl Weick has done seminal work in experiential learning in groups and institutions. Weick's sense-making model refers to concepts of making sense of chaotic, unknowable events because he believes that managers are faced with unmanageable situations. Institutions such as business schools are part of sense making because they shape signification (meaning-making) via interpretation and communication (Giddens 1984, 29) and sensible structures.

Three modifications to contextual apparatuses by which institutions affect sense making and learning are: (1) providing social cues; (2) editing sense making through social feedback processes; and (3) trigger sense making (Weber and Glynn 2006). Together, they allow us to show a fuller view of the role of context in sense making and thereby embracing the requisite richness (Figure 2.1).

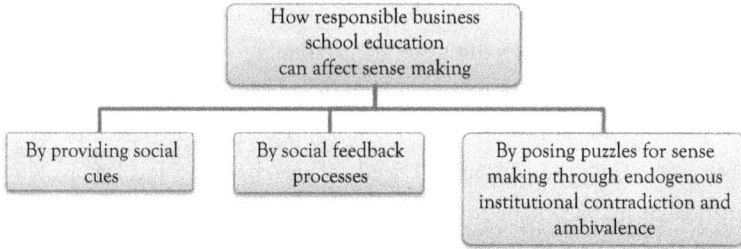

Figure 2.1 *Mechanisms relating institutional context to sense making*

The Methodological Approach for Responsible Management Education

The core elements of a high impact postgraduate education include the development of intellectual powers and capacities; ethical and civic preparation; and personal growth and self-direction (Kuh 2008; Barth 2012). Responsibility and management require a systemic "big picture" and asking "big questions" perspective to fully comprehend the myriad issues that are being faced by today's managers and leaders (Feng 2012; Frisk and Larson 2011; Hansen, Dann, and Kerr 2012; Porter and Cordoba 2009; Chun 2009). An important and proactive approach to aid responsible management learning amongst business management students is through the use of high impact educational practices (HIEP) (Hansen, Dann, and Kerr 2012; Kuh 2008).

Building on Kuh's (2008) HIEP, cross-disciplinary and multiple course perspectives may also be integrated into environmental sustainability, responsible management, and ethical understanding and education (Feng 2012; Yarime et al. 2012). Collaborative projects, writing intensity, research, community, service-oriented practices are all experiential and are recommended for sustainability education practices (Ferreira, Lopes, and Morais 2006; Bergeå et al. 2006; Sipos, Battisti, and Grimm 2008). Integration of the aforementioned arguments enabled us to create the integrative framework for responsible management education (Figure 2.2).

Case Method and Responsible Management Education

Case-based teaching (Corey 1998) has been defined as a key learning strategy from which students extract meaning and understanding from course materials and experiences (Warburton 2003). Case-based teaching is designed to go beyond intellectual development becoming more transformational,

Principle of Responsible
Management Education (PRME)
1. Purpose
2. Values
3. Method
4. Research
5. Partnership
6. Dialogue
(Addendum – Operations)

Effective learning dimensions
Integrative learning
  Integrating ideas or information from various sources
  Including diverse perspectives in class discussions/writing
  Putting together ideas from different courses
  Discussing ideas with faculty members outside of class
  Discussing ideas with others outside of class
Higher order learning
  Analyzing the basic elements of an idea, experience, or theory
  Synthesizing and organizing ideas, information, or experience
  Making judgments about the value of information
  Applying theories to practical problems or in new situations
Reflective learning
  Examining the strengths and weaknesses or your own views
  Trying to better understand someone else's views
  Learning something that changed how you understand an issue
  Applied what's learned in a course to personal life or work
  Enjoyed completing a task that required a lot of thinking and
  mental effort
Source: Nelson et al. 2008.

Stakeholder learning outcomes
Students
  • Academic gains and school connectedness by students
  • Building nondiscipline, personal and social competencies of
    students.
  • Staying in school to completion
  • Broadened career exploration for students.
  • Building social capital for students
Schools
  • Building social capital for school's greater civic engagement
    of students helping to build "town-gown" relationships
  • Greater retention rates and higher quality relationships
    between students and school
  • Informing faculty research
Communities
  • Expertise and creative solutions to immediate issues
  • Greater civic engagement by students

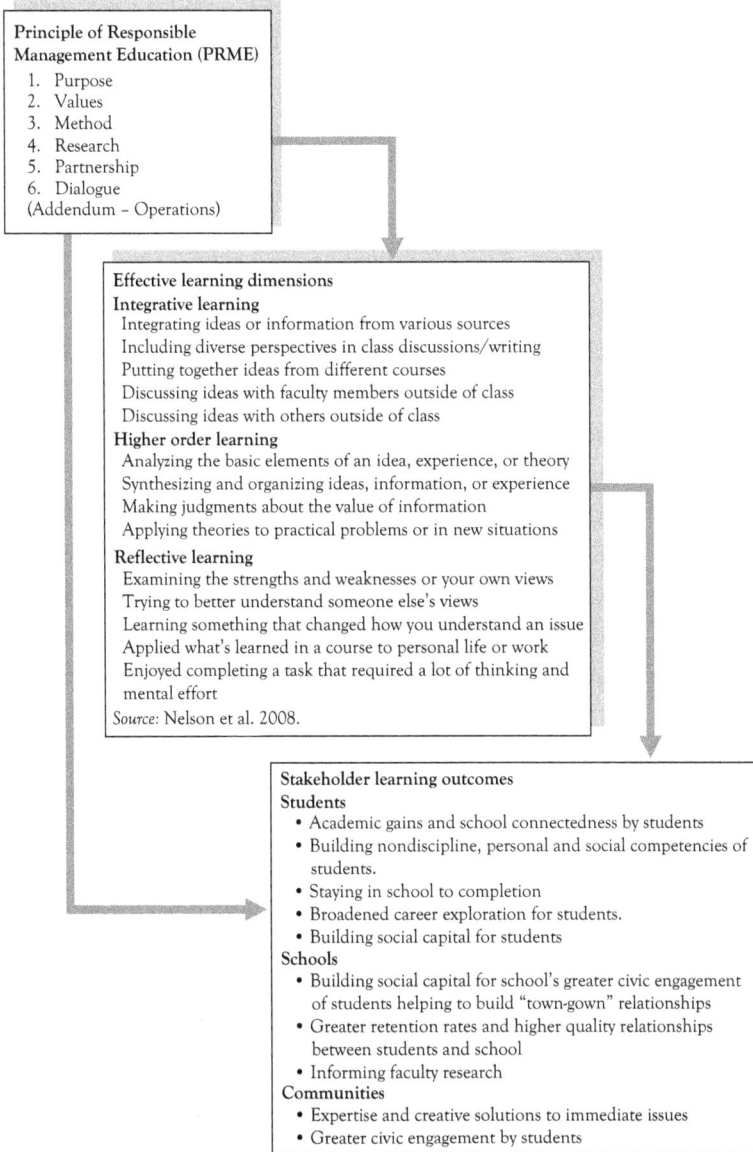

Figure 2.2 An integrative framework for responsible management education

which includes physical, emotional, aesthetic, moral, social, personal, and spiritual growth (Bentz 1992; Grauerholz 2001; Miller 1999; Stirling 2010). Case-based teaching and contingency theory have deep connections and contingency theory can be considered as a precursor to case-based teaching (Christensen and Carlile 2009).

There are various variants of contingency theory and it is the context that determines which one is most appropriate (Fiedler 1964).

In the context of changing global business environment, a combination of optimism (in face of uncertainty) and technology-enabled leadership (in the face of diversity) are required.

Project and Dialogue with Stakeholders

The management education can be facilitated by adopting project-based learning where the real life projects and business problems are dealt with using stakeholder perspective. For example, a project titles as "How to sensitize a particular industry about the harmful effectives of its waste disposal system?" The students can select a problem, collect data from the firm and other stakeholders, analyze the results, draw conclusions, and prepare and share the report with the management of the firm. Also, they can suggest alternative methods for managing the waste disposal system or process. This project will help develop knowledge, analytical and problem-solving skills along with competencies of responsible management (CAMB discussed in Chapter 1).

Other methods can be in the form of field visit, action projects, or internships. Further, the objectives and approaches of the framework envisage:

- Accelerate learning by challenging students to work with the real-world "clients" on sustainability projects, including nonprofit organizations, community, social as well as business organizations.
- Leverage multidisciplinary and intercultural diversity in the student teams to enhance team skills (Sarala 2010).
- Develop analytical and critical thinking by requiring the students to conduct comprehensive analysis of the behavior of people in an organization regarding recycling waste and developing a practical strategy and action plan to foster sustainable behavior (Gentile 2010).
- Integrate the knowledge gained from courses in accounting, finance, marketing, operations management, and in an interdisciplinary form to promote "responsible management" for sustainability (Benbunan-Fich et al. 2001).

Addressing Challenges and Opportunities Through Responsible Management Education

Besides developing the skills, the management schools, through their students and faculty, can address other challenges which are facing the organizations and societies across geographies. A suggestive list is given below:

1. Global warming: how to respond to this phenomenon in a responsible manner?
2. Transparency and accountability in public and private sector organizations.
3. How to integrate affective (emotional and social) competencies in the curriculum while retaining focus on the conceptual and analytical courses?
4. How to enhance well-being in an organization and a society?

All these challenges offer opportunities to students in business schools to develop competencies for responsible management to drive business with responsibility for a sustainable future.

Summary

The chapter encapsulates the changing context of management education and the challenges faced by business organizations to underline the need for paradigm shift in management education. With this in view it supports PRME principles and highlights some measures to integrate it into management education through change in curriculum and andragogy. It points to a growing need for institutionalization of what might be seen in the future as a key catalyst for the transformation of management education to create a more responsive and responsible economy and society. One of the critical ways in which the framework presented in this chapter furthers the field of management education is by combining the real-life projects and business problems with the perspectives of stakeholders dealing with those problems. It would help the management students and educators to delve deep into the issues that lie at the intersection of sustainable development, responsible management education, and higher educational institutions by responsibly combining theory with practice. It also provides vistas in future management research.

Discussion Questions

1. Identify and discuss the challenges faced by business organizations in your cultural context.
2. Do you think the present management education equips the students to face the current and future challenges of business? Present your arguments in favor or against.
3. In your view, what are the competency requirements for managers of the future?
4. How could values of responsible management be inculcated among management students?
5. Identify measures to make management education relevant to changing business and social environment in your cultural context.

References

Aggarwal, S. 2006. "The Workplace of the Future." Tata Group. www.tata.in/article/inside/xTlZ3G8Rit8=/TLYVr3YPkMU= (accessed on February 14, 2011).

Aiken, M.W., and J.S. Martin. 1994. "Requisite Skills of Business School Graduates: Perceptions of Senior Corporate Executives." *Journal of Education for Business* 69, no. 3, p. 159.

Aiken, M., J. Martin, and J. Paolillo. 1994. "Requisite Skills of Business School Graduates as Perceived by Senior Corporate Executives." *Journal of Education for Business* 69, no. 3, pp. 159–62.

Allen, I.E., and J. Seaman. 2003. *Sizing the Opportunity: The Quality and Extent of Online Education in the United States, 2002 and 2003.* Needham, MA: Sloan-C. Retrieved from http://sloanconsortium.org/publications/survey/sizing_the_opportunity2003 (accessed on December 22, 2011).

Amiot, C.E., D.J. Terry, and V.J. Callan. 2007. "Status, Equity and Social Identification During an Intergroup Merger: A Longitudinal Study." *British Journal of Social Psychology* 46, no. 3, pp. 557–77.

Angwin, D., and E. Vaara. 2005. "Introduction to the Special Issue. 'Connectivity' in Merging Organizations: Beyond Traditional Cultural Perspectives." *Organization Studies* 26, no. 10, pp. 1445–53.

Arensdorf, J. 2009. "The Perceptions of Employability Skills Transferred from Academic Leadership Classes to the Workplace: A Study of the FHSU Leadership Studies Certificate Program." Retrieved from http://hdl.handle.net/2097/1348 (accessed on January 23, 2012).

Barth, M. 2012. "Social Learning Instead of Educating the Other." *GAIA-Ecological Perspectives for Science and Society* 21, no. 2, pp. 91–94.

Bentz, V.M. 1992. "Deep Learning Groups: Combining Emotional and Intellectual Learning." *Clinical Sociology Review* 10, pp. 71–89.

Benbunan-Fich, R., H. Lozada, S. Pirog, R. Priluck, and J. Wisenblit. 2001. "Integrating Information Technology into the Marketing Curriculum: A Pragmatic Paradigm." *Journal of Marketing Education* 23, no. 1, pp. 5–15.

Bergeå, O., R. Karlsson, A. Hedlund-Åström, P. Jacobsson, and C. Luttropp. 2006. "Education for Sustainability as a Transformative Learning Process: A Pedagogical Experiment in Eco Design Doctoral education." *Journal of Cleaner Production* 14, no. 15, pp. 1431–42.

Chun, R. 2009. "A Corporate's Responsibility to Employees During a Merger: Organizational Virtue and Employee Loyalty." *Corporate Governance* 9, no. 4, pp. 473–83.

Christensen, C.M., and P.R. Carlile. 2009. "Course Research: Using the Case Method to Build and Teach Management Theory." *Academy of Management Learning & Education* 8, no. 2, pp. 240–51.

Dumas, C. 2002. "Community-Based Service-Learning: Does It Have a Role in Management Education?" *International Journal of Value-Based Management* 15, no. 1, pp. 249–64.

Conrad, D., and R. Newberry. 2011. "24 Business Communication Skills: Attitudes of Human Resource Managers Versus Business Educators." *American Communication Journal* 13, no. 1, pp. 4–23.

Corey, R. 1998. *Case Method Teaching*. Boston: Harvard Business School 9-581-058, Rev. November 6, 1998.

Conrad, D., and R. Newberry. 2012. "Identification and Instruction of Important Business Communication Skills for Graduate Business Education." *Journal of Education for Business* 87, no. 2, pp. 112–20.

Eberhardt, B.J., S. Moser, and P. McGee. 1997. "Business Concerns Regarding MBA Education: Effects on Recruiting." *Journal of Education for Business* 72, no. 5, pp. 293–96.

Feng, L. 2012. "Teacher and Student Responses to Interdisciplinary Aspects of Sustainability Education: What Do We Really Know?" *Environmental Education Research* 18, no. 1, pp. 31–43.

Ferreira, A.J.D., M.A.R. Lopes, and J.P.F. Morais. 2006. "Environmental Management and Audit Schemes Implementation as an Educational Tool for Sustainability." *Journal of Cleaner Production* 14, no. 9, pp. 973–82.

Fiedler, F.E. 1964. "A Contingency Model of Leadership Effectiveness." In *Advances in Experimental Social Psychology*, ed. L. Berkowitz, Vol. 1, 149–90. Academic Press.

Frisk, E., and K.L. Larson. 2011. "Educating for Sustainability: Competencies and Practices for Transformative Action." *Journal of Sustainability Education* 2, pp. 1–20.

Gartner. 2010. "Gartner Says the World of Work Will Witness 10 Changes During the Next 10 Years." www.gartner.com/it/page.jsp?id=1416513 (accessed on February 12, 2011).

Garvin, D.A. July–August 1993. "Building a Learning Organization." *Harvard Business Review*, pp. 78–79.

Gentile, M. 2010. *Giving Voice to Values: How to Speak Your Mind When You Know What's Right.* Yale University Press.

Giddens, A. 1984. *The Constitution of Society: Outline of the Theory of Structuration.* 1st ed. Berkeley, CA: University of California Press.

Goulet, P., and D.M. Schweiger. 2006. "Managing Culture and Human Resources in Mergers and Acquisitions." In *Handbook of Research in International Human Resource Management,* eds. G.K. Stahl and I. Björkman, 405–29. London: Edward Elgar Ltd.

Grauerholz, L. 2001. "Teaching Holistically to Achieve Deep Learning." *College Teaching* 49, pp. 44–50.

Hansen, L.T., S. Dann, and J.M. Kerr. 2012. "A Critical Learning Cycle Model for Sustain-Ability Education: Two Case Studies of Water Conservation Programs in Jordan." *Journal of Sustainability Education* 3.

India's Population. 2011. www.indiaonlinepages.com/population/india-current-population.html (accessed on March 4, 2011).

Knight, J., and H. de Wit. 1999. "An Introduction to the IQRP Project and Process." In *Quality and Internationalization in Higher Education.*

Kolb, D.A. 1984. *Experiential Learning: Experience as the Source of Learning and Development.* Englewood Cliffs, NJ: Prentice-Hall.

Kuh, G.D. 2008. *High-impact Educational Practices: What They Are, Who Has Access to Them, and Why They Matter.* Washington, DC: Association of American Colleges and Universities.

Larkin, T.J., and S. Larkin. 1996. "Reaching and Changing Frontline Employees." *Harvard Business Review* 74, no. 3, pp. 95–107.

Larsson, R., and S. Finkelstein. 1999. "Integrating Strategic, Organizational, and Human Resource Perspectives on Mergers and Acquisitions: A Case Survey of Synergy Realization." *Organization Science* 10, no. 1, pp. 1–26.

Levenburg, N. 1996. "General Management Skills: Do Practitioners and Academic Faculty Agree on Their Importance?" *Journal of Education for Business* 72, no. 1, pp. 47–51.

Miller, W.R. ed. 1999. *Integrating Spirituality into Treatment.* Washington, DC: American Psychological Association.

Olson, G.M., and J.S. Olson. 2000. "Distance Matters." *Human-Computer Interaction* 15, no. 2, pp. 139–78.

Olson, G.M., A. Zimmerman, and N. Bos. eds. 2008. *Scientific Research on the Internet.* Cambridge, MA: MIT Press.

Porter, T., and J. Cordoba. 2009. "Three Views of Systems Theories and Their Implications for Sustainability Education." *Journal of Management Education* 33, no. 3, pp. 323–47.

Robinson, J.S., B.L. Garton, and P.R. Vaughn. June 2007. "Becoming Employable: A Look at Graduates and Supervisor's Perceptions of the Skills Needed for Employability." *NACTA Journal* 51, no. 2, pp. 19–26.

Sarala, R.M. 2010. "The Impact of Cultural Differences and Acculturation Factors on Post-Acquisition Conflict." *Scandinavian Journal of Management* 26, no. 1, pp. 38–56.

Seo, M.G., and N.S. Hill. December 2005. "Understanding the Human Side of Merger and Acquisition: An Integrative Framework." *The Journal of Applied Behavioral Science* 41, no. 4, pp. 422–43.

Sipos, Y., B. Battisti, and K. Grimm. 2008. "Achieving Transformative Sustainability Learning: Engaging Head, Hands and Heart." *International Journal of Sustain-ability in Higher Education* 9, no. 1, pp. 68–86.

Stirling, A. 2010. "From Enlightenment to Enablement: Opening Up Choices for Innovation." In *The Innovation for Development Report,* ed. A. Lopez Claros, 199–210. Basingstoke: Palgrave MacMillan.

Terry, D.J., V.J. Callan, and G. Sartori. 1996. "Employee Adjustment to an Organizational Merger: Stress, Coping and Intergroup Differences." *Stress Medicine* 12, no. 2, pp. 105–22.

Verville, A.L. 1995. "What Business Needs from Higher-Education." *The Educational Record* 76, no. 4, pp. 46–50.

Very, P., M. Lubatkin, R. Calori, and J. Veiga. 1997. "Relative Standing and the Performance of Recently Acquired European Firms." *Strategic Management Journal* 18, no. 8, pp. 593–14.

Warburton, K. 2003. "Deep Learning and Education for Sustainability." *International Journal of Sustainability in Higher Education* 4, no. 1, pp. 44–56.

Weber, K., and M.A. Glynn. 2006. "Making Sense with Institutions: Context, Thought and Action in Karl Weick's Theory." *Organization Studies* 27, no. 11, pp. 1639–60.

Weick, K.E. 1995. *Sensemaking in Organizations.* Thousand Oaks, CA: Sage.

William, J.W. December 2002. "Department Chairs' Perceptions of the Importance of Business Communication Skills." *Business Communication Quarterly* 65, no. 4, pp. 60–72.

Yarime, M., G. Trencher, T. Mino, R. Scholz, L. Olsson, B. Ness, and J. Rotmans. 2012. "Establishing Sustainability Science in Higher Education Institutions: Towards an Integration of Academic Development, Institutionalization, and Stakeholder Collaborations." *Sustainability Science* 7, no. 1, pp. 101–13.

CHAPTER 3

The Future of Corporate Governance

Christian Strenger

Corporate Governance—Its Background and Essentials

Corporate Governance is today best described as the "art of good house-keeping" for and at companies. Its aim is to deliver a framework for the running and the control of corporations to achieve sustainable well-being and progress for its stakeholders—the shareholders, the employees, the clients, and the environment they act in. How did it become an important part of the economic life?

After severe company failures already in the 1970s and 1980s, the necessity for a new set of rules led to first steps toward codified governance with the first code in the United Kingdom, named after its father Sir Adrian Cadbury (Cadbury Code). The UK Governance Code[1] is the precursor for most official governance codes that are commonplace in the world (except the United States which only has guidelines of large pension funds). Today's codes generally follow international best practice standards that are determined by international standard setters such as the Organization for Economic Cooperation and Development (OECD),[2] the International Corporate Governance Network (ICGN),[3] and the big institutional investors.

---

[1] Financial Reporting Council (2012).
[2] OECD (2015).
[3] ICGN (2015).

Most governance codes follow a self-regulatory approach: Companies listed on a stock exchange that relies on risk capital provided by outside sources (= shareholders) have to disclose at least annually whether they comply with the code. If not, they have to explain why they deviate. This "comply or explain" principle should give the capital markets sufficient information on the governance structure and attitude of a firm.

Conceptually the market participants, and here in particular the investors, express their appreciation of the governance situation of a company by purchase or sale transactions. The ensuing price reactions for the shares (and also the bonds) then produce the concurrent effect of raising or lowering the cost of capital of the firm.

Why We Have to Rethink Today's Corporate Governance

To achieve good and improving governance, a wide array of laws and self-regulatory codes has been devised in the past two decades. While the majority of the proposals were of self-regulatory nature, there is also no shortage of binding governance laws. Good examples are the Sarbanes–Oxley Act of the United States[4] and the 2006 UK Companies Act. The latter obliges company directors to:

1. pursue a long-term approach in their decision making;
2. consider the interest of the company's employees;
3. foster business relationships with suppliers, customers, and others;
4. observe the impact of the company's operations on the community and the environment;
5. maintain high standards of business conduct; and
6. act fairly for all shareholders of the company.

---

[4] The Sarbanes–Oxley Act (SOX) came into force in June 2002. The SOX deals with compliance and corporate governance issues and augments the existing Federal laws. A major focus is on the auditing of companies and audit firms themselves.

Although this law was enacted in good time before the financial crisis in 2008, it had no real effect on the behavior of the directors of three UK banking institutions that had to be saved by £37 billion of public money.[5]

- Equally, laws and codes did not prevent spectacular corporate failures like Enron, Parmalat, Satyam, and WorldCom that cost investors many billion Euros and had severe implications for the economic and financial system.
- Particularly legally binding regulation has shown limited effects in prescribing fairness and appropriate corporate behavior. It appears that laws regulate transgressions with sanctions but seem to encourage going to their limits instead of leading to a holistic approach for sustained corporate performance.
- The manifold prescriptions were accordingly not able to keep so many companies and the system of the social market economy (= "educational capitalism") in satisfactory health. However, as there is no better system in sight (as all other approaches have failed or at least massively underperformed), fresh avenues for better governance on a global basis have to be found urgently.

What Has Not Worked and Needs Repair or Change

What were and in many cases are still the main deficits for this unsatisfactory picture:

- *Insufficient alignment of the interests of the company* with the demands of the shareholders, other stakeholders, and executives. This includes:

---

[5] In 2008, The Royal Bank of Scotland, HBOS, and Lloyds TSB needed recapitalization of £37 billion, http://news.bbc.co.uk/2/hi/business/7666570.stm (20/09/2015).

o *excessive management remuneration* with bonus systems incorrectly devised or granted by the supervisory boards.[6] Equally substantial farewell payments for failed executives (golden handshakes) can still be found instead of a "zero compensation rule";

o *short termism by investors* that are either too greedy or too fearful of short-term underperformance although they should know that only a longer-term investment horizon can deliver steady outperformance; and

o *insufficient economic knowledge* of other stakeholders that raises exaggerated expectations for wealth redistribution.

- *Independent but incompetent or inactive supervisors:* The banks that lost billions individually and trillions collectively did not have supervisory boards that asked the right questions and stopped outlandish profit-making exercises. These directors were perhaps formally independent but not in a professional sense. And even worse: many of the directors that had the professional knowledge were quiet when they should have said "No!" to the managers betting the house with speculative undertakings.[7]

- *Disregard of sensible code provisions and internal rules:* This happened also in renowned companies when well-founded principles for age limits and board succession of the supervisory directors were ignored by the same people that first set the rules, but did not apply them when it concerned them personally some years later.

- *Widespread failure of proper risk management:* Not only according to a 2010 report from the OECD, boards were, in a large number of cases, not aware of the risks that the company was

---

[6] The recent "welcome" package for the new CEO of BG group in the UK totaling £14 million and a £12 million "one off" hello payment is another confirmation of unwarranted pay exuberance.

[7] Prominent examples: The three UK banks (see Footnote 4) and the German steel company ThyssenKrupp that lost €8 billion (equaling 2/3 of its equity) in Brazilian and U.S. steel projects.

facing. This shows that too often the boards did not fulfill
their duties for conducting and overseeing the risk management and other control functions.

- *Disregard of a stated "zero tolerance policy"* for misdemeanor
  by employees and management that put the credibility of
  the corporate policies into question. One also had to observe
  insufficient pursuit of wrongdoing (recently exemplified by
  very modest court fines for past executives of the badly hit
  Landesbanken).

- *Deficient compliance structures* for cartel and corruption matters that were not sufficiently corrected by management and
  supervisors. This has already led to fines of several hundred
  million euros in several European cases.[8]

- *Oversight failures of auditors*: Some auditors deriving substantial parts of their total revenues from one firm, mainly
  through intensive and well-paid advisory services, had an
  obvious incentive to overlook illegal practices of the executives.[9] In addition, client centricity instead of providing independent control services to the shareholders and stakeholders
  led to uneven control quality.

- *Reliance on regulatory details and an abundance of figure work*
  in the expectation that these would avoid serious wrongdoing.
  The belief that even more regulation will save future bailouts
  by the taxpayers is a myth of politicians. This will be falsified

---

[8] Inter alia: Südzucker, Siemens, ThyssenKrupp.

[9] The auditor of Lehman Brothers earned $185 million in the year before the
bankruptcy in 2008. The German Landesbanken who collectively lost about
€150 billion mostly through packaged U.S. mortgages bonds, have never been
stopped in this by their auditors as their politically dominated boards were certainly not equipped to prevent this. See: International Monetary Fund (IMF):
Global Financial Stability Report, April/October 2010. The latest example is the
€4 billion insolvency case of the Banco Espirito Santo Group that rattled the Por-
tuguese financial system and was only saved by the EU-bailout-program: there
the auditor was the sole outside control body that audited a complex web of
60 subsidiaries and financial vehicles with long undetected cross guarantees to
third parties.

by the next crisis that certainly comes from an unexpected source not covered by existing regulation.

- *Professional shareholders ignoring their fiduciary responsibility*: Many institutions did and still do not act as responsible owners. As they run risk-diversified portfolios with smaller individual shareholdings,[10] a serious governance effort too often does not exist with some investors not even voting at annual meetings. Their portfolio managers often follow short term considerations like the next mergers and acquisitions (M&A) deal and higher dividends that are seen more important than sound governance practices. Quite often they also have too much leeway resulting from a wide design of their mandates, leading to deficient accountability.[11] Only now the EU Commission[12] and many supervisory authorities are putting more emphasis on having institutional investors fulfill their fiduciary duties by actively voting and pursuing the interests of their millions of pension clients.

- *No clear definition and communication of the firm's corporate values*: Simply posting advertisements like "Our reputation is our most valuable asset" failed to reach the intended recipients (employees and the clients) due to the apparent lack of authenticity. In the extreme, this can lead to the finding of the German philosopher Nietzsche: "I am not upset that you lied to me, I am upset that from now on I cannot believe you."

- *Failure to apply high ethical standards*: The 2010 OECD report "Corporate Governance and the Financial Crisis" identified that the ethical standards displayed by the board failed to respect the expectations and the interests of stakeholders. They have also the duty of ensuring that high ethical

---

[10] See: Law Commission of the Houses of Parliament (2014); FRC (2012).

[11] For a correct mandate design, see: "ICGN Model Mandate Initiative: Model Contract Terms between asset owners and their fund managers," 2012.

[12] EU Commission (2015).

standards are applied on board level and within the rest of the company.[13]

In essence, the responsible individuals have missed to understand and apply a fundamental imperative: not everything that is legal is also legitimate.

These points show the inability of the existing written regulatory governance environment—whether by law or self-regulation—to stop widespread wrongdoing with serious implications for individual companies, countries, and the global economic system. Realistically, even the best codes and laws can only provide a framework but not their correct application and corresponding behavior. They are not an end in itself but only important tools to a satisfactory end.

Conclusion: It appears that business has to show a different attitude and commitment that goes much further than fulfilling externally imposed compliance obligations. There seems to be a fundamental need to pursue governance and ethics in a holistic way with corresponding behavior by the responsible managers and supervisors. They will have to accept that corporate excellence on a sustainable basis can only be achieved by the integration of a suitable governance framework with ethical, credible, and responsible behavior. This should also be governed by Plato's finding that "Good people do not need laws to tell them to act responsibly while bad people will find a way around them."

New Approaches for Better Governance in the Future

Less Rigid Regulation

As every major economic crisis came from a new, unexpected angle that even the savviest economists or politicians were and will not be able to foresee, the hope that even more regulation can stop serious wrongdoing and ensuing government bailouts with public money is futile. It does not take too much imagination to foresee the presently unchecked high frequency trading in unregulated "dark pools" (that today represent at

---

[13] Kirkpatrick (2010).

least 60 percent of all equity turnover) and other "shadow banking" variations running the financial system into fresh trouble.

A similar picture prevails for individual governance issues. Here are just two examples of over-regulation by law that German politicians introduced to win favor with their electorate:

- *The German "Cooling off" law for executives*: Today they can become supervisory board members only after a fixed two-year hibernation requirement. The generally good idea of not letting past executives control their poor management decisions as a supervisor should not be determined by a fixed time period. What is rather required is an individual assessment of the personal suitability of each candidate. So the rules should give general guidance with a provision that the past CEO cannot become the governing chairman for at least two years.[14]

- The much debated issue of a *female quota*: A fixed percentage prescribed by law for every listed major company (but excluding firms incorporated as Sociétés Européennes (SE) like Allianz, BASF, and SAP) may be right for certain companies but is certainly wrong for others. To achieve the certainly necessary higher diversity of boards in such a rigid fashion is too simplistic and has not worked even in Norway as evidenced by recent studies.[15] The current draft law of the German ministries contains in Part two the better solution for all companies of a certain size, similar to the German Code recommendation of 2009. It prescribes that firms have to determine themselves the percentage of women in their management and supervisory boards as well as in the upper management ranks. This has to be published and is therefore subject to the control of the general public—a much more customized and

---

[14] See: principle 2.3 of the ICGN Global Corporate Governance Principles: www.icgn.org/images/Global_Governance_Principles_2014.pdf
[15] See: Bertrand et al. (2014); Dittmer and Ahern (2012).

self-regulatory way for companies to integrate the undeniable qualities of women for management and supervision.

Simpler Governance Rules

- The unsatisfactory experience with the proliferation of more minute regulation and codes also asks to reconsider the intention to regulate in every detail. To achieve less wrongdoing and sustainable value creation, it could be preferable to rein in on obvious prescriptions in favor of more concise solutions. In this vein, the German Government Code Commission started last year a review process to eliminate code recommendations that have become outdated or fully accepted norms. While such a process should continue, it should not endanger the code concept to give a complete picture of what good governance should constitute in the country proper.
- What are *examples for necessary reductions*?
  - *Code listing of basic tasks for directors*: The requirement of the latest UK Governance Code revision[16] that asks directors to give a detailed explanation in the annual report how have they assessed the prospects of the company, what period the assessment covered, and why this period was appropriate. These basic tasks should be ingrained in every director right from the start and should not be generalized in the Code as they provoke standardized, risk-avoiding answers. On the long-term viability issue, a well-reasoned statement by the independent auditors about the future viability of the company is of sufficient relevance.
  - *Overly detailed interim reporting for listed companies*: Full reporting for cents and euros on a quarterly basis employs too many company and auditor resources without adding real insight. But it is not only the volume of reporting but also its frequency: quarterly reporting can put executives

---

[16] See: Provision C.2.2. of the UK Governance Code, 2014.

under pressure to deliver positive results as often as possible. A better alternative would be to follow the UK approach with an "Interim Management Statement"[17] that focuses on major new developments and deviations from previous guidance.

○ *Excessive transfer of board responsibilities to annual meetings:* The April 2014 draft for the EU Shareholder Rights Directive prescribes that related party transactions exceeding (only) five percent of a company's assets have to be approved by the Annual general meeting and transactions exceeding one percent have to be publicized in great detail without delay. Apart from the organizational effort and the costs involved for shareholder meetings, this would substantially undermine the board's primary responsibilities to manage and control the affairs of the company. A more sensible approach would be detailed and prompt reporting for transactions exceeding three percent and shareholder meeting approval for transactions of ten percent and more (except for countries like Germany that have strict legal sanctions against improper benefits from insider transactions).

○ *Listing of group entities* that are not material for the full group picture and should be available permanently on the website.

○ *Reporting on insider transactions with too low thresholds* (increase to a cumulative 100,000 EUR per fiscal year suggested).

---

[17] An IMS is a trading update that has to be published between ten weeks after the beginning and six weeks before the end of the first and second six months of the financial year. It is a non-testified explanation of essential/substantial events and transactions that influence the financial situation of the company and describes generally the performance of the company. It can be substituted by quarterly reports, see: http://www.theaic.co.uk/sites/default/files/uploads/files/AICDTRseminarslideswebsite.pdf and for further details: www.fsa.gov.uk.

Integration of Corporate Governance Into a Customized Corporate Culture

- As every company is different and individual by its background and corporate nature, its governors—the managers and the supervisors—have to define precisely its corporate culture. Only then trust and lasting relationships can be built and maintained with all stakeholders.
- The main benefits of a convincing corporate culture are:
  - Companies with high levels of trust benefit from lower bureaucracy, simpler procedures, and higher productivity—evidenced by Larcker and Brian.[18]
  - They will also be able to attract and keep better qualified personnel that relates to the culture and values of the firm.[19] To achieve a better understanding and observance of the corporate culture and the governance of the firm, corporate behavior testing of applicants for management positions and mentoring programs for young management candidates should become standard procedures.
- Novel approaches for the improvement of the corporate culture:
  - Colin Mayer has recently suggested to establish a "trust company"[20] with explicit values. Its board has to ensure compliance with these values and to balance the various stakeholder interests. This concept would require investments of a different nature than the purchase of equipment, building of plants, and the next acquisition. It must go beyond nice words and donations for a concert or even a kindergarten. It requires changing the mindset of companies and of the people working for them. Only with the preparedness for such change will people see the wisdom

---

[18] Larcker and Brian (2011).
[19] Collins and Porras (2014).
[20] Colin (2013).

of Suchanek's "Golden Rule"[21] that it pays to invest in societal cooperation as all sides can emerge as winners—the classic win-win approach.

o A "soft line" approach has been proposed with the "Nudge-Theory" developed by Thaler and Sun Stein in 2008.[22] This has gained attention also by governments (i.e., the British Government with the "Behavioral Insights Team" and the German Government that has also set up an academic working group).[23] The Nudge-Theory follows a libertarian paternalism philosophy[24] and seeks to find alternative ways to influence people's behavior by subtle incentivization.[25] It does not limit the choices but intends to induce people to accept a better choice by "nudging" them in the right direction through subtle measures.

o A more direct solution is to achieve "connectivity" through relating compensation to the executive's compliance with the ethical culture of the firm. This was first applied by

---

[21] Suchanek (2001).

[22] Thaler and Sunstein (2008).

[23] See for UK: www.gov.uk/government/organisations/behavioural-insights-team and for Germany: www.spiegel.de/spiegel/print/d-129211274.html.

[24] Libertarian paternalism (sometimes also: soft paternalism) is a term that was firstly used by Thaler and Sunstein in their article 'Libertarian Paternalism' in the *American Economic Review* in 2003 and introduces a new form of paternalism, in which a superior force (state, parents etc.) restricts the behavior of someone to the good of the him/her by limiting the alternatives to choose from. See also: http://econweb.ucsd.edu/~jandreon/Econ264/papers/Thaler%20Sunstein%20AER%202003.pdf (Article in American Economic Review)

[25] Examples for successful "Nudging" are:- getting U.S.-employees to have their retirement contribution automatically increased in line with their compensation increases instead of them having to adjust the retirement plan themselves; putting fruits and vegetables on eyelevel in cafeterias and moving unhealthy products further away to cause people to prefer healthy food; a simple case of positioning; Corporate Governance is linked with "Nudging" by the elements of reputation, trust, credibility, honesty and integrity. The comply-and-explain principle could thus be regarded as a "Nudge"-tool for Corporate Governance.

Deutsche Telekom with part of its long-term variable compensation plan in 2010.[26]

○ A new approach to measure a company's contributions to a wider societal purpose is the so-called "Common Good Matrix" with the "Common Good Balance Sheet" derived from this matrix, developed by the Terra Institute.[27] These two instruments apply 17 Key Performance Indicators that measure the company's corporate behavior and its effects on society. Companies can earn points for good behavior (like improvement of societal and ecological standards within the sector, ethical customer relationship management, etc.) up to a maximum of 1,000 points but they will also lose points for bad behavior (like violation of ILO standards, tax avoidance, excessive income spread, etc.). This "societal" second balance sheet is already applied by some 200 Austrian, German, and Swiss companies.[28]

If such approaches would be increasingly applied in the corporate world and become an integral part of business life, rigid regulation could be increasingly replaced by self-incentivized behavior.

The way forward: To realize an optimum solution instead of pursuing the maximum gain imperative with only one winner, an individualized corporate culture must be designed and lived. To achieve lasting success, a solid framework of corporate governance must be carefully integrated with the corporate culture. Coupled with the mindset of the "royal merchant" (der

---

[26] See: Annual Report Deutsche Telekom AG 2013, p. 28; http://www.geschaeftsbericht.telekom.com/site0412/de/konzernabschluss/konzern-anhang/sonstige-angaben/index.php?page=281-01-text#/282

[27] The Terra Institute is a European competence and advisory network for development and implementation of sustainability strategies in corporations: www.terra-institute.eu/en/gemeinwohl-matrix-bilanz/gwo/gemeinwohl-matrix-gemeinwohl-bilanz.

[28] See: Bryant (2014).

"ehrbare Kaufmann") and lived in an authentic style, a stable basis can be laid for lasting credibility and trustworthiness.

The necessary investments in matching competencies and supporting structures should be quickly recovered through reduced bureaucracy, simpler procedures, and ensuing higher productivity.

The structures and processes need to be part of a holistic approach that combines an appropriate and sustainable corporate culture with customized corporate governance of high quality (rather than formal code acceptance). Directed by an ethical compass ("Ethischer Kompass"), this change in approach and mindset will not produce immediate improvements but it offers the chance for better long-term performance, also with more operational freedom through less oversized regulation. This is, however, entirely dependent upon the realization by the people in charge that it is their own responsibility to change!

Summary

This chapter leads the way toward a refined understanding and appreciation of corporate governance. After a brief background on the essentials and its emergence, the relevance of an updated approach for corporate governance is made clear. The reasons for a rethink are addressed with numerous examples for new approaches.

In the future there should be less rigid regulation (including alternatives for cooling-off of executives moving into control positions and gender quotas), simpler rules such as avoidance of overly detailed reporting, no excessive transfer of board duties to annual meeting approvals, and lower thresholds for reporting of insider transactions.

A holistic integration of and thorough compliance with corporate governance is crucial for a convincing and trustworthy corporate culture. In order to achieve improved compliance structures and responsible behavior, investments and structural changes will be necessary. The main responsibility for achieving such changes, however, lies with the people in charge: they need to be fully trained and compliant with the change in cultural behavior. Furthermore, they need to follow a sound ethical compass and have a strong enough stature.

Discussion Questions

1. Do you know relevant examples of corporate misconduct where a proper understanding of good governance was missing?
2. Which additional aspects do you find important for implementing good governance in the corporate culture?
3. What are your expectations for a responsible executive?
4. Is good governance still a "nice to have" in the company in question or has it a "must have" status?

References

Bertrand, M., S.E. Black, S. Jensen, and A. Lleras-Muney. 2014. *Breaking the Glass Ceiling? The Effect of Board Quotas on Female Labor Market Outcomes in Norway. IZA DP* No 8266. Cambridge, MA: National Bureau of Economic Research.

Bryant, C. 2014. "A Corporate Balance Sheet with a Little Added Love." *Financial Times*, p. 10.

Colin, M. 2013. *Firm Commitment: Why the Corporation Is Failing Us and How to Restore Trust in It.* Oxford: Oxford University Press.

Collins, J., and J. Porras. 1996. Review 2014. "Building Your Company's Vision." *Harvard Business Review* 74, no. 5, p. 65.

Dittmer, A., and K. Ahern. 2012. "The Changing of the Boards: The Impact on Firm Valuation of Mandated Female Board Representation." *Quarterly Journal of Economics* no. 1, pp. 137–97.

EU-Commission. 2015. "Draft for the new EU Shareholder Rights Directive." http://eur-lex.europa.eu/legal-content/EN/TXT/?qid=1398680488759& uri=COM:2014:213:FIN (September 20, 2015).

Financial Reporting Council. 2012. "UK Corporate Governance Code." www.frc. org.uk/Our-Work/Codes-Standards/Corporate-governance/UK-Corporate-Governance-Code.aspx (November 20, 2014).

Financial Reporting Council. 2012. "The UK Stewardship Code." www.frc.org. uk our-work coes-standards corporate-governance UK-stewardship-code. aspx

ICGN (International Corporate Governance Network). 2015. "Global Corporate Governance Principles."

IMF (International Monetary Fund). 2010. "Global Financial Stability Report."

Kirkpatrick, G. 2010. *Corporate Governance and the Financial Crisis.* Paris: OECD-Publication.

Larcker, D., and T. Brian. 2011. *Corporate Governance Matters*. Sanford: Pearson Prentice Hall.

Law Commission of the Houses of Parliament. 2014. "Fiduciary Duties of Investment Intermediaries."

OCED (Organization for Economic Cooperation and Development). 2015. "OECD Principles of Corporate Governance." www.oecd.org/corporate/oecdprinciplesofcorporategovernance.html (20/09/2015).

Suchanek, A. 2001. *Invest in the Conditions of Social Cooperation for Mutual Advantage*, 79. 'Ökonomische Ethik', Tübingen.

Thaler, R.H., and C. Sunstein. 2003. "Libertarian Paternalism." *American Economic Review* 93, no. 2, pp. 175–79.

Thaler, R.H., and C. Sunstein. 2008. *Nudge: Improving Decisions about Health, Wealth and Happiness*. London.

CHAPTER 4

Redefining Functions of a Manager

Roger Nion Conaway

Corporate social responsibility *(CSR) implementation "represents an incremental process and provides a strong foundation" for organizations (ABN AMRO bank 2014).*

A large international bank based in Amsterdam exemplifies the journey toward responsible management and demonstrates how to redefine management functions. ABN AMRO bank has dedicated itself to sustainability management throughout the organization and, according to Lindgreen, the bank is "committed to continuously improving the integration of sustainability into its working environment and business processes." The bank managed 4,500 branches in 53 countries in 2011 with assets over 999 billion euros and employed over 110,000 people. The bank is a significant multinational enterprise with sustained commitment to integration of sustainability in management functions. ABN AMRO's 2013 annual report gives specifics of this commitment to integration:

- Its employees volunteered 11,707 times in social projects.
- Its Foundation has undertaken 358 volunteer projects in 2013.
- It has reduced its energy consumption by 16 percent.
- It has saved approximately 4 million sheets of paper by digitizing products and processes.

How can other enterprises integrate responsibility management functions into their working environments and business processes and create savings similar to ABN AMRO bank? This chapter takes the journey toward answering that question. Key terms that frequently appear are *integration* and *commitment* when redefining management functions. In 2015 Laasch and Conaway emphasized the three dimensional perspective, "responsible management assumes responsibility for the triple bottom line (sustainability), stakeholder value (responsibility), and moral dilemmas (ethics)." A responsible manager manages those three domains of sustainability, responsibility, and ethics with a commitment to integrate throughout the organization.

Henry Fayol's Traditional Managerial Functions

First, we must begin with an overview of the five primary classical management functions of planning, organizing, commanding, coordinating, and controlling offered by Henri Fayol in 1949. These traditional functions have been used as the basis for management education for decades and nearly all basic management classroom textbooks today present Fayol's basic functions for teaching undergraduate business students. Today, commanding and coordinating are often seen as merging the one manager function of leading. It's important to draw a distinction between managing and leading, and we believe managerial functions are distinguished by its day-to-day operations that meet business objectives and delegate responsibilities and assign tasks, while leading primarily communicates the vision and mission of the organization. Other words used for leading are coaching, inspiring, and effectively communicating. Thus, the commanding and coordinating functions integrate into managerial functions, but may prove to be longer-term leadership functions.

Carroll and Gillenre evaluated Fayol's five classical functions and concluded they "still represent the most useful way of conceptualizing the manager's job, especially for management education." Still, alternative views have been provided. Henry Mintzberg proved influential by criticizing tradition functions of management. Through daily observations of managerial behavior, he named three different managerial functions of interpersonal, informational, and decisional business activities. According to Mahoney, Jerdee, and Carroll, Fayol's functions could be expanded into eight functions, identified as "PRINCESS" factors (Planning,

Representing, Investigating, Negotiating, Coordinating, Evaluating, Supervising, Staffing). A scholar named Allen provided a different perspective by examining 932 managers' *actual use of time* during the day. Interestingly, 90 percent of the managers spent time preparing budgets for projects and 84 percent spent time developing economic forecasts, placing these activities as top priorities. The least amount of time (32 percent) according to Allen was spent writing "the sequence or steps that will be carried out in achieving objectives," and next to least amount of time (59 percent) was "evaluating performance by comparing the results achieved with performance standards." Apparently, these time-related tasks fall under planning and controlling responsibilities of Fayol. To summarize our point in an easy way, we agree that Fayol's five classical functions may best represent the most useful way of conceptualizing the responsible manager's job.

Redefining Traditional Functions into Responsible Management

Thus we ask, how may each of Fayol's traditional management functions be redefined responsibly? Consider this point for a moment: Do the traditional conceptualizations of classical administrative functions appear to elevate *the economic bottom line* above the social or environmental bottom line, a perspective that aligns with Nobel Prize Laureate Milton Friedman's argument, "the business of business is business." Lindgreen suggested:

"A key driver of CSR integration is the notion that it can become deeply embedded in an organization's policies, practices, and processes."

We describe each traditional management function and explain how it can be redefined. We then focus on what experience, knowledge, skills, and abilities a responsible manager must have.

Planning

The United Kingdom's Tesco competes as a successful retailer in Asia and Europe by operating in 70 countries and employing over 500,000 personnel. The retailer's long-term CSR planning function appears prominently in its 2014 annual report:

In May 2013 we set out our new corporate responsibility strategy. We committed to using our scale and capabilities as a global, multi-channel retailer to create greater value for society.

Such planning requires the work of determining a current course of action and forecasting or anticipating a future plan of action. Both present and future activities are involved in the managerial function of planning. It is the "process of making decisions about goals and activities that will be pursued in the future" (Laasch and Conaway 2014, 39). Responsible decisions must be implemented throughout the planning process and developed with long-term organizational strategy to achieve competitive advantage for the organization. Short-term decisions made on a daily basis will evolve from the longer-term strategies. Most responsible manager decisions occur on a day-to-day basis.

We cite another example of the responsible planning function. European-based Schneider Electric is a multinational enterprise headquartered in France. Schneider produces installation components for managing energy and distributing electricity. Because reducing energy costs has become a top priority for retail businesses, Schneider Electric provides a *Sustainability Roadmap* for retails as a practical guide for responsible management in retail environments. The roadmap helps businesses create competitive advantage through responsible management and helps support core business goals. Schneider's Roadmap report cited an amazing statistic concerning energy savings:

> The retail industry has the potential of up to 21% for super-markets and up to 41% for retail stores. Based on the retail industry's $20 billion spent on energy a year, a 15% potential energy reduction represents a $3 billion dollar opportunity to reduce costs.

According to Schneider, a retail store typically operates at a 4 percent profit margin and average energy costs run around 5.5 percent of operating costs. Schneider states that if stores see a 15 percent reduction in energy consumption, their profit margins will increase from 4 to 4.75 percent, which represents an 18.7 percent increase in profits. Schneider's roadmap energy management plan illustrates the responsible manager's function of long-term planning that integrates with the economic bottom line.

Process of Responsible Decisions

The process of making responsible decisions from goals and activities will involve different planning functions of the manager. We adapted Allen's seven responsibilities to show what experience, knowledge, skills, and abilities a responsible manager must have:

- Forecasting future conditions that are framed in terms of responsible management.
- Developing responsible objectives that define the results to be achieved.
- Programming a sequence of steps that will be followed in pursuit of responsible objectives.
- Developing time schedules for carrying out responsible projects.
- Budgeting and allocating resources for future responsible activities.
- Implementing policies and establishing standards for dealing with repetitive problems.
- Developing standardized procedures for responsible work.

We urge one caution about understanding the planning process for a responsible manager. The *cultural* context of decisions determines *how* planning decisions are made. In the United States, for example, decision making generally follows linear thinking that follows John Dewey's seven-step reflective thinking process. Dewey strongly influenced Western culture and its style of making management decisions. The process positively emphasizes effective communication in teams and workgroup decision making. Yet Dewey's process is rational, sequential, and promotes cultural efficiency and effectiveness. The step-by-step linear steps prescribed how to make decisions were as follows:

1. Define the problem.
2. Analyze the problem.
3. Determine criteria for optimal solution.
4. Propose solutions.
5. Evaluate proposed solution.
6. Select a solution.
7. Suggest strategies to implement the solution.

This sequential efficiency was made popular by reducing it to five popular steps and applying it to management decisions. University professors across the United States have taught the process. In contrast, non-Western cultures may not process decisions rationally, sequentially, and efficiently in a way that follows Dewey's steps. Decision making in Asian cultures may be circular, collaborative, and interactive with employees. Decisions are made in such a way that reflects intuition and collective nonlinear thinking. Haley emphasized how the responsible manager's decision-making process must incorporate cultural awareness and cultural sensitivities.

Organizing

The second managerial function of organizing has been defined as the process of "building the structure, systems, and culture needed to implement a strategy" (Laasch and Conaway 2014). When managers perform the organizing function, they create a configuration in which middle managers and employees can responsibly recruit future employees, direct the workforce to perform their jobs responsibly, and facilitate the running of the business. We refer to *organizational structure* as the framework organizations adopt to control how managers and employees conduct their activities and move toward organizational goals. The similar term *organizational architecture* refers to the totality of organizational structure. Managers may consider two primary, but different forms of organizing by developing either a machine-like design or an "organic" design. Today most organizations in industrialized countries have moved beyond the classical, bureaucratic models.

Let's consider a contrast for a moment in terms of responsibility. Picture a long continuum with classical, mechanistic designs on one end and a very different organic design on the other. Organic designs exhibit flexibility and adaptability to change, relatively low levels of complexity, flat structures, and fewer rules and less clear job responsibilities. Organic designs have few formal policies and procedures and more informal communication. Mechanistic designs, on the other end of the continuum, are formal, highly centralized, and complex. Communication follows through the organization's formal channels in a vertical, highly structured hierarchy. Workers in this formal structure may be treated like "cogs in a well-oiled machine" who function efficiently when commanded and controlled. Humane and ethical treatment of employees typically takes low priority for managers who adopt the mechanistic design. To achieve maximum profit, workers may be pushed toward greater performance in less time and, as a result, do not perform according to expectations and are dismissed. Other workers with lower pay are hired to do the work.

Because machine-like management typically centers only on efficiency, effectiveness, and performance, profit is placed as a priority above environmental, social, or community activities and, in essence, circumvents responsibility management. We recommend responsible managers incorporate organic design structures. The less-structured design enables ethical treatment of employees, creates sustainable activities that develop the triple bottom line, and reflects responsible management throughout the structure. Changing organizational design to form an organic structure takes time but will promote responsible management.

Commanding

The third managerial function of commanding was defined by Fayol as assigning specific tasks for employees and developing unity of command. Indeed, responsible managers who command their employees engage in personal supervision and inspire subordinates to work together to achieve organizational goals and objectives. When responsible managers have clear, specific performance goals that engage workers in sustainable activities, the triple-bottom line of the organization exhibits sustainable development. Such managers demonstrate consistent unity of command by enforcing ethical codes for employees, treating new employees equally through the hiring process, conducting transparent and open-performance evaluations, and awarding fair performance-based pay increases.

Besides, those important areas of responsible management take on unique functions in developing unity of command in today's multicultural organizations. Managers often are required to supervise culturally different nationalities who speak English as a second language. That is, managers must communicate effectively with diverse workers. Multicultural employees have unique views that differ than those of their managers. Multicultural employees typically have different religious beliefs or racial perspectives than those of their supervisor. Multicultural employees have distinctive ways of thinking, a mentality which requires cultural understanding by managers.

Today, cultural sensitivity has become an essential element of the commanding function. Human resource managers and other CSR managers must demonstrate effective communication skills and exhibit cultural skills when implementing CSR policies of hiring. Demonstrating cultural sensitivity with the people who work for them is necessary. In the commanding function, responsible managers must set a good example with ethical leadership. Cultural sensitivity ties in closely with effective communication. The responsible manager may need to eliminate colloquialisms and certain types of cultural humor and focus on clear communication. They develop the skill of interacting with workers and asking for responses to confirm clear understanding of the message.

Another aspect of the commanding function directs the responsible manager to select key positions within the organizational structure and assign individuals to handle certain responsible activities. These activities may be delegated to an individual or department, depending on the size of the organization. We offer the following six suggestions for the responsible manager to consider for key positions in an organic, responsible structure:

- Name a single chief sustainability officer (CSO) at the corporate level in large enterprises. Small medium enterprises (SMEs) may ask either line or staff personnel to oversee specific responsible, ethical, and sustainable activities.

- Identify individuals who are responsible for specific sustainable programs, including eco-efficiency or diversity programs, or who direct a sustainability office.
- Direct an individual to oversee a code of ethics or an office of ethical performance. This office will facilitate transparency and dialogue with stakeholders to improve responsible business performance.
- Assign an individual to supervise a community service office responsible for specific groups of people, such as the elderly, disabled, or those who cannot afford medical or dental care. This volunteering process requires strong organization with a concrete series of actions that lead to these social outcomes.
- Identify an individual who will develop anonymous communication tools such as whistleblowing hotlines to support employees or to report discrimination activities against employees.
- Assign a manager to oversee an office that directs the production of the company's annual sustainability reports, which may be included in the annual report.

Coordinating

The fourth managerial function of *coordination* directs all efforts toward a common goal. This function harmonizes or synchronizes workers toward mutually shared organizational objectives and activities, a function which overlaps coordination with each of the other managerial functions. We view commanding and coordinating as closely related because each involves directing employees toward specific goals of the organization. Primarily, the coordinating function involves clear communication with workers about specific ethical guidelines and sustainable goals.

A well-known Latin American movie chain illustrates responsibility in its integrated marketing communication (IMC). *Cinépolis* demonstrates the coordinating function through sustainability activities. The company competitively maintains its status as the largest movie theater chain in Latin America, based on sales and number of patrons, and exists as the fourth largest movie theater chain in the world. *Cinépolis* manages

a social foundation which helps poor and elderly people with eye diseases and who cannot afford a doctor's care. This social activity is related
to the company's core purpose of good eyesight when watching movies and managing healthy personal eye care. Called "Love Gives Birth to
Eyesight" (*Del Amor Nace La Vista*), the campaign effectively coordinates
employees' time with foundation activities among government agencies,
various eye doctors' associations, and medical assistants in the field of eye
care. The entity's organized IMC creates consistent messages with patrons
in the movie theater lobbies and in 30-second "trailers" that appear before
movies, advertisements, and website communication. Stakeholders and
investors read the same message in annual reports. As a result, the movie
chain has branded itself in the media and public as a sustainable company
and the branding has enhanced its economic bottom line.

Controlling

The fifth managerial function of *controlling* means the responsible manager ensures everything is working in accordance with accepted goals.
Laasch and Conaway define controlling as "the process of assessing and
steering business activities and outcomes within a set of predefined goals."

Responsible managers will realize the controlling function for responsible managers is more complex than the mainstream controlling function.
Ethical performance standards, for instance, may be less clear than manufacturing performance standards for a line employee. The controlling
function directs responsible managers to evaluate performance with social
activities and appraise environmental impact of the activities. Responsible managers may often ask, "What is the value created in this activity?"
Performance evaluations answering the question of value may find difficulty in precise, agreed-upon definitions.

Johnson & Johnson enterprise comprises a conglomerate of approximately 250 companies worldwide and totals an estimated $62 billion
in sales (Clark 2011). The company is the world's largest health care
company, ranking number 3 on *Newsweek's* list of Biggest Green Companies. An eco-leader employed by Johnson & Johnson is senior director of
Worldwide Health & Safety, AlIannuzzi, whose responsibilities include
green marketing programs across the conglomerate. Johnson & Johnson

began with sustainability goals in place since the early 1990s. Today, new sustainability goals are written every five years. In 2009 the company built Earthwards, a product stewardship initiative, to help make "their products greener based on lifecycle thinking and to get good, science-based, greener claims to market" (Clark).

The Earthwards initiative illustrates four distinct stages of the controlling function, listed as follows in bold print followed by an example from Johnson & Johnson. Examples are adapted from the Earthwards initiative website.

1. **Define performance standards**: Every new product must deliver on Johnson & Johnson's high standards and achieve regulatory compliance.
2. **Measure performance**: Johnson & Johnson sets a target for measuring impact on world health by stating "All our products that address diseases of the developing world achieve WHO prequalification." The company measures performance with this criterion, "Our TB medicine is included in World Health Organization (WHO) interim policy guidance on the treatment of MDR-TB issued in June 2013."
3. **Assess performance fulfillment**: Johnson & Johnson seeks to identify at least three 10 percent improvements in key footprint categories (Clark 2011).
4. **Take corrective actions**: Green products must undergo a review by a board of internal and external experts (Clark).

An Option Not to Manage Responsibly?

We conclude this chapter with examples of how the journey toward responsible management may experience difficulty along the way. Today's multinational enterprises (MNCs) illustrate how these experiences are hindered because of an occasional lack transparency in accounting practices, missed procedural justice with employees (in areas such as performance appraisals), or infrequent discrimination against employees in their organizations that create public relations nightmare.

Bloomberg News has positively characterized Apple, Inc. as a sustainable enterprise (Krosinky), yet the company has experienced difficulty.

A major supplier for Apple, HonHai Precision Industry Co., in Shenzhen, China, has received in 2012 accusations of excessive use of overtime, publicity of employee suicides, and employment of underage interns. Similarly, the familiar history of Nike's manufacturing plants in Indonesia provides another example, where child labor, low wage per hour issues, and poor factory working conditions were not addressed by Nike. The company managed to turn around its poor corporate image of unsustainability and today it has integrated responsible management functions throughout its organization. Generally, Nike is known as a responsible company.

Finally, Britain's Serious Fraud Office (SFO) opened a formal criminal investigation into accounting errors at Tesco, the UK's largest retailer, and widely known for its sustainable development. *The Guardian* in 2011 wrote that Tesco has established a strong record and is now matching that record "with some even more impressive targets to grow sustainably." Tesco plans to become a zero-carbon business by 2050 without purchasing offsets. Yet accounting errors have created public relations trouble. These examples show how responsible managers still encounter difficulties along the path to sustainable development, but the end of the journey is well worth the responsible manager's performance.

Summary

If you are a manager, this chapter will challenge your thinking about your everyday responsibilities or functions and help you to redefine these functions responsibly. You may have been taught in a business school the traditional business functions of planning, organizing, commanding, coordinating, and controlling. Yet in most organizations these day-to-day operations appear to elevate the economic bottom line above the social or environmental bottom line. We describe each traditional management function and explain how it can be redefined. We then focus on what experience, knowledge, skills, and abilities a responsible manager must have, using global examples. Finally, we address the question whether managers have an option not to manage responsibly and discuss difficulties they may encounter. In the end, the journey is well worth the responsible manager's performance.

Discussion Questions

1. How would you redefine the five traditional managerial functions into responsible management functions?
2. How would you contrast a classical, mechanistic designed organization with an organization operating with an organic design in terms of communication and treatment of workers?
3. Why would the commanding and coordinating functions be considered as the one function of leading?
4. Do managers not have the option to manage responsibly?

References

ABN AMRO Group N.V. 2013. *Annual Report 2013*. Retrieved November 7, 2014. www.abnamro.com/en/images/035_Social_Newsroom/010_Press_releases/2014/Files/ABN_AMRO_publishes_2013_Annual_Report_and_Sustainability_Report.pdf

Allen, L.A. 1981. "Managerial Planning: Back to Basics." *Management Review* 70, no. 4, pp. 15–20.

Burns, T., and G.M. Stalker. 1994. *The Management of Innovation*. Oxford: Oxford University Press.

Carroll, S.J., and D.I. Gillen. 1987. "Are the Classical Management Functions Useful in Describing Managerial work?" *Academy of Management Review* 12, no. 1, pp. 38–51.

Clark, A. 2011. "Johnson & Johnson's Strides Toward Sustainable Healthcare." *Greenbiz.com Blog*. Retrieved November 7, 2014 from www.greenbiz.com/blog/2011/04/15/johnson-johnson-strides-toward-sustainable-healthcare

Dewey, J. 1933. *How We Think: A Restatement of the Relation of Reflective Thinking to the Educative Process*. Vol. 8. H. Fayol. 1949. *General and Industrial Management* (C. Storrs, trans.). London: Pitman and Sons.

Fisher, B.A. 1970. "The Process of Decision Modification in Small Discussion Groups." *Journal of Communication* 20, no. 1, pp. 51–64.

Haley, G.T. 1977. "A Strategic Perspective on Overseas Chinese Networks' Decision Making." *Management Decision* 35, no. 8, pp. 587–94.

Johnson & Johnson. 2010–2014. "Product Stewardship/Earthwards." Retrieved November 19, 2014 from www.jnj.com/caring/citizenship-sustainability/strategic-framework/product-stewardship-earthwards

Krosinsky, C. 2011. "Is Apple the Model of a Sustainable Company?" *Bloomberg News*. Retrieved November 12, 2014 from www.bloomberg.com/news/2012-06-13/is-apple-the-model-of-a-sustainable-company-.html

Laasch, O., and R.N. Conaway. 2014. *Principles of Responsible Management: Global Sustainability, Responsibility, and Ethics.* South-Western College Publishing.

Lindgreen, A., S. Valérie, D. Harness, and M. Hoffmann. 2011. "The Role of 'High Potentials' in Integrating and Implementing Corporate Social Responsibility." *Journal of Business Ethics* 99, no. 1, pp. 73–91. doi:10.1007/s10551-011-1168-3

Lindgreen, A., S. Valérie, and F. Maon. 2009. "Introduction: Corporate Social Responsibility Implementation." *Journal of Business Ethics* 85, pp. 251–56.

Mahoney, T.A., T.H. Jerdee, and S.J. Carroll. 1965. "The Job (s) of Management." *Industrial Relations: A Journal of Economy and Society* 4, no. 2, pp. 97–110.

Manzur, P. December 18, 2012. "Foxconn Workers Say, 'Keep Our Overtime.'" *The Wall Street Journal,* Retrieved December 17, 2012 from http://online.wsj.com/news/articles/SB10001424127887324296604578175040576532024?mod=djkeyword&mg=reno64-wsj#articleTabs=article

Mintzberg, H. 1999. The Nature of Managerial Work. New York: Harper&Row as cited in Meskill, M., S. Mouly, and S. Dakin. 1999. "Managerial Disturbance Handling: A Case–Study Approach." *Journal of Managerial Psychology* 14, no. 6, pp. 443–454.

Schneider Electric Report. 2014. "$3 Billion Opportunity: Energy Management in Retail Operations." Retrieved November 6, 2014 from http://oreo.schneider-electric.com/flipFlop/556458495/files/docs/all.pdf

Tesco and Society Report. 2014. Retrieved November 7, 2014 from www.tescoplc.com/files/pdf/responsibility/2014/tesco_and_society_review_2014.pdf

The Guardian. May 26, 2011. "Tesco—Britain's Biggest Retailer Targets Green Growth." Retrieved November 12, 2014 www.theguardian.com/sustainable-business/britain-biggest-retailer-green-growth

Waller, R.L., and R.N. Conaway. 2011. "Framing and Counterframing the Issue of Corporate Social Responsibility the Communication Strategies of Nikebiz.com." *Journal of Business Communication* 48, no. 1, pp. 83–106.

Wren, D.A., A.G. Bedeian, and J.D. Breeze. 2002. "The Foundations of Henri Fayol's Administrative Theory." *Management Decision* 40, no. 9, pp. 906–18.

CHAPTER 5

Goal Setting and Decision Making

Roberto Quaglia

We live in an era of continuous change and cross-cultural organizations, in which the future seems to be less extrapolation of the past, and companies do not need to simply achieve a temporary competitive advantage, but need to build healthier and sustainable organizations. In order to do so, managers play a crucial role in the decision-making process, and all the people in the organization are crucial to strategy execution, to build a responsible competitiveness. Every manager, in fact, needs to have knowledge of internationally recognized standards/practices to be able to conduct business with responsibility and ethics. Creating a common code of language will enable organizations to deal with the accelerating complexity in a sustainable and responsible way.

Two elements are particularly important to build a sustainable competitive advantage: to set clear goals when motivating people and to have a structured decision-making process.

Clear Goals and People Motivation

The concepts of goals and motivation are strictly related, as stated by Robbins and Judge (2012): "The processes that account for an individual's intensity, direction, and persistence of effort toward attaining a goal." *Intensity* refers to how hard a person tries to do something; *direction* refers to where you focus your efforts; *persistence* refers to how long a person is able to keep doing his effort. Therefore, motivation is "a reason or a set of reasons for acting or behaving in a particular way." Everyday we base our behaviors on our assumptions about motivation, both in professional and private life, for reaching a goal. It is very important, from an ethical perspective, not to set immoral goals, as role modeling—that is, providing a good example for colleagues, employees, and clients—is the first step that leads to responsible management and responsible competitiveness.

According to Hellriegel, Slocum, and Woodman (1992), the most important purposes of goal-setting are:

- Guide and direct behavior
- Provide clarity
- Provide challenges
- Improve performance
- Increase the motivation to achieve
- Increase self-confidence

Furthermore, people who do goal setting properly, suffer less from stress. They are more concentrated and they are more self-confident. In order to build a healthier organization, goal setting should take into consideration the social, the environmental, and the economic perspectives the organization is facing, as well as the employees conditions, the workforce diversity, and the entire competitive scenario.

SMART Model

Leaders shall approach goal setting in a structured and effective way in order to have all the organization aligned: responsible management, in fact, could lead to profitability and sustainable effectiveness. The key challenge here is to make sure leaders can explicit their goals and communicate them effectively. Doran (1981) offers a framework based on five criteria, called SMART, which helps leaders in their goal-setting process:

- S, Specific: Goals should be clear and concrete, not too general.
- M, Measurable: establish criteria for how a goal is to be achieved.

- A, Action-oriented: be proactive in taking actions to reach the goal.
- R, Realistic: strive for attainable goals, considering the resources as well the constraints you have.
- T, Timely: define a reasonable deadline to complete each goal.

Other guidelines are important to remind in setting effective goals: (1) Express goals positively, (2) Be precise in identifying what is to be achieved, (3) Set priorities, (4) Write goals down, (5) Share goals, and (6) Keep goals achievable.

Furthermore, a number of key questions shall be kept in mind while setting goals: What skills do I need to achieve this? What information and knowledge do I need? What resources do I need? What constraints do I have? Is there a better way to do things?

A positive thinking attitude helps leaders not only in goal setting, but also in redefining goals. In the case goals are not met, managers have a big responsibility—toward themselves, the stakeholders, the company—and they should focus on the opportunity to improve either goal setting itself or strategy execution. A sound feedback culture is a key pillar, for allowing organizations to learn and to readjust their goal setting and strategy execution.

Goal-Setting Theory

Locke proposed his Goal-Setting Theory in 1968, according to which specific and difficult goals, together with a good feedback, lead to higher performance, that is, profitability and efficiency. The research of Locke leads to consider goal setting as part of a goal-performance relationship, which is particularly relevant to management practice.

The goal–performance relationship is influenced by four factors:

1. *Possibility to obtain feedback*: People will do better when they get feedback, because it helps identify gaps between what they have done and what they still have to do.
2. *Goal commitment*: It helps people not to lower or abandon the goal.
3. *Self-efficacy*: It is the individual's beliefs that he or she is capable to perform the task.

4. *Task characteristics*: Goal-Setting Theory seems to be more effective when tasks are simple and clear.

A sustainable organization, in fact, should be made by sincere people, looking for responsibility, open to feedback and improvement sessions: only through organization and alignment it is possible to change for better companies.

Management by Objectives

The Management by Objectives (MBO) is a systematic implementation of the Goal-Setting Theory and it is defined by Robbins and Judge (2012) as "a program that encompasses specific goals, set in a participative way, for an explicit time period, with feedback on goal progress." More specifically, MBOs shall have four characteristics:

1. *Goal specificity*: MBO program set objectives that should be tangible, verifiable, and measurable—we add that goals should also be ethic and consider the social environment.
2. *Participative decision-making process*: Managers and employee should jointly choose the goals and agree on how to measure them.
3. *Explicit time-period*: Each objective should have a specific time period in which it is to be completed (i.e., 3, 6, 12 months).
4. *Performance feedback*: MBO seeks to give continuous feedback on progress toward goals; review meetings should be programmed regularly.

Example

At General Electric during Jack Welch's leadership as CEO (1981 to 2001), he implemented MBO motivation techniques called "stretch target," or "stretch goals," which can be defined as goals that cannot be achieved with what is known and how is worked today, as they aim for something that is impossible today. As Welch used to say: "by reaching for what appears to be the impossible, we often actually do the impossible.

And even when we do not quite make it, we inevitably wind up doing much better than we would have done." The concept of stretch goals was applied to improve long-term view, and stimulate breakthrough ideas, relating to profitability as well to sustainability. An example of stretch goal? Let us assume you want your company to grow by 20 percent next year, you will set a stretch goal aiming for 40 percent growth!

A Structured Decision-Making Process

Leaders face the challenge to leverage theory for solving management problems in a more and more complex context. They need to rely on structured and scalable processes, which allow them and their organizations to take decision on a daily basis, considering their sustainability in the long term. Being challenged by dozens of problems every day, managers need to adopt a structured and replicable process, in order to be able to consistently deliver efficiency and sustainability.

Four Steps for Decision Making

Decision-making shall be viewed as any business process, which is scalable and it can be delegated to a number of people within an organization. As such, the process must be structured and replicable. Quaglia and Viotto firmly believed that alignment in the decision-making process throughout the entire organization allows people to act efficiently, not wasting time and efforts, and working toward sustainability. Quaglia and Viotto have leveraged concepts such as "the hypothesis-driven problem solving" and they have developed a four-step approach for decision making (see Figure 5.1):

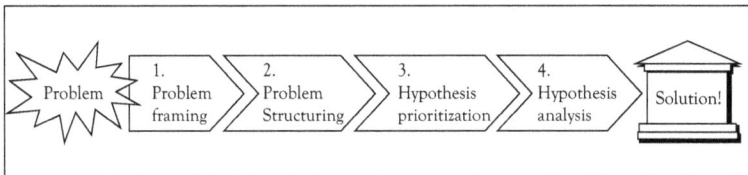

Figure 5.1 Four steps for decision making

1. Problem framing
2. Problem structuring
3. Hypothesis prioritization
4. Hypothesis analysis

1. **Problem framing.** The very first step deals with defining the problem. Problem framing means making sure that criteria of success, constraints, and the key elements of context are clear and explicit. It is a sort of "contract" with key stakeholders, in which we make sure that we do work at solving the right problem. Such process consist of interviews and information exchanges with decision makers and key stakeholders in order to clearly define:

- The statement of the problem
- The context
- The success criteria
- The constraints

Figure 5.2 suggests a framework, which synthetizes the key elements of problem framing. The final objective is to avoid doing a great job at solving either the wrong problem or a marginal aspect of it.

A typical situation:

...when I saw that sales was not on target, I decided to reduce prices, but only later on I realized that the problem was on the quality of the product..., by then my call center was already jammed with complaints.

Let's take a very simple and basic example, in order to let understand the framework proposed.

Example: Mr. and Mrs. Smith want to move to a new house and ask their 21-year-old kid John, currently studying architecture, to let them know in which part of the city he suggests to move. John interviews his parents and frames the problem as in Figure 5.3.

Statement of the problem		
Context	Success criteria	Constraints

Figure 5.2 Framework for problem framing

Statements of the problem		
Mr. and Mrs. Smith want to rent a new house in Paris, for reducing Mr. Smith's travel time to work. Before any action they want to understand in which part of city they should search for the new house.		
Context	Success criteria	Constraints
• The Smiths live and work in Paris, with two children of 21 and 19 years old. • Mrs. Smith is a housewife, Mr. Smith works in town (11th Arrondissement), while the two children are students at Paris Sorbonne (6th Arrondissement). • Mr. Smith's office is in place de la République, 45 min away from home with public transport. • The family income is of 96,000 € net per year. • They do not have a car, as they prefer public transport, taxis, and occasionally car renting for weekends. • They currently live in Paris near Montparnasse and rent for 3,0000 € per month a 100 sqm flat.	• Reduce Mr. Smith's travel time to work to less than 30 min	• Mr. Smith's want to do the home-office travel with Paris "Metro" (the underground) or RER (suburban train) • Having either a garden or a terrace allowing them to have meals outside at summer time • Having at least three bedroom and a double living room • Budget: maximum 3,000 € per month • A supermarket at walking distance

Figure 5.3 Example of problem framing

2. **Problem structuring.** Problem structuring aims at developing possible solution hypothesis, by decomposing the problem with logic trees. We can identify two types of logic trees (see Figure 5.4 for an example):

- *Hypothesis trees*, useful when people already have a strong hypothesis about the solution. The solution hypothesis is decomposed by answering the question "why" and leads to a list of subhypothesis to be tested.
- *Issue trees*, useful when people do not have a strong hypothesis about the solution. In this case, they start from the problem, decompose it in subproblem by answering the question "how or what," until the subproblems are simple enough in order to have a hypothesis of solution; the end game is the same as the hypothesis tree; that is, to arrive to a list of hypothesis to be tested.

The branches of both hypothesis and issue trees are mutually exclusive and collectively exhaustive: in other words, one shall be decomposed into a sublist, which is exhaustive (e.g., How shall I dressed to go to office:

Issue tree (how?)   Hypothesis

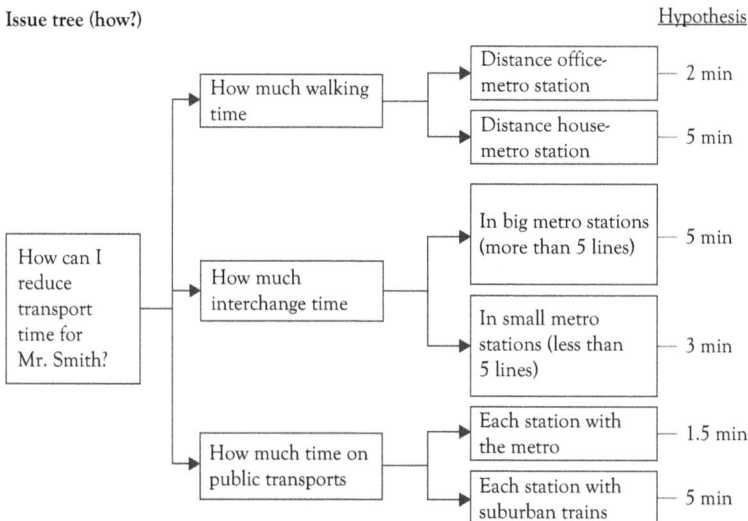

Figure 5.4 Example of issue tree

underwear, socks, shoes, shirt, tie, and suit) and items must be mutually exclusive (e.g., if I mention a suit in my list of clothes, I shall not mention trousers, as they are included in the dress). The latter is a very important condition in order to be able to delegate hypothesis testing and analysis to different people, while avoiding that they walk on each other's feet.

A typical situation: "...the problem is too complex...we began to work on it into subgroups, but in the end everyone worked on the same processes..."

Example of *issue tree* for the Smith family

How can I satisfy Mr. Smith's criteria of success, while meeting Smith's family constraints? How can I decompose home-office transportation time?

1. How much walking time?
2. How much interchange time?
3. How much time on public transports?

John is now ready to develop some macro hypothesis based on the analysis of any Paris underground map (see Figure 5.5).

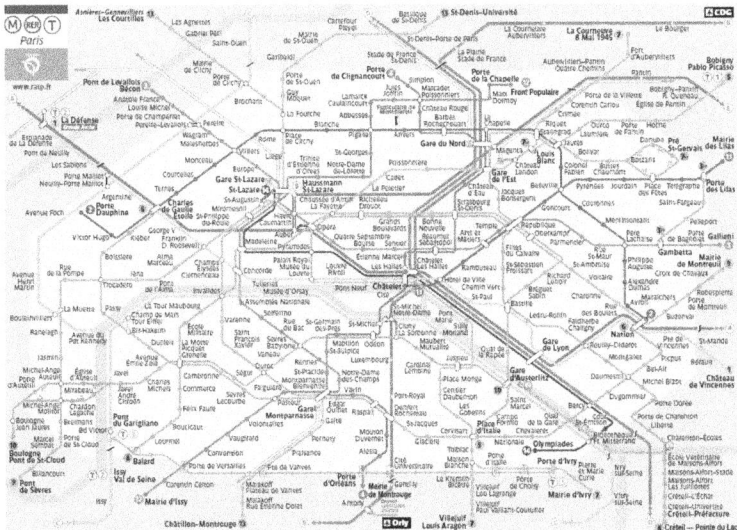

Figure 5.5 Paris metro plan

NB: If John's hypothesis hold true, the new house shall be either:

- Maximum 12 metro stations away from Place de la République if on a direct metro line, or two to six stations closer per each interchange (depending on the size of the interchange station)
- Maximum two stations away from Gare du Nord or Les Halles, using RER B.

For example, he may develop some hypothesis with direct lines 3, 5, 8, 9, 11, or with RER B or one or two line changes on the metro (see Figure 5.6 for an example).

Example of *hypothesis tree* for the Smith family:

How can I satisfy Mr. Smith criteria of success, while meeting Smith's family constraints?

My hypothesis is that they shall move to the suburb of Bois de Vincennes:

1. Because it is 10 stations away with one interchange in a small station, under the following hypothesis:
   a. 2 minutes from office to République metro station
   b. 4.5 minutes to hotel de ville station via Metro #11

Hypothesis tree (why?)

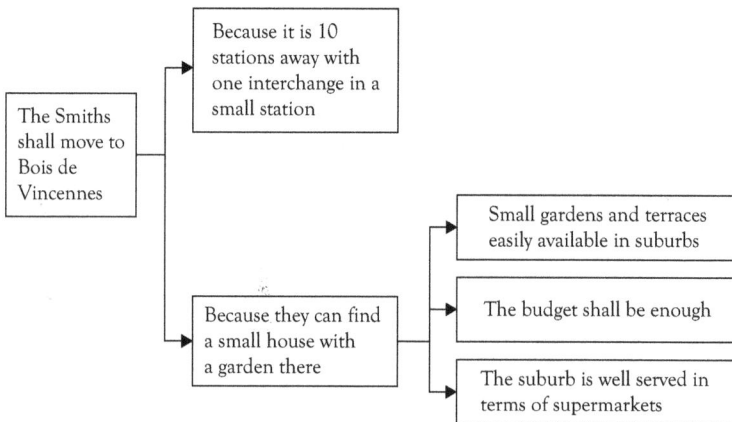

Figure 5.6 Example of hypothesis tree

    c. 3 minutes interchange time

    d. 9 minutes on Line 1 to Porte de Vincennes

    e. 14.5 minutes available for either walking home or continuing on Line 1 for another station or two

2. Because I can find a small house with a garden there, which satisfies our constraints

    a. Small gardens and terraces shall be easily available in suburbs

    b. The budget shall be enough

    c. The suburb is well served in terms of supermarkets

3. Prioritization of hypothesis: Prioritization of hypothesis refers to selecting the hypothesis to be tested before conducting any further analysis. The selection shall satisfy both criteria of success and constraints. The process consists of selecting two prioritization variables, the first based on the most important criteria of success and the second based on a key constraint or variable synthetizing constraints. Hypothesis are, then, summarized on a matrix with four quadrants and axes are placed in order to have enough hypothesis to hold true and solve the problem with best effectiveness and efficiency. All necessary analysis and calculations shall be approximated with appropriate criteria (e.g., orders of magnitude, to the million euro, to the minute, etc.): the objective being to prioritize hypothesis to be tested first, not to analytically test the hypothesis. An 80/20 approach is key in this phase: put 100 percent of the effort on the 20 percent of the analysis, which solves 80 percent of the problem. The top right quadrant of the matrix shall include hypothesis to be tested first (see Figure 5.7 for an example of priority matrix).

A typical situation: "...we do not know where to start, there were thousands of tasks to accomplish, thousands of options from which to choose..."

Example of priority matrix for the Smiths family; the case of the Smiths *issue tree*.

Having completed his issue tree, John defines his prioritization variables. As per the criteria of success, he chooses the number of minutes of travel time. As per the constraints, he defines an index, which takes into consideration the probability to comply with all constraints. More specifically, John's index sets a probability of compliance per constraint and

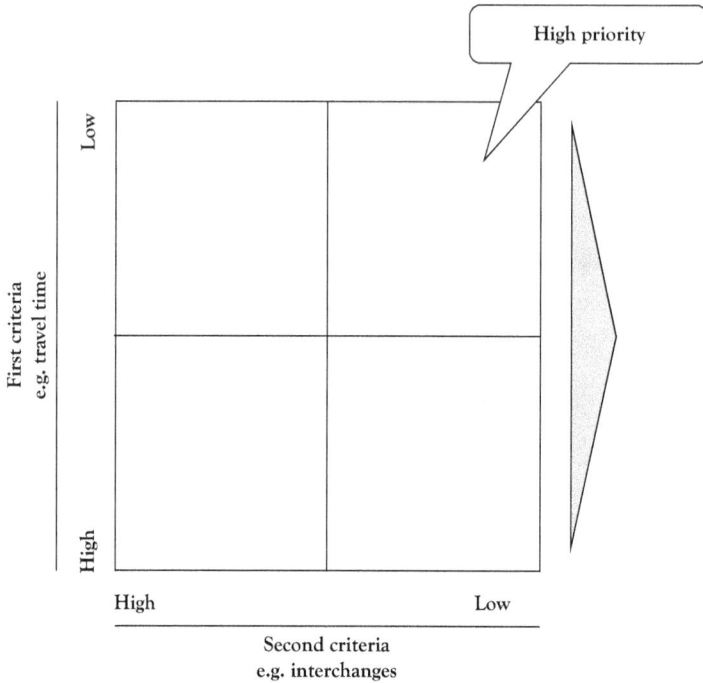

Figure 5.7 Example of priority matrix

then he calculates a weighted average. See Figure 5.8 for prioritization matrix:

4. *Hypothesis analysis*: Hypothesis analysis deals with testing the higher priority hypothesis, doing all necessary analysis for either retaining the hypothesis or rejecting it. Each hypothesis shall be decomposed in terms of open elements to be tested, the underlying hypothesis, rationale, analysis needed, and sources (see Figure 5.9). This leads to a work plan with all analysis needed, which can be easily delegated to team members.

A typical situation: "…we knew exactly which we had to do, but with no plan, we got lost…"

Example of hypothesis analysis for the Smith family.

One of the hypothesis selected by John is to look for a new house near Parmentier; concerning this hypothesis, he has a number of open issues to analyze; one of them is the availability of houses with terraces or small gardens within the assigned budget.

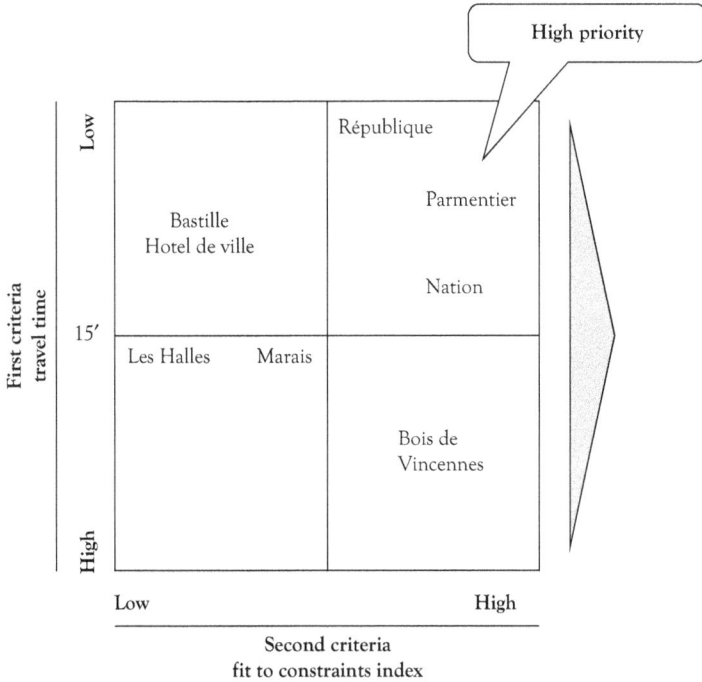

Figure 5.8 *Example of priority matrix for the Smith family*

Open element	Hypothesis	Rationale to support hypothesis	Information/ analysis needed	Sources of information
Parmentier: is it possible to rent a 3 bedroom apartment with a terrace or garden for 3,000 € per month?	Yes, with a terrace, as gardens are rarely available in town center	A friend from school just moved there in an apartment with similar characteristics	Check real estate websites selecting the following criteria: price 3,000 € Max, 3 bedrooms, metro Parmentier	http://www.seloger.com/ http://www.pap.fr/ http://www.logic-immo.com/ http://www.parisattitude.com/ http://www.avendrealouer.fr/ http://www.Airbnb.com/

Figure 5.9 *Framework for hypothesis analysis*

In conclusion, we can argue that a proper goal setting and a structured decision-making process are very much interconnected. A proper goal setting is key for aligning an organization toward the same objectives. Structured decision making allows an organization to work at achieving objectives, with an efficient process, avoiding useless analysis or worst addressing the wrong problem. All this is surrounded by a background of efficiency, sustainability, and ethics, three characteristics of corporate social responsibility in modern companies.

Summary

Being challenged by dozens of problems everyday, managers need to adopt a structured and replicable process in taking their decisions, in order to be able to deliver efficiency and sustainability, as well as to conduct business with responsibility and ethics. Two elements are keys: setting clear goals when motivating people and having a structured decision-making process.

To set clear goals allows people to be aligned and motivated; the SMART model suggests to have Specific, Measurable, Action-oriented, Realistic, and Timely goals. A sustainable organization should have people open to feedback and improvements.

Quaglia and Viotto believed that alignment in the decision-making process allows people to act efficiently; they have developed a four-step approach:

1. *Problem framing*: Defining what is the problem, the context, the success criteria, the constraints.
2. *Problem structuring*: Decomposing the problem through *hypothesis trees* or *issue trees,* answering the question "how or what" until the subproblems are simple enough.
3. *Hypothesis prioritization*: Selecting the hypothesis to be tested before conduct any further analysis.
4. *Hypothesis analysis*: Testing the higher priority hypothesis, doing all necessary analysis for retaining the hypothesis or rejecting it. This leads to a work plan which activities can be delegated to team members.

Discussion Questions

1. Which are the five criteria of the SMART framework for setting clear goals?
2. Which are the four steps of the problem-solving approach?
3. How it is possible to prioritize hypothesis creating a four quadrants matrix? Please explain.

References

Doran, G.T. 1981. "There's a S.M.A.R.T. Way to Write Management's Goals and Objectives." *Management Review. Ama Forum* 70, no. 11, pp. 35–36.

Hellriegel, D., J.W. Slocum, Jr., and R.W. Woodman. 1992. *Organizational Behavior.* 6th ed. St. Paul: West Publishing Company.

Locke, E.A. 1968. "The Effects of Knowledge of Results, Feedback in Relation to Standards, and Goals on Reaction Time Performance." *American Journal of Psychology* 81, no. 4, pp. 566–74.

Locke, E.A., and J.F. Bryan. 1968. "Goal-Setting as a Determinant of the Effect of Knowledge of Score on Performance." *American Journal of Psychology* 81, no. 3, pp. 398–407.

Locke, E.A., N. Cartledge, and J. Koeppel. 1968. "The Motivational Effects of Knowledge of Results: A Goal-Setting Phenomenon?" *Psychological Bulletin* 70, no. 6p1, pp. 474–85.

Quest, F. 1996. *Discovery Focus on Your Values and Accomplish Your Goals.* Salt Lake City, UT: Franklin Quest Co.

Robbins, S.P., and T.A. Judge. 2012. *Organizational Behaviour.* Pearson: The Oxford Dictionary.

Welch, J. April 24, 1991. *Speech to the General Electric Annual Meeting.* Charlottesville, VA.

CHAPTER 6

Corporate Responsibility as the Avoidance of Relevant Inconsistencies*

Andreas Suchanek

Introduction

The topic of corporate responsibility has gained prominence in the academic field of business administration over the last 25 years or so. Globalization and digitalization have unlocked new opportunities for firms to enter new markets, exploit economies of scale and scope, and drive costs down. However, this development has also created new challenges due to the lack of a stable regulatory framework. Regulations are necessary for maintaining fair competition which fosters societally desirable value creation instead of unsustainable and short-term oriented races to the bottom at the expense of third parties, and sometimes also the competitors themselves.

These changes in the conditions of doing business have led to an increase of societal inquiries about the role of business. Companies have had to react to the public desire to understand not only how they create monetary value for their shareholders but also, how they contribute to society.

The academic discussion about an appropriate understanding of corporate responsibility has generated deeper insight into how corporations are embedded in society and the possible organizational and

---

* I'm grateful for an anonymous reviewer's comments.

institutional consequences thereof. Nonetheless, there is still no widely accepted systematic approach to corporate responsibility.[1]

In this chapter, some basic ideas of such a systematic approach are outlined. *Corporate responsibility is defined as the fulfillment of legitimate trust expectations*, or the avoidance of relevant inconsistencies between these expectations and the corporation's actions, respectively. The core idea is to accentuate an intimate connection between responsibility and trust, where trust is understood as a necessary prerequisite for both successful cooperation and value creation. At the same time, trust is seen as an asset for a firm; untrustworthy companies rarely find partners who readily engage with them in cooperative ventures. In cases where partners have no choice but to cooperate with such companies, these partners will reduce their cooperative efforts to a minimum in order to protect themselves from any (potential) negative consequences of the venture, thereby increasing transaction costs and the probability for failed cooperation.

This idea of corporate responsibility as maintenance of a corporation's (generalized) trustworthiness will be systematically developed and then the practical implementation thereof will briefly be discussed. But first, some background considerations are briefly outlined.

Fundamentals

As a starting point for understanding corporations' societal role, the following definition is helpful: "Society is a cooperative venture for mutual advantage" (Rawls 2005, 4). This understanding of society refers to values such as solidarity, justice, and sustainability, which form the basis of successful cooperation as well as to everyday forms of cooperation. Everyday

---

[1] This is not only a challenge for academia, it also poses problems for corporations: in an increasingly complex world, there is a need for unambiguous criteria for "good" behavior. With regard to practice, this problem is partially solved by initiatives like the UN Global Compact, the International Standard ISO 26000, or the Global Reporting Initiative. However, these practical orientations leave open a conceptual definition of corporate responsibility and therefore also a tangible and generally shared heuristical yardstick for a reasonable corporate behavior that encompasses normative values and principles as well as considering the empirical conditions that constrain this behavior.

cooperative ventures include the purchase of bread from the baker, or an insurance policy from an insurance salesman, or offering a complex software solution for a company, and so on. Furthermore, it may refer to the daily duties of a judge, engineer, journalist, or business ethicist, who all contribute to social cooperation for mutual advantage, but also get something in return for doing so. Likewise, this view of society incorporates the larger goals of tackling social problems like climate change, poverty, or corruption as effectively as possible.

Hence, social cooperation for mutual advantage is based on contributions of practically all members of a society as well as supporting structures, rules, and other conditions, of which markets and organizations are obviously an important part.

The guiding ethical principle, which can serve as a normative orientation for everyday life as well as a realization of corporate responsibility, is a reformulated and an advanced version of the Golden Rule. Classically, the Golden Rule is a moral norm that can be found all over the world and expresses the logic of reciprocity. A typical version is "do not do unto others what you do not want them to do unto you." Here, this norm is adapted to business life and supplemented by the idea that socially desirable actions need supporting (institutional) structures. Thus, the Golden Rule that is used here runs: "*Invest in the conditions of social cooperation for mutual advantage*" (Suchanek 2007).

With regard to corporate responsibility, this norm demands from economic agents to establish and maintain conditions which are conducive to future value creation processes. Special emphasis will be given to a specific asset that is often neglected: trust.

Another conceptual tool which aids in understanding and implementing corporate responsibility is the so-called practical syllogism which guides decision makers to relate (1) normative statements in terms of their goals and values to (2) empirical assertions about the realities of the situation which may hinder the realization of goals and values with the aim of deriving (3) enlightened yet realistic expectations or judgments about one's own actions or those of others.

The practical syllogism (cf. Figure 6.1) is a helpful conceptual tool because it connects values and empirical conditions, thereby offering insights not only about the feasibility of goals, but also guiding our

| (1) Goals/values: fairness, respect, well-being, profit |
| (2) Reality: constraints, conflicts, empirical conditions |
| (3) Expectations/judgments about possible actions |

Figure 6.1 The practical syllogism

thinking as to which investment should be undertaken in order to change reality such that we are one step closer to our goals and values. Therefore, it can be seen as an important complement to the aforementioned Golden Rule, especially with regard to clarifying the (empirical) conditions that one should build up or maintain, if they are conducive for social cooperation, or avoid, if they are detrimental. Equally, it helps to specify trust expectations, thereby changing the concept trust from an abstract idealized notion to a realistic assessment in concrete situations, taking into account that managers as well as a firm's stakeholders are self-interested (in different ways) and face manifold constraints in everyday life like budget or time constraints, competition, regulations, and many more.

Value Creation as the Societal Task of Corporations and the Making of Profits

In the past few decades, the prevailing viewpoint in many companies was that their contribution to society is tantamount to increasing shareholder value. Given a set of specific conditions, it can be argued that shareholder value—appropriately defined—can indeed serve as a kind of focal point. However, as many crises and scandals have shown, the sole focus on shareholder value may not provide companies and managers with a sound orientation because all causes that do not traceable contribute to this value are in danger of being neglected.

Hence, in this conceptualization of corporate responsibility, shareholder value is seen as a criterion that can be used to check whether a firm is on track. It is not, however, a goal. Taking a single, concrete measure as a goal to be reached is always connected with the risk that other dimensions of value, that are not directly recognized as contributing to this goal, may be neglected.

Therefore, the societal goal (or task) of corporations is defined here in a more abstract way, namely as value creation in a way that can find societal consent, thus maintaining the corporation's license to operate. This idea will be further specified subsequently by defining that a corporation must not violate legitimate[2] trust expectations. To put it positively: the social responsibility of corporations is to organize structures which coordinate and motivate individual contributions for a "social cooperation for a mutual advantage." An important requirement of this social responsibility—which will be of particular relevance throughout this text—is to organize these processes in ways that ensure that the legitimate interests of third parties are taken into consideration.[3]

The importance of preventing harm has to be emphasized given that corporations must act under the constraint of competition. This constraint puts them under pressure to cut costs, amongst others, and this pressure can lead to an externalization of costs. Therefore, one might ask whether competition is socially desirable.[4]

The answer is positive due to the fact that competition forces corporations, firstly, to orientate themselves toward the preferences of others—as these necessary cooperation partners will otherwise migrate to competitors—and, secondly, to use their resources efficiently. This includes the continuous search for new opportunities to improve on both the fulfillment of cooperation partners' wishes and the efficiency of their use of resources.[5] However, in order to have this kind of socially desirable competition, two conditions have to be met: (1) corporations have to act responsibly, and (2) appropriate rules need to exist which create a "level playing field" and make sure that corporations that act responsibly are not disadvantaged by other irresponsible firms.

---

[2] This addition is important since not all trust expectations are legitimate. Trust exists also in criminal organizations.

[3] Otherwise, one could legitimize organizations such as the Mafia which engages in value creation processes as well, but does so at the expense of third parties. This definition of social responsibility principally demands that every member of society can consent to the existence of corporations as long as no fundamental rights and legitimate interests are violated.

[4] It is a basic task of business ethics (or in a more practical view: of business management) to give consideration to the ambivalence of competition.

[5] See in this regard Homann 2014.

The second condition is a necessary, but not a sufficient one. Rules always leave some leeway for action—and actually should do so in order to have the socially desired freedom which is not only an elementary source of individual well-being but also very important for innovation (Hayek 2013).

This is why the first aforementioned condition, using one's freedom responsibly, is equally important. Rules cannot be so detailed and specific that they exclude the possibility of any irresponsible behavior. That is to say, there are various ways to make profits.

The ordinary way of doing business is to create value by some form of cooperation for mutual advantage: collaboration, trade, division of labor, and so on. This is typically a win-win-scenario where one can assume—given appropriate rules—that the rights of third parties are respected. However, there are also many situations where a corporation can make profit by withholding important information, delivering low quality, exploiting suppliers or employees, breaching rules, corruption, and many more ways, which are irresponsible (cf. Figure 6.2).

The fundamental question is then: why should a firm abstain from making these profits?

From a normative perspective, the answer is obvious: because it is irresponsible. But this is an abstract thought which does not gain real power of persuasion in practical life as long as one has to fear being systematically disadvantaged by acting responsibly (not making profits may give competitors an edge).

Thus, the systematic answer is that not making irresponsible profits, however can be an *investment*. The next section aims at explaining this form of investments.

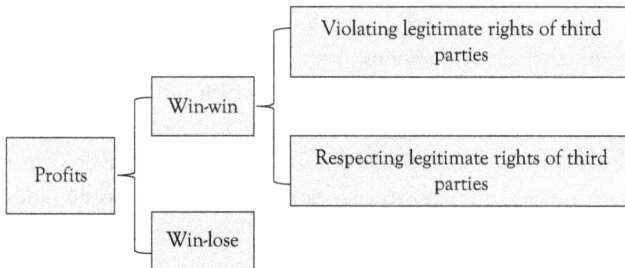

Figure 6.2 Ways to make profits

Corporate Responsibility as an Investment in Trust (Worthiness)

Investments can take many forms. In the business world, investments are typically thought of in the form of monetary costs, either directly when an asset is purchased or indirectly when an opportunity that seems to be profitable in the short-term is nonetheless abstained from given the expectation that the engagement may be associated with long-term costs. Either way, an investment involves the use of one's freedom and depends on one's intentions as well as capabilities. Often, investing is tantamount to doing something[6] one is not keen on doing now, but which one expects to appreciate later, thereby avoiding future regretfulness.[7]

This personal character of investments becomes especially relevant in the context of corporate responsibility as the asset that is built up through these investments is trustworthiness. The following graphic captures this structure (cf. Figure 6.3).

In order to create value, any corporation needs partners: customers, employees, suppliers, investors, and others. Since these partners, as a rule, cannot be forced to cooperate, they have to be won for cooperation by offering them *quid pro quos* for their contribution to value creation: goods

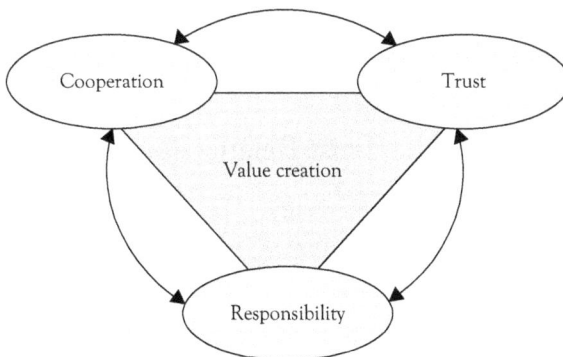

Figure 6.3 Investments in trust as responsible behavior

---

[6] Or sometimes: abstaining from doing something or even accepting situations without trying to circumvent them.

[7] It is a characteristic feature of irresponsible behavior that it goes hand in hand with the *creation of (ethical) risks*, that is, the potential that one will regret this behavior later.

and services for customers, salaries and attractive careers for employees, timely payments to suppliers, high returns and low risks for investors, and so on. These offers are *promises*, done via not only commercials and job postings, but also annual reports, presentations, and in many other ways.

However, promises alone are ineffective unless an essential condition is fulfilled: the respective partners have to *trust* that these promises will be kept. It is important to recognize these promises only function if trust expectations are positive.

Trust expectations do not rely exclusively on the trustworthiness of the corporation. Expectations, particularly in economic relationships, are safeguarded by the conditions and institutions that frame the situation, such as legal regulations, contractual arrangements, or other incentive specifications. Thus, trust itself transforms into "system-trust" (cf. Luhmann 2009, 59 ff.).

Nonetheless, as mentioned earlier, rules alone cannot safeguard that the trustor's vulnerability cannot be exploited. As trustees, corporations have a number of alternative courses of action; they have freedom. What is more, under the conditions of globalization and digitalization, options for action vary more than ever before. This increases the uncertainty (of behavior) and hence, creates a greater demand for trust.[8] This explains why the topic of trust in corporations—parallel to CSR—has gained in prominence in recent years.

The Trust Relationship

In order to understand what is meant by "investing in trust,"[9] it is helpful to look at the basic aspects of a trust relationship (cf. Figure 6.4).

The trust relationship, in its most simple form, is defined as a relationship between a trustor and a trustee. The trustor has the option to enter the relationship, thereby putting trust in the trustee and making himself dependent on the trustee's actions. This dependence is critical since it goes

---

[8] See in this regard Giddens 2008.

[9] Or more specifically: investing in trustworthiness, since in the following we will deal mainly with the corporation as a trustee.

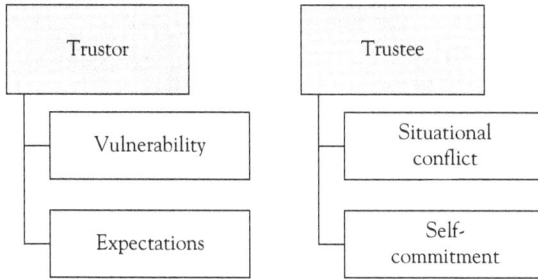

Figure 6.4 The trust relationship

hand in hand with the possibility of being harmed by the trustee's action, that is, the trustor is *vulnerable*. As a consequence, they will only enter the relationship if they *expect* the trustee to be sufficiently trustworthy.

The trustee, on the other hand, often faces situations where he can profit at the expense of the trustor—for example, by concealing defects of a good, externalizing costs, or exploiting the vulnerability in another way which amounts to the *quid pro quo* arrangement not coming to fruition as promised. Since the trustor will have some knowledge about this situational conflict and will only enter the relationship when they expect the trustee to be trustworthy—that is, they expect not to be exploited— the trustee has an incentive to *signal their self-commitment* by, in turn, constraining himself to a course of action that meets the trustor's expectations. The three basic forms of self-commitment are:

Keeping one's promises
Adhering to rules
Respecting moral values

ad (1): *Promises* are, by definition, made voluntarily and are thus an expression of the intention of the person who has given it. In the business context, promises are regularly made to win others for cooperation. The essential problem of every promise is its credibility, which depends on the trustworthiness of the one who gives the promise. However, the promise's credibility can be strengthened or weakened depending on the incentives and constraints that define the particular situation.

ad (2): *Rules* are the strongest means of supporting reliability since they are usually backed by third parties, mainly governments. Rules prescribe or forbid specific actions thereby helping to create expectations about others' behavior. In order to be credible, they need to be monitored and, in case of a breach, to be sanctioned. In the context of corporate responsibility, it is the attitude toward (adhering to) rules that has to be emphasized.

ad (3): *Values* are, on the one hand, mere words. On the other hand, they can become a very powerful tool to enable and support cooperation by defining criteria of action that are generally accepted because they help to realize common interests. Typical values are *respect, fairness, or sustainability*.[10] As values which refer to individuals' actions, they express an attitude as to *how* actions are performed. Actors who have a reputation for acting according to their values are trustworthy because they respect the trustors' interests.

Relevant Inconsistencies

(Corporate) Responsibility means fulfilling legitimate trust expectations, that is, keeping one's promises and adhering to rules and values. In everyday life, however, it is often not possible to do all that; one has to compromise due to empirical conditions.[11] A plane's delay, a misunderstanding, or generally: unforeseen contingencies (Kreps 1990) may result in promises not being able to be kept or even in rules not being precisely observed. Another obvious reason as to why not all promises are kept or contracts and rules are broken, is rooted in human nature, that is, in the manifold trade-offs and conflicts of everyday life. Usually, trustors adjust their expectations accordingly. One knows that business persons, as everyone else, are not saints. Nonetheless, one has to rely on others and the more one can do that, the better the chances to realize gains from cooperation become.

---

[10] Respect, fairness, and sustainability are interpreted here as values which refer to individuals' attitude about how to act with regard to others.
[11] This is why the practical syllogism (see above Section 2) becomes important as an analytical tool in business ethics.

And this is also the reason why the disappointment of trust expectations may become costly for the trustee's reputation. This happens to be the case, when *inconsistencies* between trustor's expectations and trustee's actions become *relevant*, that is, when legitimate claims are deliberately neglected, positions of power are exploited or costs are externalized (etc.) at the expense of the trustor or third parties. These are examples of actions that are typically seen as irresponsible behavior.

Accordingly, in practice, corporate responsibility can be defined as the avoidance of relevant inconsistencies. More concretely, corporations have to build up the respective *competencies* which are: identification, diagnosis, prevention, and therapy of relevant inconsistencies.

> In order to *identify* relevant inconsistencies, one may use the aforementioned focal points—keeping promises, adhering to rules, and respecting moral values—and do a so called consistency check: does the firm keep the promises that were given to its stakeholders (and if not, are there acceptable explanations for that)? Does the firm adhere to the relevant rules and regulations (compliance)? Are the values appropriately respected and lived in day-to-day operations?
>
> It is not enough to identify potential or actual relevant inconsistencies; one should also be able to *diagnose* the causes. Examples of root causes of the violation of legitimate trust expectations might be: a lack of candor, appropriate guidelines or value orientation in the corporate culture, a firm management that provides negative role models, insufficient risk management systems, a lack of critical feedback, high pressure of competition without strong, reliable rules or, finally, managerial myopia.
>
> The more it is known about possible root causes, the better one can *prevent* them. The most important aspect from an ethical perspective is to recruit suitable managers and employees, offer them qualified training and support and give them positive and negative feedback regarding to what extent their actions are in line with the values, rules, and promises.
>
> Even if various precautionary measures are taken to prevent relevant inconsistencies, they may happen. In this case, *how* a firm reacts is critically important since this is one of the most significant signals

regarding its trustworthiness. If a firm is able to demonstrate in such a situation that its values are a guide for its behavior, that it doesn't try to escape reality and that it cares for those trustors whose rights and interests have been violated, chances are that it can regain its trustworthiness and sometimes even strengthen it.

Concluding Remark

The basic idea of corporate responsibility, as it is presented here, is rather simple: honor legitimate trust expectations. In real life, however, it is often quite demanding to follow this ideal due to the complexity of situational conditions. Therefore, it is all the more important that not only firms, but also their stakeholders, invest in the ability of moral discernment as the most elementary prerequisite for sustainable social cooperation for mutual advantage.

Chapter Summary

Even after decades of intensive discussion, the concept of corporate responsibility is still not yet clarified. In this article, it will be argued that corporate responsibility can be defined as the (corporate) intention and capability to honor legitimate trust expectations, which are a prerequisite for sustainable social cooperation for mutual advantage. This definition will then be operationalized as prevention of relevant inconsistencies, which are defined as a violation of legitimate trust expectations. In the course of that, specific models, such as the practical syllogism, are presented in order to provide tools that aim at helping to develop the ability of moral discernment, what is crucial for trust and sustainable value creation.

Discussion Questions

1. What are examples of investments in trust, or in conditions of social cooperation for mutual advantage?
2. What are examples of *relevant* inconsistencies? And why are they relevant for the trustee?

3. Think of examples of inconsistencies between the actions of a corporation (trustee) and the expectations of a trustor and try to deploy the models of the practical syllogism and the trust relationship in order to identify if it is a relevant one.

4. Apart from the recruitment of suitable managers and employees, what are conducive conditions in a corporation enabling a prevention of relevant inconsistencies?

References

Giddens, A. 2008. *The Consequences of Modernity*. Cambridge: Polity Press.

Hayek, F.A. 2013. *The Constitution of Liberty: The Definitive Edition*. Vol. 17. London: Routledge.

Homann, K. 2014. *Sollen und Können*. Tübingen: Mohr Siebeck.

Kreps, D.M. 1990. "Corporate Culture and Economic Theory." *Perspectives on Positive Political Economy* 90, pp. 109–10.

Luhmann, N. 2009. *Vertrauen*. 4th ed. Stuttgart: Lucius and Lucius.

Rawls, J. 2005. *A Theory of Justice*. Cambridge, Mass.

Suchanek, A. 2007. Ökonomische Ethik. 2nd ed. Tübingen: Mohr Siebeck.

CHAPTER 7

Ethics in Business

Positive and Negative Practices Exploring the *"Rocket Singh"* Parable

Kemi Ogunyemi

Introduction

Organizations are made up of human beings and human beings' deliberate actions always have a moral character (Melé 2012), especially once examined with due regard to their purpose and the circumstances. A lot of harm has been caused to victims all over the world because of low ethical standards of people running businesses (Ogunyemi 2014b) and there is a lot to be done in order to minimize such occurrences in future. This chapter endeavors to unbundle ethical and unethical practices within organizations according to the ways they occur in different organizational functions and within different relationships into which the organization enters. It is deliberately written in very simple language in order to lend itself more easily to teaching and learning purposes of the book. The suggested texts for further reading go deeper into the issues and can be taken up by interested parties who wish to do a more in-depth study of the issues.

Many ethical duties are specified for professions in some code. Codes for business professionals may be largely unwritten but this does not diminish their validity and importance. Our perspective will embrace many stakeholders, starting with the ones who are internal to the organization and spend most of their day within its premises. These are the people who form the immediate community of the organization and need to find in it a space for growing and flourishing. Having at the back of our minds, Melé's framework as a reference point for stakeholder relationships could be a rewarding approach to teasing out the corresponding ethical duties of the parties (Melé 2014). The framework espouses five organizational levels for human quality treatment within organizations. These levels, in ascending order, are maltreatment, indifference, justice, care, and development (Melé 2014). Using Melé's own definitions, we set out the content of the levels below:

> Maltreatment (Level 1): Blatant injustice through abuse of power or mistreatment. Indifference (Level 2): Disrespectful treatment through lack of recognition of people's personhood and concern. Justice (Level 3): Respect toward persons and their rights. Care (Level 4): Concern for people's legitimate interests and support for them in resolving their problems. Development (Level 5): Willingness for favoring people's human flourishing. (Melé 2014, 463)

Melé was talking about the way employees treat their employers. In this chapter, without being exhaustive, we will expand the analogy to include the way any of the stakeholders in the firm treats the others. The lower levels can be subsumed into the higher ones for our purposes, that is, justice presupposes that there is no mistreatment or indifference, while care and development come after and include justice. This chapter concentrates on justice and care considerations.

In order to be ethical, the employer and any other party to mutual relationships must at the very least be at the level of justice, since injustice is by definition unethical. When extended to other stakeholder relationships, we expect justice between shareholders and managers; shareholders and employees; employees and customers; customers and the company (represented by the managers); the company and suppliers; employers (the managers) and the employees. We will in fact begin our ethical analysis with the last group mentioned. In order to stay within the limits of the topic, we will not focus on the stakeholders external to the firm except insofar as it helps us to analyze the ethical duties of the stakeholders within the firm.

Our illustrations for the discourse will be taken mostly from the film, *Rocket Singh* used as a parable in this context of a discussion of ethics in a business organization. The ethical issues are those common to most organizations and thus, even though the film brings them together as a specific case study set in a distinct cultural framework, the lessons learnt are generalizable. It is not necessary (though it could be a useful precourse exercise when teaching) for the reader to have watched the film—a brief description of the story follows: Harpreet Singh Bedi, a young idealistic graduate from a humble religious background applies to work as a salesman in At Your Service Computers (AYS). He very soon experiences a clash of values—this organization believes in bribery, in delaying payments to creditors, in trampling over others to climb up, in denigrating colleagues, and in exploiting customers. At AYS, profitability is the most important thing and must be attained by any means including unethical practices. Naively, Harpreet antagonizes a client to whom he refuses to give a bribe. This makes him *persona non grata* in AYS. He is ostracized and is obviously on his way back into the job market and most likely without a good reference. Bitter and rebelling against his circumstances, Harpreet builds a new organization, Rocket Sales Corporation (RSC) using AYS's resources and list of dead clients and recruiting other disgruntled AYS employees to partner with him. RSC grows very fast because of its ethical strategies and policies and soon begins to compete with AYS. It is however discovered by Puri, the CEO of AYS, and he takes over RSC and gets rid of Harpreet and his team. Subsequently, Puri discovers that it is impossible to work with customers who are used to the high ethical standards and customer-centric style of RSC. After asking Harpreet to come back to work with AYS-RSC and getting a refusal, he returns RSC to Harpreet and his partners.

The next segment following this introduction will include a general discussion of underlying principles behind ethical and unethical practices and this will be followed by segments focusing on different aspects of the firm's relationships. An attempt will then be made to discuss loyalty expectations in general before adding on a conclusion to the chapter. Finally, some study questions are proposed and further reading recommended.

Ethical Responsibilities in Justice and Related Breaches

One of the first ethical responsibilities of a person, whether human or corporate (a collection of humans) is to do no harm. This is classically framed as "Good is to be pursued and evil is to be avoided" (Melé 2012). As humans, we are responsible for our actions and should specifically respect the rights of other human beings to a meaningful existence. Another duty is that of promise keeping. This duty derives both from the duty of truthfulness which demands that we should not harm others by inducing a false belief in them and from the duties of fairness and justice which demand that we give others their due. The demands of justice and fairness are expressed differently by different peoples and cultures, for example through the golden rule of not doing to others what one would not like to be done to oneself, but they are universally accepted. Limiting ourselves to these basic ideas, we can further translate them into brief but hopefully succinct practical implications governing the relationships within the ambit of business, as follows.

For the employer and the employee, the ethical responsibilities of employer and employee one to the other include the following:

- Fulfillment of the explicit terms of the contract: Pay, work hours, and so on.
- Fulfillment of the implicit terms of the contract: This includes respect for the other person, fairness considerations, and so on.
- Loyalty: It includes the above two and extends to duties of care especially when the same is expected from the other party

Toward the client, the organization (both employers and employees) owes a duty to fulfill the terms of the contract; duties not to mislead or deceive through advertising or through product descriptions; and the ordinary duties of care as well. With regard to suppliers and other creditors, the organization must pay their bills or interest on loans and should not take undue risks with the money, for example, moneys borrowed for one purpose should not be used for another much riskier purpose.

What about duties toward the society? According to Babalola (2012, 39) "A firm cannot ignore the problems of the environment in which it operates." At the very least, they must refrain from harming society and the environment. In this way they exhibit justice toward present and future generations. One of the ways not to harm the society is to obey the laws of the country. Another is to avoid and fight corruption, which destroys the very fabric of fair play and trust in society by unfairly appropriating what is meant for the common good to one person's use. Yet another is to respect the personal time of their employees—this is not only fairness to the employees but also fairness to society since the families of the employees and the rest of society also have a stake in the way the employee uses time outside work. They refrain from harming the environment by minimizing their impact and doing what they can to repair any collateral harm caused by their business activities. Once they have fulfilled their primary duties toward shareholders, employees, customers, and suppliers, they should also consider their positive responsibilities as good citizens to give something back to the society from where their resources come and as good neighbors to help others in need. This could be done with a small proportion of the profits they make.

Finally, shareholders are the residual owners of the organization. They have duties of justice to all the other stakeholders—even though the managers represent them in the actual carrying out of these duties, they are not excused from the duty to ensure that they are indeed carried out. They, especially those appointed as directors, have the task of oversight. They therefore can be held at the very least morally responsible for the actions of their agents. Directors can be held legally responsible to an extent. They in turn are owed duties of justice by the management team of the company and all who are paid to work there—a duty to earn, for the shareholders, optimal returns on their investment. In the following paragraphs, the ethical duties of justice and care are discussed in a bit more detail.

Employment Contracts and Internal Customers—The Human Resource Function

It has been pointed out that organizations need to behave ethically toward their employees as well as toward their clients (Paine and Dimanche 1996). As human beings and therefore of much more value than mere nonhuman assets, employees deserve respect and fairness from the very moment of recruitment to that of disengagement. Unethical recruitment practices could include discrimination, nepotism, and exploitative salary negotiation. Since employers control the future of their employees to a great extent and very often are not on an equal level with them, it is easy to see that they can greatly harm their employees even very early in the relationship. We see this illustrated in Rocket Singh where the employee is desperate for a job and is afraid of being let go without a reference. Harpreet accepted a job where there was no medical cover, no gratuity, and presumably no training plan included in his employment package. It was clear that this was the standard practice of the organization. While one could argue that the employees did agree to such contracts and cannot claim they were cheated strictly speaking, it is also accepted expectations that employers, in order to be ethical, should pay a living wage which ordinarily includes the standard benefits that normally accrue in employment relationships. Further on in the course of employment, there could occur other injustices such as neglect to provide a safe work environment, lack of access to fair hearing, denial of due promotion, unfair reward systems, and the fostering of unhealthy competition among employees. Where the employer sets out to be as exploitative as possible, it would not be surprising if employees paid back in the same coin. Similarly, it would not be surprising that an employer who treats employees exploitatively may act the same way toward customers, suppliers, and even shareholders.

There is a lot of disrespectful treatment of people in AYS, in contrast with the RSC approach. The instances observable in AYS exemplify what should not occur in a business where there is a concern for ethics—employees are abused and called names (Mishra is called cup-plate and Harpreet is called a donkey and a zero); targets are set arbitrarily and without regard to what is realistically achievable (and doubled when commissions are decreased); positive values are scorned; women are stereotyped (Koena is told that her role is to attract customers because of being a pretty woman); there is no attention to ensuring meaningful work or job fit (Koena is kept back as a receptionist though there is a vacancy for office manager for which she is qualified and in fact she does all the work), and so on.

Appraisal and reward systems can also lend themselves to unfair and unethical practices—AYS employees are unhappy because they feel unfairly compensated while the managers go for trips abroad. In addition, employers need to provide adequate training and development so that the employee can deliver on the job. Disengagement can also at times be laced with a lack of ethics—either because it is unfair in itself or because the manner of its implementation is unfair.

The burden is not totally one-sided. Employees are hands-on agents who could do considerable damage to the interests of their principals, whether we take these to be their employers or, ultimately, the sharehold-ers. They very often know more about the business than their managers and they control the latter's access to information and access to custom-ers. They also have ethical responsibilities toward their employers. Once the person is employed, the terms of employment bind both parties in justice. Most of the issues behind this are rooted in conflict of interest situations. While it is not possible to predict and avoid all situations in which one's interest may conflict with the organization's, it is important when in a position of trust to be able to put the company's interest above personal interest. The possible unethical actions range from very sim-ple ones to things which could cost the employer a lot. For example, an employee's unethical actions in this line could include using the workday for personal interests. Illustration: Early in the film, we discover that Giri spends his time at the office watching porn and sleeping. Watching porn is bad for him personally, but even if he had spent the time doing some-thing that would ordinarily be good for his personal flourishing, he would still be wrong to steal from the time he owes to the office. This is time he should have dedicated to working toward achieving the company's objectives. Later, he and the other RSC staff use office time to advance RSC work rather than AYS's. Employees, within reason, may need to do something personal during the time they spend in the office, for example, check makeup. This should usually be done with the approval, explicit or implicit, of the organization and should not be taken advantage of immoderately, for example, checking makeup should not take an hour. Despite Harpreet's good intentions and his plan to return the equivalent of all he used from AYS with the prevailing bank interest rate, his actions at that point are not justifiable. He should have resigned, and the others also, and competed with AYS from outside the organization rather than from within.

In practice, there are many other unethical practices that employees may engage in, at times because they feel unfairly dealt with by the organization. For example, employees may exploit loopholes in their companies' policies to their advantage; swindle customers of commissions and fringe benefits; abuse sick leave policies; deliberately underperform to slow down the rate of work; sabotage other employees' efforts and dampen morale; connive with other employees or with customers and external bodies to defraud the organization, the list is long.

Sales and Marketing: In the Course of Business

Firms provide products or services to their clients (at other times referred to as customers). Front office people and marketers deal directly with customers and are the face of the company. Ethical issues that arise in the course of sales and marketing are numerous and the ways to deal with them have been given a lot of attention in research (Dubinsky and Loken 1989). The company should be truthful with its customers and should deliver value in return for the money paid. Failure to deliver at the time agreed by the parties detracts from the value of the service or product and is unfair to the customer. RSC and AYS diverge totally here. AYS lies to its customers, overbills them for minor repairs, and fixes exorbitant prices not founded on value addition. RSC makes a solid value proposition and backs it up with on-time delivery and after sales service tailored to the convenience of the customer. One operates on a win-lose paradigm with the customer and the other on a win-win paradigm. A company that operates on a win-win paradigm with the consumers it serves is likely to be more profitable in the long run because of its ethics (Paine and Dimanche 1996). For how long would AYS be able to take advantage of the ignorance of the customer or of its unethical way of influencing the contracts it gets? It is easy to see which is the more sustainable approach to business as well as the more ethical.

Operations: On-Time Service Delivery

Both product and services have to be delivered on time and in good condition and at the level of quality contracted for. This consideration is only one of the many that people in operations research and management must have in mind in order to fulfill their moral responsibilities and carry out their work in an ethical manner (Kunsch, Kavathatzopoulos, and Rauschmayer 2009). The possibility of achieving this is to a great extent dependent on the nonclient-facing staff, at times referred to as backoffice people. Because AYS has no interest in the good of the customer, there is little or no concern to ensure that the operations work in such a way as to deliver value to the customer. Thus, artificial bottlenecks are created—Giri does not lift a finger to do his job when he should—and service after sales is close to nil. In contrast, RSC is customer-centric and determined to fulfill any promise made to the customer. The company values truthfulness and reliability so much that rather than compromising their integrity, they are ready to take a step which at first glance would reduce their profits—they decide to take on a new team member, Mishra. In the long run, this means greater capacity and therefore more business for the growing firm. Companies must be careful to ensure that their operations are configured in such a way as to make it easier for employees to be ethical. At times, the duty laid on the company extends to sensitivity to the practice of ethics along its supply chain (Maloni and Brown 2006).

Financing; Suppliers' Money and Loyalty

The firm very often uses other people's money to do business—creditors' money or suppliers' money. It is only just that such providers of capital be given a fair return for the risk they have taken. To ensure this and minimize negative outcomes that could possibly result from conflicting interests, governance structures may need to be placed within organizations (Mintz 2005). It could prove easier to achieve this in the case of equity and debt financing than in that of working capital financing provided by suppliers. Yet, suppliers' money is also used in the business. Harpreet gets his initial supplies on credit and he pays back and also repays the trust placed in him by this supplier, going beyond the demands of justice, by remaining loyal to him even when they get overwhelmed with orders and have to go slowly. In doing this, Harpreet also goes beyond the demands of justice, reciprocating care with care. In justice, the supplier did not owe it to Harpreet to give him goods on credit when there was no prior relationship between them. In justice, Harpreet does not have to stick with the same supplier. However, because of the loyalty exhibited by the supplier, Harpreet saw clearly that he had to reciprocate with loyalty. This can be contrasted with the case of Nitin who, with the help of Koena was avoiding all calls from creditors whom AYS did not want to pay.

Citizens Within a Society—Social Responsibility and Sustainability

The social responsibility of companies has been given a lot of importance in recent times (Maloni and Brown 2006). The laws laid down within a given society are usually vehicles for ensuring the common good of the whole society. People belonging to the society are obliged to obey the law and not free-ride on the others who do so. They thereby contribute to the common good from which they also benefit. This is the case, for example, with laws governing tax and intellectual property. Companies, as well as individuals, would be unethical if they did not pay their tax or if they violated others' intellectual property rights. The latter is illustrated again in the case of AYS where the company usually did not buy the original software but ordinarily used pirated versions—Giri was amazed that Harpreet would consider reducing possible profit by using original software.

A company's ethical stand on corruption also impacts the society either positively or negatively. When companies give bribes in order to get contracts, as AYS does, a number of things go wrong. The competition for getting the job is unfair and others in the same industry are being cheated of a fair selection process. The client company may not be getting the best person for the job since the selection criteria have been disregarded in order to favor the person who gave the bribe. The person collecting the bribe is further corrupted since he becomes a worse person and finds it easier to continue putting his personal interest ahead of his company's. The cost to the client company is higher since usually the bribe has been built into the cost of the project—AYS in fact connives with the client's agent to fix the price as well as the "commission" to the client's officer. In addition, the onus on the company to do the job well is lowered. Apart from lowering of trust in the system when it is manifestly unfair which often then leads to higher costs of transactions, the price of the questionable payment is ultimately transferred to third parties. These could be either the customers of the client company who have to pay more for the products or services so that the client company can be profitable, or other beneficiaries who get substandard products or services and have to compensate at their own cost. Thus, for example, a patient may have to pay more for drugs because the physician has been bribed to prescribe expensive ones, or a business center may charge its customers more because of what it has cost to put in the computers bought from an AYS, or people may have to pay more get water because the boreholes sunk by a contractor have been badly done and do not supply as much as they should.

Businesses that seek to practice ethics also demonstrate good citizenship by, after being fair to other stakeholders, contributing some small proportion of their earnings to the betterment of the environment in which they operate. If such a company is in fact guilty of having compromised the sustainability of the Earth and its peoples through its (the company's) activities, then it needs to quite literally clean up its act as well as engage in other acts that demonstrate corporate social responsibility (CSR). A number of organizations find this a difficult undertaking (D'Amato, Henderson, and Florence 2009). Some of these are of the opinion that they are only responsible to the shareholders and do not have to spend shareholders' money in favor of the society. Regardless of their views on other forms of CSR, host communities expect companies to take responsibility for the impact of their economic activities on the societies and their immediate environment especially when these impact social and environmental sustainability negatively. CSR is only one of the ways to do this. As explained by van Marrewijk and Werre (2003), sustainability is "an organization's activities, typically considered voluntary, that demonstrate the inclusion of social and environmental concerns in business operations and in interactions with stakeholders." Every organization must find its own ways to work toward sustaining the society and the environment that all benefit from. To do otherwise may in fact mean free-riding on the common goods created and sustained by other individual and corporate citizens.

Shareholders—Corporate Governance and Fair Returns

Long term, the company owes returns to the people who own equity in it (Mintz 2005). Unethical practices in managing the organization may make its profitability unsustainable. This is bad for the owners. In addition, it may cause the destruction of the organization's value instead of its enhancement, as has happened, for example, in the well-known cases of companies going down due to scandals—Enron, News of the World, and so on. Agency relationships have an inbuilt disparity. Corporate governance mechanisms help to reduce the chances of having the company's management get away with unethically diverting the company's resources. However, fostering trust and actively demanding integrity in the way the company is run may go a long way to resolve issues that are beyond the reach of even the most elaborate governance structures. If the company's owners are manifestly not interested in ensuring that the company's business is run based on ethical standards, they can hardly be surprised if the people they put in charge of their business lack ethical values in relating with them as well. AYS shareholders appear to have been complacent regarding Puri's way of doing business. Now they have a problem because Puri's methods are not sustainable in long term. The RSC client that he tried to bribe told him that his old method of doing business no longer worked. The customers want to deal only with companies that have integrity and are therefore reliable partners in the quest to create and share value.

Fairness to Competitors?

Does an organization owe any ethical duty toward its competition? The idea of fairness to competition is a very old one (Knight 1923) and it applies very strictly in some spheres of life, for example, in sports. In relation to business, it could be summed up into the duty of maintaining a level playing ground. Ultimately, this is important for the good of the customers now and in the future. For example, if an organization cheats or bribes in order to get a contract, the fairness of the transaction is compromised. This same scenario of cheating may be compared to students cheating in an exam or to corporate sabotage. The level of trust and the cost of business are affected as already discussed in the section talking about society's vulnerability. Also, there is the more general duty not to harm one's fellow human beings. Going back to the *Rocket Singh* story, Nitin pushing the salesman of another company out of a lift also fits here. Deliberately setting out to harm another is always wrong.

Organizational Culture and the Strategic Imperative

The whole organization ultimately suffers when unethical practices become rife. Structures such as ethics codes (de Colle and Gonella 2002) and ethics committees (Svensson, Wood, and Callaghan 2010; Svensson and Wood 2011) help to sustain an ethical culture by making it easier for employees and the whole organization to avoid unethical practices (Wimbush and Shepard 1994). If bribery becomes the norm in the company, there is no way to control the misappropriation of monies by employers since bribes and other questionable payments such as facilitation and extortion are not receipted. In AYS, Nitin has been using fraudulent documentation to siphon funds, and Mishra is able to threaten him with this when he got to know about RSC. Once an organization lacks the structures, policies, and processes that encourage ethical behavior, rationalizations abound and the employees more easily engage in unethical behavior (Gellerman 2003) and can also raise the legal and reputational risks for the company.

Also, a negative culture of disrespect reinforces itself and quickly spreads to others in the organization. Employees of AYS are treated badly and they in turn treat one another badly. However, RSC's employees are treated well and they are able to work well and respectfully together and achieve a positive synergy that constantly enhances their operations and service delivery. This impacts the organization positively and makes it more profitable. The fact that the same set of people experiences both cultures and reacts negatively and positively respectively shows the power of establishing a culture in which people flourish. Ultimately, this may be put down to the people strategy and profit orientation behind the top management of AYS (to see people are tools and in order to grow and attain profit by all means, one must step on others) and of RSC (people as fellow human beings with whom one partners in order to achieve the company's goal of ethical profit). The ethical strategy of a company there-fore goes a long way to influence its culture and its propensity to gather either people who impact the organization positively or those who destroy it with regard to ethics. It should not be left to chance.

Loyalty Expectations and the Element of Care

When an organization expects loyalty from employees, customers, and suppliers, it must take cognizance of the fact that loyalty is likely to be expected by these parties as well. It would be difficult to demand loyalty from an employee who is treated badly (Ogunyemi 2014a). Thus, for example, Puri had no reason to expect his employees to be loyal to AYS. He also could not expect loyalty from customers once they had discovered a superior value offering or the way AYS had been cheating them.

In addition, when the relationships are maintained within the strict bounds of justice, then the loyalty expectations of the employer from the other parties should also remain within the same bounds (Ogunyemi 2014c). Otherwise it would be unfair and unethical to demand loyalty that goes beyond justice to care from an employee, a supplier, or a customer while refusing to reciprocate. Care is an element of loyalty insofar as loyalty often means going beyond what is due in strict justice to demon-strate an affective attachment to the other (Ogunyemi 2014c), as would happen, for example, when an employer shows interest in the well-being of the employee beyond the contractual terms or when an employee is sometimes expected to attend to customer demands that may be out of the ordinary or be made outside of working hours. We thus include in this category of care the duties that do not necessarily derive from justice, but which are good for an ethical organization to undertake because they contribute to human flourishing.

Harmful Consequences

Apart from the obvious harm done in the different instances of unethical practices discussed earlier, we also have the perhaps more insidious harm done to each person involved in unethical actions. Much the same way as being ethical builds up the person and his or her character, acting unethically destroys the person. Nitin is a good example. He was like Harpreet at first, but gradually the company's unethical culture changed him into a different kind of person, far from the person he would actually want to be. He became a person who was selfish and likely to in turn destroy other persons—witness his coaching of Harpreet into unethical practices and the dubious means he uses to obtain information when in the client's premises. Eventually he is happier when he rediscovers his lost self.

When there are unethical practices in business, the harm done could be considered with a threefold perspective. First, the people themselves who carry out these practices are harmed. They become worse people, humanly speaking, people who do not have regard for other human beings. In a way, they become less human themselves because they disregard people who share their nature. Perhaps this is why, when we find evil in its most blatant form, we often describe it as inhuman. Next, the other party to the transaction in question is harmed. This could be the employer who is cheated, the employee who is victimized, the supplier who does not get his money back, the people living in the environment that gets polluted, the shareholder whose returns are depleted, or the customer who gets an inferior product delivered late, the person who is personally "corrupted" when he or she is persuaded into bad behavior. Finally, third parties are harmed—the shareholders behind the cheated employer, the family and other dependents of the unhappy and stressed employee, the dependants of the cheated supplier, the descendants of the people who get sick from the pollution, the shareholder whose company gets a bad reputation or loses customers due to bad management, or the people who buy from the customer something made with the inferior product, the general public who have to travel on bad roads and suffer car damage to their vehicles because of contracts poorly executed by those who paid bribes to get them, and so on.

At times however, harm could result without one wanting it. Tests of the validity of such a situation include establishing whether there is a proportionate cause, whether other alternatives are available, and whether the protagonist has done all that is possible to mitigate the resulting harm.

Conclusion

The world of business is a very complex one, with relationships crisscrossing in many directions. Yet, it is possible to very quickly see the negative impact of unethical practices and the positive impact of ethical ones. The practice of ethics in business devolves on all the different stakeholders in different ways. In this chapter, the spotlight has been on those internal to the organization (employers—management—and employees) and those more intimately linked to it (customers, suppliers, creditors, shareholders, and society). If these stakeholders act with mutual respect and establish mutual loyalty based on good ethical practices, the effect is likely to be greater profitability for the shareholders and greater value to customers, a healthier and more rewarding work environment for employees, fairer competition and happier suppliers, and enhanced benefits to the society. It is our hope that businesses will see that they have a great role to play in ensuring an order of justice and fairness in the world and make as much effort to increase their ethical competence as well as their technical competence in their effort to strategize and compete effectively in a global and changing world.

Summary

As happens in their daily lives, the people working in organizations make many decisions that have moral implications; hence one could say the day-to-day running of any organization is fought with ethical and unethical practices. These practices impact the various stakeholders in the company—both internal and external, and affect the company's brand, reputation, profitability, and overall moral character. This chapter, using illustrations from a film, "Rocket Singh: Salesman of the Year," examines the ethics of organizational practices and how they affect the stakeholders—employers, employees, shareholders, customers, suppliers or creditors, and the society at large. The lesson learnt is that ethical practices constitute a competitive advantage and can lead to both employee and customer loyalty and to sustainable profitability. Organizations that exploit their employees, suppliers, and customers, may actually end up suffering for it, not the least because they are vulnerable to new entrants who are able to offer the market the same or higher quality with integrity and reliability.

Discussion Questions

1. Find two companies in which ethical and unethical practices appear to have been pervasive. Give reasons for identifying these companies as such.
2. Trace the trail of harm caused by a single unethical practice in order to show all the parties affected, no matter how remote.
3. Explain in what ways one person's unethical practice within an organization may lead others to act likewise.
4. Share any personal experiences you have of an organization's lack of justice with its employees, customers, or suppliers.
5. Watch Rocket Singh and identify practices that characterize Melé's five organizational levels with regard to the different stakeholders, especially the employees. Which level is dominant in AYS? Which level should they aspire next and how could they move there? Which level is dominant in RSC? Which level should they aspire next and how could they move there?
6. Discuss the positive impact of ethical practices within organizations.

References

Babalola, Y. 2012. "The Impact of Corporate Social Responsibility on Firms' Profitability in Nigeria." *European Journal of Economics, Finance and Administrative Sciences* 45, no. 1, p. 41. Retrieved from www.eurojournals. com/EJEFAS.htm

D'Amato, A., S. Henderson, and S. Florence. 2009. *Corporate Social Responsibility andSustainable Business: A Guide to Leadership Tasks and Functions*, 1. North Carolina: CCL Press.

De Colle, S., and C. Gonella. 2002. "The Social and Ethical Alchemy: An Integrative Approach to Social and Ethical Accountability." *Business Ethics: A European Review* 11, no. 1, pp. 86–96.

Dubinsky, A.J., and B. Loken. 1989. "Analyzing Ethical Decision Making in Marketing." *Journal of Business Research* 19, no. 2, pp. 83–107.

Gellerman, S.W. 2003. "Why 'Good' Managers Make Bad Ethical Choices." *Harvard Business Review on Corporate Ethics*, pp. 49–66.

Knight, F.H. 1923. "The Ethics of Competition." *The Quarterly Journal of Economics* 37, no. 4, pp. 579–624.

Kunsch, P.L., I. Kavathatzopoulos, and F. Rauschmayer. 2009. "Modelling Complex Ethical Decision Problems with Operations Research." *Omega* 37, pp. 1100–8.

Maloni, M.J., and M.E. Brown. 2006. "Corporate Social Responsibility in the Supply Chain: An Application in the Food Industry." *Journal of Business Ethics* 68, no. 1, pp. 35–52.

Melé, D. 2012. *Management Ethics: Placing Ethics at the Core of Good Management.* New York: Palgrave MacMillan.

Melé, D. 2014. "Human Quality Treatment: Five Organisational Levels." *Journal of Business Ethics* 120, no. 4, pp. 457–71.

Mintz, S.M. 2005. "Corporate Governance in an International Context: Legal Systems, Financing Patterns and Cultural Variables." *Corporate Governance: An International Review* 13, no. 5, pp. 582–97.

Ogunyemi, K. 2014a. "Justice, Care and Benevolence as Spurs to Employee Loyalty." *International Journal of Academic Research in Management* 3, no. 2, pp. 110–25.

Ogunyemi, K. 2014b. "Teaching Ethics across the Management Curriculum." In *Teaching Ethics across the Management Curriculum: A Handbook for International Faculty,* ed. K. Ogunyemi. New York: Business Expert Press.

Ogunyemi, K. 2014c. "Employer Loyalty—The Need for Reciprocity." *Philosophy of Management* 13, no. 3, pp. 21–32.

Paine, D., and F. Dimanche. 1996. "Toward a Code of Conduct for the Tourism Industry: An Ethics Model." *Journal of Business Ethics* 15, no. 9, pp. 997–1007.

Svensson, G., G. Wood, and M. Callaghan. 2010. "A Corporate Model of Sustainable Business Practices: An Ethical Perspective." *Journal of World Business* 45, no. 4, pp. 336–45.

Svensson, G., and G. Wood. 2011. "A Conceptual Framework of Corporate Business Ethics across Organisations Structures, Processes and Performance." *The Learning Organisation* 18, no. 1, pp. 21–35.

van Marrewijk, M., and M. Were. 2003. "Multiple Levels of Corporate Sustainability." *Journal of Business Ethics* 44, nos. 2–3, pp. 107–19.

Wimbush, J.C., and J.M. Shepard. 1994. "Toward an Understanding of Ethical Climate: Its Relationship to Ethical Behavior and Supervisory Influence." *Journal of Business Ethics* 13, no. 8, pp. 637–47.

Additional Readings

Elegido, J.M. 1996. *Fundamentals of Business Ethics: A Developing Country Perspective*. Ibadan: Spectrum.

Elegido, J.M. 2013. "Does It Make Sense to Be a Loyal Employee?" *Journal of Business Ethics* 116, no. 6, pp. 495–511.

Melé, D. 2001. "Loyalty in Business: Subversive Doctrine or Real Need?" *Business Ethics Quarterly* 11, no. 1, pp. 11–26.

Melé, D. 2009. *Business Ethics in Action: Seeking Human Excellence in Organisations*. London: Palgrave Macmillan.

Ogunyemi, K. 2013. *Responsible Management—Understanding Human Nature, Ethics and Sustainability*. New York: Business Expert Press.

Paine, L.S. 2003. "Managing for Organisational Integrity." *Harvard Business Review on Corporate Ethics*, pp. 85–112.

Schwartz, M.S. 2002. "A Code of Ethics for Corporate Code of Ethics." *Journal of Business Ethics* 41, nos. 1–2, pp. 27–43.

CHAPTER 8

Promoting Responsible and Sustainable Organizations Through Ethics Committees

Consuelo García-de-la-Torre and Gloria Camacho Ruelas

Introduction

Stakeholders' pressures regarding greater support of human rights and natural environment, more dialogue, more disclosure about the impacts of firms' operations, among others (Logsdon and Wood 2005) have made that firms integrate economic, social, and environmental issues in their business strategies as an attempt of doing business in a more human, ethical, and sustainable manner (Kärna, Hansen, and Justin 2003; van Marrewijk 2003).

Firms try to include concepts such as corporate social responsibility (CSR), triple bottom line (TBL), and sustainability in their business ethics (Svensson, Wood, and Callaghan 2010) through the implementation of ethics programs (Jose and Thibodeaux 1999). Ethics programs are instruments that allow firms to implement CSR (Brenner 1992) as a promoter of corporate sustainability (Portales and García-de-la-Torre 2012): "The ongoing commitment to ethical behavior contributes positively to economic development as well as to the improvement of quality of life of all" (Francis and Armstrong 2003, 377). Hence, the purpose of this chapter is to present the role of ethics committees, which are part of firms' ethics programs, to promote responsible and sustainable firms.

This chapter is structured as follows: First, we present an introduction. Second, we present a general definition of ethics programs, and then we focus specifically on ethics committees, their functions, and their importance within a firm. In addition, we present examples for an international perspective. Finally, we offer a summary of the chapter and some exercises that will enrich the student development of knowledge in this topic.

Definition

An ethics program is understood as "the values, policies, and activities which impact the propriety of organizational behaviors" (Brenner 1992, 393). It defines corporate values and it is useful to spread them within the organization. In addition, it provides guidelines for stakeholder engagement (de Colle and Gonella 2002). Ethics programs have different components (Table 8.1).

One of the main explicit components is the code of ethics. It is "a document which states the fundamental ethical principles or values that a company is committed to follow in the relationships with all its stakeholders" (de Colle and Gonella 2002, 87). Once that a firm has developed its code of ethics, it is important to develop formal mechanisms, such as ethics committees, that promotes ethical decisions within organizations (Murphy 1988).

For this chapter, we focus our attention on ethics committees, because they are formal mechanisms that are helpful to develop trust within a firm

Table 8.1 Ethics program components

Component	Elements
Explicit components	Codes of ethics Policy manuals Employee training materials Employee orientation programs Ethics seminars Ethics committees
Implicit components	Corporate culture Incentive systems Promotion policies Performance measurement systems

(Svensson, Wood, and Callaghan 2010) and to manage and to monitor ethical business practices (Svensson and Wood 2011). An ethic committee is defined as "a committee with responsibility for implementation and monitoring a code of conduct or ethical matters in general" (Moore, Slack, and Gibbon 2009, 177).

According to Weber (1981, 50 as cited in Wood 2002), the primary functions of the ethics committee are: the discussion of ethical issues; the clarification of ethics code and its review; the communication of this code to all firm's employees; the investigation of its violations; the development of rewards and sanctions; and, the communication of the committee's actions to the board of directors. In general, there is a summary of the main ethics committees' functions: the development of ethical policies, the evaluation of employees' behaviors, and the analysis of policy violations (Weaver, Klebe, and Cochran 1999).

Exhibit 8.1 Example: Mex Group*

Mex group is a Mexican group located in the northeast of the country. It is formed by four divisions. It guides its operations on the following values: respect for the individual, integrity, responsibility, team spirit, innovation, and client focus.

Mex group has a code of ethics, which is formed by its values, ethical standards (e.g., stakeholders' relationships, handling of information, protection of assets, and conflicts of interests), and administration, such as sanctions and violations. Ethics committees deal with issues related to business ethics.

In this group there is a central ethics committee, and then each division has its own ethics committee. The main functions of these ethics committees are: to encourage the understanding and the implementation of code of ethics, to solve complaints, and to promote group's values within the whole organization.

*For confidentiality reasons, the name of the group has been changed.

Source: Elaborated by authors with information from Camacho (2012).

On the one hand, the main benefits of the presence of code of ethics and ethics committees in companies are: collaboration of employees and a higher morale of them; prevention of fraud and bribery; prevention of loss of stakeholders' confidence; better access to financial capital (de Colle and Gonella 2002); reduction of staff turnover; and enhancement of firm's reputation (Painter-Morland 2006).

On the other hand, the main risks that face ethics committees are the delegation of ethical issues by top managers and the lack of involvement from employees (Bonn and Fisher 2005). Top managers and senior managers are role models for employees in companies, thus, their support is fundamental for the implementation of the code of ethics and ethics programs (Benson 1989; Bonn and Fisher 2005; Schwartz, Dunfee, and Kline 2005).

International Perspective

Accountability has become important for firms. On the one hand, organizations have developed internal approaches that allow them to develop policies, structures, and processes in order to follow firms' values in their relationships with their stakeholders. On the other hand, firms can follow an external approach to communicate the impacts of their operations to external stakeholders through reports (de Colle and Gonella 2002). For example, sustainability reports include ethics, environmental, social issues, and financial aspects (Kolk 2006).

There are some firms that have developed a deep ethical commitment as it is shown in their structures, procedures, and policies. For example, HP has developed ethical standards that guide stakeholders' relationships. In addition, there is an audit committee that guides the activities of ethics and compliance officer, and ethics and compliance committee. Besides these explicit components of ethics programs, there are training programs in ethical issues for employees (HP 2012).

In Japan, top managers are committed to business ethics. Thus, firms have made efforts to institutionalize their ethical practices. They have developed codes of conducts and also formal mechanisms to improve transparency, such as ethics training programs, communications, and committees. For example, Japanese firms have included outside directors, or experts in business ethics as members of their ethics committees (Demise 2005).

In summary, multinationals have started to focus on board supervision and developing and structuring sustainability responsibilities, such as compliance, ethics, and verification (Kolk 2006).

Conclusions

There is a need for responsible business practice. Firms need to "nurture the skills and passions and talent for everyone in their organization to deliver real and positive change" (Rake and Grayson 2009, 398) in order to move firms toward sustainability. Ethics committees are formal mechanisms that will be helpful to create awareness for ethics and sustainability issues within organizations.

Exercise

In the next paragraphs we describe the simulation game titled "Game Cubes," which is helpful for our students to understand development and social capital problems (see Table 8.2). This simulation game is about injustices in the distribution of wealth and living conditions, and how the development process can solve this problem by relying on social capital and human capital.

Table 8.2 Simulation game elements

Elements of simulation game	Description
Objective	To build the greater number of paper cubes with the best quality in the time indicated by the facilitator.
Audience	From 18 years of age, students, adults.
Number of players	Minimum 10 players are needed. If there are more than 25 players, it is recommended that there are 1 or 2 facilitators who observe and take notes about players' reactions.
Duration	Game: From 30 to 60 minutes depending of the size and characteristics of the audience. Evaluation: From 30 to 60 minutes depending of the desired level of analysis.

Source: www.iadb.org/es/noticias/articulos,2360.html

Participants need to be divided into groups of four people maximum (each representing a country or socioeconomic status of a country, but are not told anything about it) and each group is assigned a number, table, and chairs for work (you can also work on the floor if it is carpeted).

Each group receives at the start of the game an envelope with materials to manufacture the paper cubes. For this simulation you need envelopes, sheets of papers, scissors, rulers, glue or tape. In the next table, there is an example of the distribution of materials for six groups formed by four participants.

In Table 8.3, we can see that Group 1 has superabundant resources, Group 2 is self-sufficient, Group 3 lacks of scissors which are a basic tool to build the paper cubes. Groups 4, 5, and 6 are in shortage. Groups 5 and 6 lack of a fundamental raw material. They need to think how to solve this situation. For example, one possible solution for them is to associate with others, negotiate, borrow, ask for donations, remove from anywhere other inputs to the cubes, and so on.

Envelopes must be prepared earlier by the facilitator in order to introduce large disparities in the distribution of resources: For example, there are sufficient papers for everyone, but it is poorly distributed. There are scarcity of some supplies such as rules and pencils, but they are replaceable.

After each group receives its envelope, the facilitator indicates the amount of fame time. Then, after surprise and complains, all groups start to work. The facilitator must keep absolute silence address all questions

Table 8.3 Simulation game materials

Groups (countries)	Paper sheets	Rules and pencils	Scissors	Glue or adhesive tapes
1	3	2 rules 2 pencils	1	2
2	1.5	1 rule 1 pencil	1	1
3	1	1 pencil	0	1
4	½ wrinkle	0	0	1
5	0	1 pencil	0	0
6	0	0	1	0

Source: www.iadb.org/es/noticias/articulos,2360.html

and demands: Why we do not have this material? Can we use other tools to make cubes? The facilitator should allow each group to take its own decisions. The only thing that is forbidden is leaving the classroom to get missing materials.

It is important that the facilitator underline the notion of "competition" and the need to "win" to stimulate the spirit of competition between groups. You can tell to the group that the winning group will receive a special prize by the jury, which is formed by the facilitator and any observers. In addition, the facilitator also indicates how long they have left to play to "make up the pressure," wanders between groups and notes what happens in silence. Upon completion time, each group must submit to the facilitator and the other participants their cubes.

After the groups finish their cubes, then the assessment phase starts. There are some questions that can guide the discussion:

- What happened? How would you deal with those feelings senses during exercise?, What?, Did immoral behavior take place during the game?, What ethical values are shown throughout the game?, and so on.
- This game is the illustration of what real-life situations are: at graduate level, at the country level, and the world.

Finally, at the end, participants were asked: Why did they not use the first five minutes to meet among all groups, distributed equitably materials, and coordinate loans for the entire duration of the game? How could we describe a human group that has this behavior from the beginning?

What we lack in this exercise, in general, human beings behave rationally, justice and solidarity among all?

In the next exhibit, you will find some advices and helpful instructions for the facilitator.

Exhibit 8.2 Game cube simulation suggestions

- Provide sheets of papers of different colors.
- Do not feel uncomfortable about the unfair initial distribution of materials. The game will be more interesting.

- Do not explain anything about the meaning of the game to participants before they play the game.
- It is important to note loan agreements (glue, scissors, etc.) and strategic partnerships between groups, and highlight the difference between a donation, a negotiated exchange, and a permanent association.
- It is important to highlight innovations and use of own resources granted in the game, which are not provided for in the envelopes and they did not imagine they can turn to other groups for what they have (there are groups that decorate your cubes with images , others using alternative tools, etc.).
- It is important to highlight the importance of resource "non-material" intelligence illustrated in this game and the ability to design and build models of cubes and eventually "sell" to another group.
- It will be useful to the participants reflect on the problem of desire to compete among ourselves: where does this desire? Can we use either socially or always end up hurting everyone?
- This game is an excellent introduction to explain the difficult notion of social capital.
- When using this game with participants with low educational level, it is preferable to draw a cube model on the board.

Source: www.iadb.org/es/noticias/articulos,2360.html

References

Benson, G.C.S. 1989. "Codes of Ethics." *Journal of Business Ethics* 8, no. 5, pp. 305–19.

Brenner, S.N. 1992. "Ethics Programs and Their Dimensions." *Journal of Business Ethics* 11, nos. 5–6, pp. 391–99.

Bonn, I., and J. Fisher. 2005. "Corporate Governance and Business Ethics: Insights from the Strategic Planning Experience." *Corporate Governance* 13, no. 6, pp. 730–38.

Camacho, G. 2012. *Exploring the Role of Marketing in Corporate Sustainability: A Case Study* (Doctoral Dissertation). Monterrey, México: EGADE Business School.

de Colle, S., and C. Gonella. 2002. "The Social and Ethical Alchemy: An Integrative Approach to Social and Ethical Accountability." *Business Ethics: A European Review* 11, no. 1, pp. 86–96.

Demise, N. 2005. "Business Ethics and Corporate Governance in Japan." *Business Society* 44, no. 2, pp. 211–17.

Francis, R., and A. Armstrong. 2003. "Ethics as a Risk Management Strategy: The Australian Experience." *Journal of Business Ethics* 45, no. 4, pp. 375–85.

HP (Hewlett Packard). 2012. "HP 2012 Global Citizenship Report." Retrieved from http://h20195.www2.hp.com/V2/GetPDF.aspx/c03742928.pdf

Jose, A., and M.S. Thibodeaux. 1999. "Institutionalization of Ethics: The Perspective of Managers." *Journal of Business Ethics* 22, no. 2, pp. 133–43.

Kärna, J., E. Hansen, and H. Juslin. 2003. "Social Responsibility in Environmental Planning." *European Journal of Marketing* 37, nos. 5–6, pp. 848–71.

Kolk, A. 2006. "Sustainability, Accountability and Corporate Governance: Exploring Multinationals' Reporting Practices." *Business Strategy and the Environment* 18, no. 1, pp. 1–15.

Logsdon, J.M., and D.J. Wood. 2005. "Global Business Citizenship and Voluntary Codes of Ethical Conduct." *Journal of Business Ethics* 59, nos. 1–2, pp. 55–67.

Moore, G., R. Slack, and J. Gibbon. 2009. "Criteria for Responsible Business Practice in SMEs: An Exploratory Case of U.K. Fair Trade Organizations." *Journal of Business Ethics* 89, no. 2, pp. 173–88.

Murphy, P.E. 1988. "Implementing Business Ethics." *Journal of Business Ethics* 7, pp. 907–15.

Painter-Morland, M. 2006. "Triple-Bottom Line Reporting as Social Grammar: Integrating Corporate Social Responsibility and Corporate Codes of Conduct." *Business Ethics: A European Review* 15, no. 4, pp. 352–64.

Portales, L., and C. García-de-la-Torre. 2012. "Evolución de la Responsabilidad Social Empresarial: Nacimiento, Definición y Difusión en América Latina [Evolution of Corporate Social Responsibility: Birth, Definition and Diffusion in LatinAmerica]." In *Responsabilidad Social Empresarial*, eds. E. Raufflet, J.F. Lozano, E. Barrera, and C. García-de-la-Torre, 1–13. México, D.F: Pearson Educación.

Rake, M., and D. Grayson. 2009. "Embedding Corporate Responsibility and Sustainability—Everybody's Business." *Corporate Governance* 9, no. 4, pp. 395–99.

Schwartz, M.S., T.W. Dunfee, and M.J. Kline. 2005. "Tone at the Top: An Ethics Code for Directors?" *Journal of Business Ethics* 58, nos. 1–3, pp. 79–100.

Svensson, G., and G. Wood. 2011. "A Conceptual Framework of Corporate Business Ethics Across Organizations Structures, Processes and Performance." *The Learning Organization* 18, no. 1, pp. 21–35.

Svensson, G., G. Wood, and M. Callaghan. 2010. "A Corporate Model of Sustainable Business Practices: An Ethical Perspective." *Journal of World Business* 45, no. 4, pp. 336–45.

van Marrewijk, M. 2003. "Concepts and Definitions of CSR and Corporate Sustainability: Between Agency and Communion." *Journal of Business Ethics* 44, nos. 2–3, pp. 95–105.

Weaver, G.R., L. Klebe, and P.L. Cochran. 1999. "Corporate Ethics Programs as Control Systems: Influences in Executive Commitment and Environmental Factors." *Journal of Business Ethics* 41, no. 1, pp. 41–57.

Wood, G. 2002. "A Partnership Model of Corporate Ethics." *Journal of Business Ethics* 40, no. 1, pp. 61–73.

www.iadb.org/es/noticias/articulos,2360.html

CHAPTER 9

Credit and Risk Assessment

CSR Tools for Local Government, Financial Institutions and SMEs

Giovanni Lombardo and Federica Viganó

Introduction

The corporate social responsibility construct (CSR), originally thought for large companies to cope with social and environmental issues for the sake of their brand and the public perception, is today relevant also for small medium enterprises (SMEs). The evolution of the concept so far, according to the last European definition (COM 2011), brought to interconnect CSR and long-term sustainability of business of all size, including SMEs. Considering the networked environment and the relations along the supply chain globally, large companies increasingly work with SMEs as suppliers, and if large companies are committed to CSR, this leads to ask their suppliers to comply with CSR too.

Moreover, the financial instability, sharpened by the crisis, when it comes to management practices in the credit-rating process, increases the attention of financial institutions about assets, securities, lending, loans, and mortgages. In this regard not only the listed companies but also SMEs defining a CSR strategy are more trustful, as they demonstrate the ability to repay their loans thus obtaining credits.

The European Commission has published a CSR Action Plan to spread good CSR principles across Europe, pushing for higher standards and best practice in this area. Moreover, the recent Directive 2014/95/EU of the European Parliament about disclosure of "nonfinancial and diversity information" for listed and large companies, stresses furthermore the relevance to provide nonfinancial information (social and environmental) into the financial reports of balance sheet. Specifically, by measuring a number of social and environmental issues, sustainable companies can better manage their risks and result in a higher credit worthiness. Despite the high number of well-known CSR standards (OECD Guidelines for Multinational Enterprises; UNI:ISO 26000; United Nations (UN) Guiding Principles on Business and Human Rights; ILO Standard; social accounting standard "Global Reporting Initiative" (GRI); Accountability 1000 (AA1000); Social Accountability 8000 (SA8000); Green Public Procurement [GPP] and Social Public Procurement [SPP] framework; COM 2011; the Report of the European Parliament 6.2.2013), at a national level, each member state developed its own CSR Action Plan.

The role played by the public actor has always been relevant, ranging from financially supporting CSR through specific policy instruments (e.g., incentives, fiscal deduction, etc.), to promoting CSR culture and attention to social and environmental impacts. The development of CSR platforms of indicators supports banks and governments in assessing companies' capabilities to create value and to manage their risks, thus obtaining a lower risk of default. We will analyze the best practice of Italy in the development of such a platform for measuring a strategic, innovative, socially, and environmentally oriented competitiveness aimed at determining the impact of companies on society.[1]

The Relation Between Responsible Business and Financial Sector

Lots of studies highlight the advantages to be a socially responsible company: increased reputation and trust of partners, lower costs related to workers and company management, increased productivity of human resources, lower contributions for insurance against industrial injuries,

---

[1] The Project has been presented in Germany and Denmark in 2014, by the Italian Regions and Ministries, as partners of "DIESIS" EU project. See www.lavoro.gov.it, www.formez.it, http://pcnitalia.mise.gov.it

improved safety in the workplace, more sales and customer loyalty, lower costs of supply, growth of the total value of the company in terms of intangibles (Berman et al. 1999; Christmann 2000; Graves and Waddock 2000; Griffin and Mahon 1997; Margolis and Walsh 2001; Moskowitz 1972; Richardson, Welker, and Hutchinson 1999; Rochlin and Christoffer 2000; Russo and Fouts 1997; Wood and Jones 1995).

Nevertheless, in the relation between businesses and the financial and public system (banks, mutual guarantee societies and guarantee funds, local government), CSR practices do not automatically lead to a positive evaluation by, for example, the financial institutions.

Therefore, the proposal of a CSR platform mapping companies' actions and providing CSR indicators for medium and small business enterprises (MNEs and SMEs), leads to recognize CSR practices as signs of credit capability, value production, and company's riskiness. The CSR platform, whose first goal is to drive companies toward a sustainable competitiveness, serves also as an instrument to detect the main risky areas of companies' value chain and operations. Socially responsible companies in fact, besides producing higher ROE and turnover per worker, are less subject to market volatility, affected by external shocks (Webley and More 2003; Wood and Jones 1995).

In the "overriding procedure" the financial sector, according to the "Basel Capital Accord," began to consider not only the quantitative data taken from financial reports, but also "collaterals," or qualitative components hugely affecting the "risk" factor in the specific sectors of activity.

The adoption of some specific CSR practices (mainly qualitative components) leads also to diminish risks such as a negative impact on cash flows, or worse relations with major stakeholders and strategic partners. A socially responsible leadership is more likely to result in lower absenteeism and turnover, it lowers training costs; by increasing employees' loyalty, it reduces strikes and disputes arising for unfair competition (Fombrun and Shanley 1990; Zyglidopoulos 2002; McWilliams and Siegel 2001); by increasing involvement of local communities and consumers, it leads to lower risks of boycotts and litigations; finally bettering health and safety conditions, it diminishes injuries and social costs (Barney and Hansen 1994; Nahapiet and Ghosal 1998; Waddock and Graves 1997).

An environmentally responsible leadership, adopting procedures and plans for managing crises, or insurances against the environmental risks, reduces costs and losses in case of specific problems in this area (Godfrey, Merrill, and Hansen 2009). Lastly, considering the risks along the supply chain, socially responsible companies controlling the supplier from an ethical point of view (e.g., adopting codes of conduct, safety standards etc.) contribute to limit risks related to safety and the interruption of production, thus providing financial institutions with a higher guarantee of their activity.

One of the main tasks of governments is to promote training programs at company level. The best investment for governments to make human capital grow on CSR is to offer education and training on environmental issues, respect for diversity and human rights, and transparent accountability. Public players are also required to implement rebalancing policies, supporting sustainable competitive system and responsible companies (e.g., incentives and financial helps) and discouraging irresponsible businesses (Albareda et al. 2007; Albareda et al. 2008).

Toward the CSR Italian Platform

The effort to encourage responsible business at regional level leads to develop a mix of compliance requirements and voluntary measures, often difficult to evaluate because of their incomparability. In 2012, the Italian government (including the Ministry of Economic Development, Labor and Agriculture, the Italian Regions, OECD-Italian National Contact Point and the Italian institute against industrial injuries [INAIL]) started a project aimed at creating a common scheme for regions willing to sustain innovative socially responsible oriented firms.[2] The project, in 2014, produced a very simple online check-board tool, through which SMEs—but also MNEs—can proceed with a self assessment, obtaining a CSR diagnosis. One of the best results of this tool is to help SMEs to

---

[2] The project has been funded by the Italian National OECD Contact Point and the Ministry of Development. The sample of SMEs and MNEs participating in the survey so far is around 7,000 companies and the project is on going.

recognize if they are already a CSR-oriented company. Very often, SMEs are unaware of what they are doing, the so called "implicit CSR" (Matten and Moon 2008) or "sunk CSR." The second result of the platform is that SMEs, recognizing their CSR profile, improve their attractiveness facilitating their involvement in the supply chain of sustainable MNEs.

The tool unifies CSR indicators for MNEs and SMEs, regional standards, INAIL standard, and key performance indicators of GRI standard in a unique platform, capable to evaluate in depth the positive externalities of business, their social and environmental performances, and the respect of requirements included in tenders, and call for funding (e.g., the EU funding program 2014 to 2020).

The Italian Platform of Actions and Indicators for a Strategic, Innovative Socially and Environmentally Oriented Competitiveness

The project was proposed by 15 Italian Regions, supported by the Ministry of Economic Development, the Ministry of Labor and Social Policies and INAIL, committed since years in fostering the social responsibility of the firms through the development of initiatives and specific policy instruments (e.g., incentives, fiscal deduction).

The most common and well-known CSR standards (OECD Guidelines, UNI ISO 26000; UN Guiding Principles on Business and Human Rights; ILO; GBS Standard, GRI, AA1000SES, SA8000; GPP-Green Public Procurement; SPP-Sustainable Public Procurement; COM 2011-A renewed EU strategy 2011–14 for CSR; other 10 regional standards) have been systematically revised in order to filter out principal areas and indicators. Results have been validated by key testimonials (Entrepreneurs, Business networks, Business Association, Academics, public actors, Trade Unions, NGOs).

The final framework recognizes six strategic areas of CSR actions:

- Business organization and administration (governance and business model)
- People and work environment

- Clients, customers, consumers
- Suppliers
- Natural environment, local community, and relation with the public government
- Innovation and competitiveness

For small, medium, and large firms (excluding only the *micro*enterprises), a set of specific indicators, namely indicators for the "management of major risks," identify five major areas of sector-specific risk:

- Food industry and agriculture
- Building, construction and manufacturing
- Pharma
- Business facilities, finance, banking, insurances
- Utilities (energy, water, electricity, gas, waste recycling)

The entire system helps companies of different size to test their CSR areas, through a material evidence: the platform provides information for firms suggesting how they can provide a "proof" of their CSR behavior (internal documents, corporate statement, policies etc.); this, in turn helps the public administrations to check the material evidence of a CSR practice. Moreover, the platform provides concrete indications to companies to enhance their sustainable competitiveness (Porter and Kramer 2006; Porter and Kramer 2011; Crane et al. 2014) by suggesting how to:

- Focus on relevant stakeholders in order to correspond efficiently their needs
- Minimize philanthropy as spot initiative, not aligned with innovation and strategy of the firms
- Select actions leading to economic advantages and competitiveness
- Establish robust relation with stakeholder and reduce their own risk (thus reducing their own capital cost, see the agreements with banks and the calculation of the probability of default, according to Basel-II financial and bank rating standard)

- Build a better reputation, foster commitment of the employees, identify new business opportunities, and reinforce productivity
- Identify the corporate contribute to the society
- Better design the "value chain," by defining organizational process and products in a CSR perspective
- Nurture innovation
- Valorizing the relation between firms, territories, and local communities
- Integrate sustainability into management, planning, control systems performance assessment methods to which are generally associated premium, strategic plans, budget, project management and "management by objective" (MBO)

The main feature of this platform is to link environmental and safety issues to the concept of risk. Risks' analysis, in fact, cannot forget indicators affecting the natural environment or health and safety, according to the sector of activity. An assessment that does not take into account the environmental and social aspects, could not figure out if a company has managed well its own risk. Any action related to ethical and sustainable business process at higher risk, may:

1. Limit the risks of the event that cause a negative impact on cash flow, such as a fine or other penalty tax, economic fine or temporary interdiction
2. Limit the possibility of abandonment of the company, by some of its strategic partners
3. Limit forms of contrast (boycott)

Regarding the usability of the Platform, it is highly company friendly, with a small number of relevant core indicators, strictly related to the core business and to the highest risky internal process. To provide an example, an SME operating in textile and garments, could check actions referred to workers conditions, customers, suppliers, and environment; the tool suggests to check actions regarding the supply chain, because in this sector the main risk concerns human rights of workers located in far countries, where health and safety conditions are not protected as in Europe. Key performance indicators following the international social reporting standard "GRI"[3] are as follows:

- "Operations and suppliers identified in which the right to exercise freedom of association and collective bargaining may be violated or at significant risk, and measures taken to support these rights" (GRI social accounting standard; "Human rights" section HR4)
- "Percentage of new suppliers that were screened using labor practices criteria" (GRI social accounting standard; "labor practices and decent work" section LA14).

In the case of "environment," as the process is recognized as the most risky:

- "Monetary value of significant fines and total number of nonmonetary sanctions for noncompliance with environmental laws and regulations" (GRI social accounting standard; "environment" section EN29);
- "Percentage of new suppliers that were screened using environmental criteria" (GRI social accounting standard; "environment" section EN32).

Companies applying this approach—that is, including environmental, social and governance indicators (ESG) or CSR criteria into Basel financial rating are among others: Generali Investment management companies (IMCO), Intesa Bank Imco, Caisse des Dépôts et Consignations, Crédit Agricole, Unep Financial Initiative.

Conclusions

Due to the inter linkage between CSR, finance and risk, the assessment that banks carry out to calculate the probability of default—based on

---

[3] Global Reporting Initiative standard n. 4, www.globalreportinginitiative.com

Basel standards—includes fields which are specifically monitored through some CSR or ESG indicators, linked to environmental, social, or security risks.

As a result, it is possible to use specific CSR indicators as an acknowledgment of the companies' capabilities to create value and have a low risk of default. Consequently, sustainable companies are more likely to obtain:

a) An interest rate on loans or financings which is lower than the market rate, and which is rewarding in comparison to what other non-CSR companies and customers are able to obtain;
b) A lower spread;
c) Lower fees on services;
d) A longer time period for repaying financing in comparison to the usual time fixed by the bank, having in this way a longer lapse of time to repay disbursed funds.

Therefore, the use of qualitative, relational, intangibles-related and environmental indicators linked to the risk assessment of companies, improves also the application of the Basel rating formula.

Summary

The chapter highlights the link, not yet deeply investigated in the literature, between CSR, risks assessment, and capability to increase trustworthiness within the credit rating processes. According to the recent Directive 2014/95/EU of the European Parliament about disclosure of "nonfinancial and diversity information" for listed and large companies, it is more evident and relevant to provide nonfinancial information (e.g., social and environmental) into the financial reports, in order to prove a good management of major risks. This applies also to SMEs as supplier of large companies.

The role played by the public actor in this context has always been relevant, from financially supporting CSR, to promoting CSR culture, and attention to social and environmental impacts. The chapter presents the Italian best practice of a CSR platform of indicators, developed by the Italian government, to map companies' actions and recognize CSR practices as signs of credit capability, value production, and company's riskiness.

Due to the interlinkage between CSR, finance, and risk, the assessment that banks carry out to calculate the probability of default—based on Basel standards—includes fields, which are specifically monitored through some CSR or ESG indicators. As a result, we suggest the opportunity to use specific CSR indicators as an acknowledgment of the companies' capabilities to create value and demonstrate low risk of default.

Discussion Questions

1. Should CSR be required by law or should it be a voluntary action? What do you think about the recent Directive 2014/95/EU of the European Parliament about disclosure of "nonfinancial and diversity information?"
2. The Italian Government has developed a platform to map CSR companies' actions. What is the main goal of this tool?
3. CSR and financial risk assessment interlinked. Why?
4. What are the GRI CSR indicators measuring risk which can be adopted in the context of bank or financial risk assessment?

References

Albareda, L., J. Lozano, and T. Ysa. 2007. "Public Policies on Corporate Social Responsibility: The Role of Governments in Europe." *Journal of Business Ethics* 74, no. 4, pp. 391–407.

Albareda, L., J. Lozano, A. Tencati, A. Midttun, and F. Perrini. 2008. "The Changing Role of Governments in Corporate Social Responsibility: Drivers and Responses." *Business Ethics: A European Review* 15, no. 4, pp. 347–61.

Barney, J.B., and M.H. Hansen. 1994. "Trustworthiness as a Source of Competitive Advantage." *Strategic Management Journal* 15, no. S1, pp. 175–90.

Berman, S.L., A.C. Wicks, S. Kotha, and T.M. Jones. 1999. "Does Stakeholder Orientation Matter? The Relationship Between Stakeholder Management Models and Firm Financial Performance." *Academy of Management Journal* 42, no. 5, pp. 488–506.

Christmann, P. 2000. "Effects of 'Best Practices' of Environmental Management on Cost Advantage: The Role of Complementary Assets." *Academy of Management Journal* 43, no. 4, pp. 663–80.

COM. 2011. "A Renewed EU Strategy 2011–14 for Corporate Social Responsibility: Communication from the Commission to the European Parliament, the Council, the European Economic and Social Committee and the Committee of the Regions." October 25, 2011. http://www.europarl. europa.eu/meetdocs/2009_2014/documents/com/com_com(2011)0681_/com_com(2011)0681_en.pdf

Crane, A., G. Palazzo, L.J. Spence, and D. Matten. 2014. "Contesting the Value of Creating Shared Value." *California Management Review* 56, no. 2, pp. 130–52.

Fombrun, C., and M. Shanley. 1990. "What Is in a Name? Reputation Building and Corporate Strategy." *Academy of Management Journal* 33, no. 2, pp. 233–58.

GRI 4 (Global Reporting Initiative). 2013. *Sustainability Reporting Guidelines.* Boston, MA: GRI.

Godfrey, P.C., C.B. Merrill, and J.M. Hansen. 2009. "The Relationship Between Corporate Social Responsibility and Shareholder Value: An Empirical Test of the Risk Management Hypothesis." *Strategic Management Journal* 30, no. 4, pp. 425–45.

Graves, S.B., and S.A. Waddock. 2000. "Beyond Built to Last. Stakeholder Relations in 'Built-to-Last' Companies." *Business and Society Review* 105, no. 4, pp. 393–418.

Griffin, J.J., and J.F. Mahon. 1997. "The Corporate Social Performance and Corporate Financial Performance Debate: Twenty-five Years of Incomparable Research." *Business and Society* 36, no. 1, pp. 5–31.

Margolis, J.D., and J.P. Walsh. 2001. *People and Profits? The Search for a Link Between a Company's Social and Financial Performance.* Mahwah, NJ: Lawrence Erlbaum Associates.

Matten, D., and J. Moon. 2008. "'Implicit' and 'Explicit' CSR: A Conceptual Framework for a Comparative Understanding of Corporate Social Responsibility." *Academy of Management Review* 33, no. 2, pp. 404–24.

McWilliams, A., and D. Siegel. 2001. "Corporate Social Responsibility: A Theory of the Firm Perspective." *Academy of Management Review* 26, no. 1, pp. 117–27.

Moskowitz, M. 1972. "Choosing Socially Responsible Stocks." *Business and Society* 1, no. 1, pp. 71–75.

Nahapiet, J., and S. Ghosal. 1998. "Social Capital, Intellectual Capital, and the Organizational Advantage." *Academy of Management Review* 23, no. 2, pp. 242–66.

Porter, M.E., and M.R. Kramer. 2011. "Creating Shared Value." *Harvard Business Review* 89, nos. 1–2, pp. 62–77.

Porter, M.E., and M.R. Kramer. 2006. "Strategy and Society: The Link between Competitive Advantage and Corporate Social Responsibility." *Harvard Business Review* 84, no. 12.

Richardson, A.J., M. Welker, and I.R. Hutchinson. 1999. "Managing Capital Market Reactions to Corporate Social Responsibility." *International Journal of Management Reviews* 1, no. 1, pp. 17–43.

Rochlin, S.A., and B. Christoffer. 2000. *Making the Business Case: Determining the Value of Corporate Community Involvement.* Newton, MA: The Center for Corporate Citizenship at Boston College.

Russo, M.V., and P.A. Fouts. 1997. "A Resource-based Perspective on Corporate Environmental Performance and Profitability." *Academy of Management Journal* 40, no. 3, pp. 534–59.

Waddock, S.A., and S.B. Graves. 1997. "The Corporate Social Performance-Financial Performance Link." *Strategic Management Journal* 18, no. 4, pp. 303–19.

Webley, S., and E. More. 2003. *Does Business Ethics Pay?* London: IBE.

Wood, D.J., and R.E. Jones. 1995. "Stakeholder Mismatching: A Theoretical Problem in Empirical Research on Corporate Social Performance." *The International Journal of Organizational Analysis* 3, no. 3, pp. 229–67.

Zyglidopoulos, S.C. 2002. "The Social and Environmental Responsibilities of Multinationals: Evidence from the Brent Spar Case." *Journal of Business Ethics* 36, nos. 1–2, pp. 141–51.

CHAPTER 10

Morality and Self-Relevance

In Search of Objective Moral Judgment in Brand Transgression

Segun Shogbanmu and Olutayo Otubanjo

Introduction

Academics who study consumer psychology and consumer behavior have found the need to discuss business ethics through the pinhole of moral reasoning as this relates heavily with consumer psychology. Over the decades, moral reasoning was predominantly explained through moral disengagement (moral rationalization), and recently moral decoupling, though these relate directly to instances of brand transgression. When a brand engages in a wrong-doing (brand transgression), consumers, in turn, get engaged in a psychological evaluation of such brands. The purpose of this chapter is not only to appraise this psychological evaluation, but also to understand what must be present to increase our chances of predicting consumer responses. As a follow up, we show that it is not only transgression relevance (relevance of wrong doing to the brand) as previously studied but also consumer self-relevance (the degree to which a consumer identifies with a product or service as a vehicle to achieving his goals or values) that drives a consumer's motivation to oppose thereby leading to a psychological process of combining judgment of morality and that of performance through a process called moral coupling, a previously unstudied moral reasoning process.

When in 2014, the Fédération Internationale de Football Association (FIFA) refused to name Luiz Suarez amongst the 23 shortlisted contenders for the Ballon d'Or, Liverpool manager, Brendan Rodgers, queried such an unfair action, arguing that the award was not a recognition for character but for performance following an outstanding 31-goal campaign that saw Luiz Suarez named Footballer of the Year and Professional Footballers' Association (PFA) Player of the Year in England. In his opinion, Brendan believed that Suarez shouldn't be made to pay for his misdemeanor in biting Italy's Giorgio Chiellini during the FIFA World Cup as the Ballon d'Or is given in recognition of outstanding skills as a footballer and not for character. In Rodgers' opinion, the decision to leave Luis out of the award was not football-related.

But really, is Brendan Rodgers correct? In as much as he has a point in his argument, it may not be the whole truth. Would anyone have argued in favor of a brand that transgressed against its consumers and expect the consumers to turn a blind eye to the immoral action by simply maintaining loyalty or even patronage status with the same immoral actor? This is most unlikely. Rodger's argument is guilty of disregard for consumer sensitivity, and the idea that performance or financial maximization is the singular metric with which to evaluate an organization or brand is moot. Considering moral as well as financial metrics so as to improve society and not just self is a (psychological) measure with which consumers gauge brands (Robert, Paul, and Jurkiewicz 2005). Often times, consumers take morality as a given until an immorality is committed.

We are interested in consumers, not merely because we ourselves are consumers, but because we want to understand what drives why some people "buy" while some others do not. What one segment of consumers considers amazing may be viewed by others as appalling for some reasons that interest us.

In general, consumers may be described or compared to other people in several dimensions. One of such dimensions is demographics—classification based on age, religion, income level, gender, or occupation for example. The other form of classification is psychographic—understanding based on consumers' lifestyles, personalities, interests that may relate to eating, clothing, or parenting, or even the manner in which consumers settle into their evenings. These classifications, as simple as they may seem, are very critical to any marketer as these determine how to segment, position, and target any product or service market.

However, after these series of deliberate activities including messaging the potential customers, professor of marketing at the Wharton School of Business, Americus Reed II believes that a marketer's delight would be to move potential consumers through five stages: awareness, consideration, conversion, loyalty, and advocacy. In as much as Reed II has a very valid submission and indeed many organizations and their representatives have focused more on pushing a close knit relationship with users of their products, just a few have taken the issue of transgression against a consumer seriously. Instead, they leave the issues in the hands of the public relations (PR) teams who often do not have as deep an understanding of markets and consumers as those who constitute the marketing department.

Since the 1950s, marketers have engaged in a careful and consistent study of consumers (Craig-Lee, Joy, and Browne 1995) and this exercise has not stopped. In fact, more marketers and academics have collaborated to understand how individuals discover, evaluate, acquire, consume, and dispose of goods and services. These adventures to understand behaviors of users of products and services have broadened the perspective of researchers into disciplines such as: anthropology, economics, sociology, and (social) psychology.

Consumers have a set of predispositions or potentials to act in certain ways at particular times but this is based on several factors that can potentially influence all the combinations of actions. Put in another way, situational factors such as contexts of purchase, availability of products and services, degree of influence of social norms, point of purchase promotion, and store atmosphere (Craig-Lee, Joy, and Browne 1995) influence the behavior of a consumer. But before behaviors, the impact of cognitive and affective experiences could shape how a consumer would react. For example, consumers who have been loyal to a brand may choose to act otherwise because they feel offended by that brand (Aaker, Fournier, and Brasel 2004) and may act in certain ways to register their distaste. This dimension of the consumer has, however, witnessed relative attention. But a critical point worthy of discourse here is an exploration of possible variables that drive peculiar moral reasoning processes, the manner in which people who patronize brands attempt to justify their choice to admonish a brand they consider to have offended them.

In the management of corporate reputation, consumer–brand relationship is critical, hence, the increased interest in the relationship paradigm. Brands seek an ideal world where consumers will always have a loyalist disposition toward them, but in reality, it is not always the case. Brands engage in wrongdoings from time to time thereby breaching the trust bestowed on them by consumers. In cases where consumers desire to maintain support for a brand, the immoral "actor," consumers maintain a reasoning that interprets the immoral act as being less immoral—this reasoning process is traditionally referred to as moral rationalization (Baumeister and Newman 1994; Ditto, Pizarro, and Tannenbaum 2009; Haidt 2001; Mazar, Amir, and Ariely 2008; Paharia and Deshpande 2009; Shu, Gino, and Bazerman 2011; Tsang 2002). However, in recent times, it has been shown that this is not always the case. A team of three researchers made up of Bhattacharjee, Berman, and Reed II (2013) demonstrated that while moral rationalization as a reasoning process redefines transgressions as being less immoral, not all consumers engage in such a self-demoralizing immorality-evaluation process. They were able to show that beyond justifying immorality as being less immoral to maintain support for a coveted brand, consumers as an alternative, may maintain their support for a coveted brand who has engaged in an immoral action by simply separating judgment of morality from that of performance through a reasoning process called moral decoupling.

In other words, while the rationalization of immoral actions is a process of explaining immoral actions as being less immoral in order to maintain support for an immoral actor, moral decoupling emphasizes a separation process where an immoral actor is supported, but not for its immoral act but for its performance. This should be easily understood when one considers consumers who maintain their support for President Bill Clinton when he was accused of lying under oath concerning an unhealthy relationship with a White House intern. His supporters argued that he may have a character flaw (judgment of morality), but that he must not be denied his virtue as an amazing president (judgment of performance), hence their continued support for him.

As a follow-up, we hereby try to identify unresolved presuppositions of this reasoning process. First, one must understand that moral rationalization and moral decoupling are reasoning processes that are devoid of consumer sensitivity for whatever reasons, justifiable or not. Second, while consumers separate the identity of a brand in a bid to admire it, the same cannot be said in situations where consumers would desire to reprimand a transgressor. We are of the opinion, as first hinted by Bhattacharjee, Berman, and Reed II (2013) that consumers would act in a manner contrary to decoupling toward a brand if they are sufficiently motivated to oppose it. The work of Bhattacharjee and his team suggests the possibility of a potential asymmetric construct to moral decoupling, which is moral coupling. This chapter, among other things, seeks to explain moral coupling and also attempts to show the factors whose presence would promote reasons why consumers would go all the way to antagonize a brand and not simply forgive or give excuses for its actions. The conversation in this chapter also attempts to clarify that it is not only the relevance of a wrongdoing (transgression relevance) to brands that determines moral (de)coupling, but also the relevance of such wrongdoing to a consumer's person. Better put, the authors are of the opinion that in a situation where the accusation of a transgression of a comedian Bill Cosby, for example, is relevant both to the self-expression of his fans and the domain of performance in question, fans' reasoning process is more likely to equate the immoral accusations of Bill Cosby with his performance as a comedian. It would be difficult, if found guilty of the allegations, for fans to "tip their hats" in love for him as a comedian but "wag their fingers" for the immoral acts.

Evolution of Consumer–Brand Relationship

Writings on building consumer–brand relationship remain very important especially considering the increase in uncertainties, and reduction in product differentiation while the pressure from competition remains on the rise (Shocker, Srivastava, and Ruekert 1994), yet experts points in the direction of encouraging firms to pursue strong ties with consumers (Keller 2001). This, therefore, created a need to understand the intricacies of such critical relationship. In as much as findings suggest the pursuance of strong consumer–brand relationship, this in itself could threaten the very existence of a brand (Johnson, Matear, and Thomson 2011). In a bid to understand this relationship, many writers and practitioners have trod the path to describe different kinds of relationship between brands and their consumers and even clarify previously ambiguous specifics (Jacoby and Kyner 1973; Dick and Basu 1994; Wernerfelt 1991; Olsen 2002). The loyalty that exists between a brand and its customer, for example, was described as the strength of the connection that binds individual relative attitude and repeat purchase (Dick and Basu 1994). This particular perspective was popularized by Jacoby and Kyner (1973) who helped to better understand that the widely accepted yet incomplete view that loyalty could be taken as a replacement for repeat purchase, should not be so. Simply put, the fact that customers keep coming to buy a particular product is not necessarily a show of loyalty.

However, understanding this admiration state of a consumer cannot be satisfying to practitioners especially when there is a gap concerning the factors that make relationships lasting and strong (Aaker, Fournier, and Brasel 2004). This then shifts the conversation from the mere relationship to the strength and duration of the relationship (Aaker, Fournier, and Brasel 2004). It is expected that a brand that wants to continuously remain in business will crave for a perpetual and deep connection between itself and its consumers. This may explain why the strength of such relationships remains the most-studied characteristics in the interpersonal relationship sphere (Fincham and Bradbury 1987). It is as critical to marketing researchers (Day and Van den Bulte 2002) as it is to managers (Gummesson 2002), but recent trends show that both academics and practitioners are increasingly interested in understanding the complexities that involve the wrongdoing of brands.

A Peep Into Discussions on Brand Transgression

As earlier mentioned, more research has gone into the conversion of positive relationships between brands and consumers (Fournier and Yao 1997; Fletcher, Simpson, and Thomas 2000; He, Li, and Harris 2011). But there have been fewer critical enquiries into situations of transgressions—direct or indirect breaches of guidelines that form the boundaries of a relationship (Buunk 1982; Metts 1994) and of the violation of trust and expectations leading to betrayal (Elangovan and Shapirio 1998). At some points, investigations in the directions of the relationship between employees and employers grew (Morrison and Robinson 1997). Not until recently did the study of violation of the norms and guidelines that define a partnership between consumer and brand begin (Price, Arnould, and Bardhi 2002; Koehler and Gershoff 2003; Aaker, Fournier, and Brassel 2004). Hence, betrayal and transgression as concepts had their descriptive origins from discussions on interpersonal relationships. However, our elaborations here are limited to the negative actions of brands and not consumers.

Brands as an identity system (Kapferer 1992) or as possessing personality or human characteristics (Epstein 1977; Rook 1985; Aaker and Fournier 1995; Swaminathan, Stilley, and Ahluwalia 2009), when in relationship with consumers, form a partnership; and ultimately, as expected with all partners in close relationships, they are not immune from acting badly (Rusbult et al. 1991) though these brands never set out to wrong consumers. However, *when good brands do bad*, there are consequences that await them, although the outcomes are often dependent on the kind of relationship formed between the brand and the consumer (Aaker, Fournier, and Brassel 2004).

Extant literatures that discourse dislocations in a customer–brand relationship have, amongst other things, focused on: the potential threats inherent in self-relevant consumer relationship (Johnson, Matear, and Thomson 2011); understanding the cause and effect of transgression on the relationship strength between the brand and the consumer (Aaker, Fournier, and Brasel 2004); influence of time and relationship strength on customer revenge and avoidance (Gregoire, Tripp, and Legoux 2009); relationship between consumer advocacy and consumer complaining through voicing and negative word-of-mouth (Chelminski and Coulter 2011); and the reasoning process of consumers who support transgressors (Bhattacharjee, Berman, and Reed II 2013). Knowing that the customer–brand partnership, just like interpersonal relationship, is bound to have relationship violations (Ries and Knee 1996), then it may be an unfair exaggeration on the part of consumers to assume a violation-free relationship (Smith, Bolton, and Wagner 1999). It may be more realistic to expect that the degree of transgression is not severe (Aaker, Fournier, and Brasel 2004) or that a prompt display of resolving such a breach in the relationship norms is demonstrated (Xie and Peng 2009).

It is observed that a violation of expectations and relationship norms between these partners is inevitable (Price, Amould, and Bardhi 2004). Further research has shown that as it is almost impossible to have a long-term consumer–brand relationship without some occasional frictions (Grayson and Amber 1999) especially considering the irony of brands seeking more interactions with consumers for purpose of brand loyalty and advocacy (Buss and Craik 1983), interdependency, self-connection, commitment, intimacy, and brand partner quality all increase (Fournier 1998), and consumer expectations change (Kopalle and Lindsey-Mullikin 2003) else this would not amount to a relationship but an isolated transaction (Bersheid and Peplau 1983). In such instances that are almost perpetually unavoidable, it is imperative that understanding the stance and reaction of consumers is critical as some could react through customer switching (Keaveney 1995) on occasions where switching cost may not be too high. So, while brands are striving not to violate their commitment to customers, brands must be proactive to understand possible scenario outcomes and how to respond to customers who are sufficiently motivated to admonish the wrongdoing of brands they may have been loyal to previously (Lee 2007; Nussbaun 2008) especially knowing that such consumers have a potential to engage in negative word-of-mouth (Richins 1983).

Although Aaker, Fournier, and Brassel (2004) have demonstrated the reaction of consumers when sincere and exciting brands breach the (psychological) contract with their consumers, this evidence should not deter brands but reinvigorate them to understand the psychology of the customers who are motivated not to continue their support for the brand, especially having empirically shown that some customers still have the courage to support transgressed brands (Bhattacharjee, Berman, and Reed II 2013). However, this consumer reaction to transgression may be heavily determined by the severity and cause of the transgression (Aaker, Fournier, and Brassel 2004), but this research interest is of the particular opinion that consumer reactions are dependent on how relevant such an act of transgression is, relative to the domains of performance of the brand (Bhattacharjee, Berman, and Reed II 2013) and how relevant the transgressed act impacts the consumer self-concept or self-image.

Understanding Transgression Relevance

The most popular opinion evident in research concerning the effect of transgression is that it is potent with inherent harm that puts the customer–brand relationship at risk (Buysse et al. 2000). As evident as this may be, it has also been shown that the degree to which a consumer considers a transgression to be significant is partly determined by the weight of its significance and discovery as wrongdoing. Put differently, a transgression is only as significant when the act itself has a high measure of importance (Fiske 1980). Transgression relevance exists when a transgression is significantly related to the domains of performance in question (Bhattacharjee, Berman, and Reed II 2013). In other words, transgression relevance relates to how a wrongdoing is related to the core business of an organization or a public figure.

The case of transgression relevance is not the same as transgression severity. Some transgressions are perceived as being relevant to performance relative to some other performance; hence, some transgressions are irrelevant within the context of performance. The use of steroids, for instance, is observed to have a high relevance for a baseball player but low relevance for a governor; while tax evasion was considered of a high relevance to a governor but of a low relevance to a baseball player (Bhattacharjee, Berman, and Reed II 2013).

As determined by Bhattacharjee, Berman, and Reed II (2013), wrongdoings with high transgression relevance reduces consumer support. This provides the logic to expect that highly relevant transgressions will increase opposition from consumers.

Understanding Self-Relevance

Self-relevance explains that products and service offerings achieve goals, values, and benefits that are important to the consumer or refers to the degree to which a consumer identifies with a product or service as a vehicle to achieving its goals or values (Houston and Walker 1996). The construct also refers to consumer–brand relationships where important aspects of consumer self-concept or self-image are established (Johnson, Matear, and Thomson 2011).

The concept of self-relevance cannot be fully understood outside brand personality. At the worst, there is great need to understand the relationship between both constructs as many researchers have used both without drawing a line of distinction. There is, therefore, a gap in literature concerning how self-relevance is different from brand personality.

Put in its most basic form, brand personality is described as that set of human qualities that has direct association with a brand (Aaker 1997). It is the personification of a brand and it derives its meaning from people who associate with that personification because they consider those human qualities *(which were created before the contact—the contact between brands and consumers)* to describe their total self or an aspect of them.

This is distinct from the utilitarian benefits derived from product-related attributes. Instead, brand personality attribute relates with the symbolic and self-expressive idea (Keller 1993). This has been observed, through earlier research, to be possible because consumers have a tendency to ascribe human features to brands (Gilmore 1919; Caprara, Barbaranelli, and Guido 2001; Aaker, Benet-Martinez, and Garolera 2001; Sung and Tinkham 2005) as a result of a deliberate construction of the marketer (Azoulay and Kapferer 2003). This personification act is typically ascribed to a brand by consumers who dress brands in human personality traits called animism (Aaker 1997), but it is also argued that this personification is a deliberate act of marketers who use celebrities to endorse brands in order to authenticate the brand with personalities of the celebrities (Azoulay and Kapferer 2003). Put differently, Azoulay and Kapferer (2003) argue that the personality of celebrities that areassociated with brands endorsed by celebrities is what consumers associate with though they also agree with Aaker (1997) disposition that brands may have over time been perceived as exudingsome personality traits.

The meaning of self-relevance points us to look in the direction of the ideal or actual self. Brands were created to appeal to either ideal or actual self because even if a consumer's actual self is not in congruity with a brand personality (the image created out of a brand), but because people perceive themselves better than they actually are (ideal self), the consumer would either find a congruity or attempt to use the personality of the brand to correct his perceived self. People prefer to perceive themselves as being honest (Mazar, Amir, and Ariely 2008) even if that isn't their actual self.

In her seminal work (Aaker 1997), five dimensions of brand personality were demonstrated to have subsumed other possible personalities. These dimensions—sincerity, excitement, competence, sophistication, and ruggedness—were shown to be broad vehicles through which consumers communicate who they are. Put in another way, brand personality is described as a communication mechanism of consumer self-expression (Aaker 1997; Belk 1988; Johar, Sengupta, and Aaker 2005), self-expression of an ideal image (Sirgy 1982; Malhotra 1988), or a specific dimension of self (Kleine, Kleine, and Kerman 1993) is central to helping a consumer communicate self to fulfill some requirements for relationships he seeks (Aaker 1997; Wallendorf and Arnould 1988) or an image that represents his understanding of himself (Aaker 1999; Sirgy 1985). In other words, a consumer's continued attachment to a certain brand is dependent on how that brand successfully mirrors the image the consumer seeks to portray. In fact, one major means through which brand personality increases consumer preference and usage (Sirgy 1982), and increases levels of loyalty and trust (Fournier and Yao 1997) is as a consequence of consistent representation of self.

To properly explain the distinctions, we have attempted four means of distinguishing both constructs: ordering, timing, measurement, and origin.

Ordering: The sequence of events is critical to understanding a distinction between these seemingly confusing constructs. Brand personality often times follows from the abstraction of self-relevance; hence, they can't possibly be the same. These human personalities are as a result of strategies executed by advertisers (Aaker 1997) to make one brand distinct from another. A congruity with self-relevance is a key function that brand personality seeks to achieve in order to promote consumer brand loyalty (Bhattacharya and Sen 2003; Park, MacInnis, and Priester 2006) and a protection against consumer defection but this is not always so as there could be self-neutral or low self-relevance (Johnson, Matear, and Thomson 2011). It, therefore, follows that if the creation of brand personality targets self-congruity as an outcome, then it must have been created with self-relevance as a target for congruity. Then, it is not the same as self-relevance.

Timing: The possibility of a difference in ordering presupposes dissimilarity of the time that either constructs are present. When advertisers are busy building a specific personality for a brand, it is not likely that such a brand already enjoys an attachment with the image of self a consumer seeks to portray although firms have a fair idea of the images that consumers would like to communicate about themselves. This is so because creating a brand personality in itself takes time to form an image on the mind of a consumer. Azoulay and Kapferer (2003) reiterate that it has been long agreed that brands could have a personality just as persons do and this is not dependent on whether consumers perceive any personality fit between that of the brand and self or not.

Measurement: Some brand personalities, for example, that connote fun and excitement (Park, Jaworski, and MacInnis 1986) do not implicate the self (Parker 2009; Aaker, Fournier, and Brasel 2004). A consumer may imbue a brand with human personality traits without seeing any congruity with self (Johnson, Matear, and Thomson 2011). In other words, low or no self-relevance doesn't presuppose lack of brand personality, it just goes to demonstrate that a brand personality has been realized but self-relevance has not been realized with certain consumers either as a result of the nature of personality (like fun and excitement as earlier mentioned) or as a result of misalignment with the personality traits a consumer would want to project about her ideal or actual self.

Origin: One of the origins of brand personality is celebrity endorsements, in that, famous personalities endorse a brand and the personality of the celebrity is associated with the brand, hence the personality of the brand. The same cannot be said of self-relevance; self-relevance has its source from an individual's attempt to be perceived in a particular light.

The greater the congruity between the human characteristics that consistently and distinctively describes an individual's actual or ideal self and a brand, the higher the preference for that brand (Sirgy 1982; Malhotra 1988; Aaker 1997). Conversely, we can also expect that the less the consistency between the human characteristics that describe self and a brand, then the least likely there will be consumer preference for such a brand.

But, in the face of acts of transgression that distort the image a consumer seeks to project, we believe that a consumer will combine her judgment of performance and that of morality (moral coupling) for the transgressed brand as a means to oppose the brand—an attempt to disassociate herself from the brand. Therefore, as a converse of Sirgy (1982), Malhotra (1988), and Aaker (1997) earlier mentioned, we also believe in this study that the less the harmony between the human features that define an individual's actual and ideal self (self-relevance) and those that define the brand, then the least likely the preference for the brand.

Theories on Moral Reasoning

Moral Rationalization

The issue of morality, like the concept of moral relativism in the domain of business ethics, has been argued by some scholars to be dependent on personal interpretation while others argue otherwise; it has become a case of moral relativism versus moral objectivism (Elegido 1994). However, our concern here is neither the objectivism nor relativism perspective on morality; instead, we are concerned about those customers who are hurt as a result of acts of violation by brands. Comparatively, we would not aim to convince customers to judge a book by its cover or not, but to understand their rationale for judging the book by its cover.

The more the fuzziness that surrounds a transgression, the higher the potential for subjective interpretation (Mazar, Amir, and Oriely 2008; Shu, Francesca, and Max, 2011). Extant literatures have tried to explain a moral reasoning process that accounts for immoral acts of others. Tsang (2002) explained this process of moral rationalization as "an individual's ability to reinterpret her immoral actions as, in fact, moral." This personal reconstruction tends to defend, reduce, exonerate, or empathize with morality (Bhattacharjee, Berman, and Reed II 2013) and as result, places limits on the moral standard of the consumer. Moral rationalization is described as the process of reconstruing immoral actions as less immoral or as the self-power of an individual to redefine her immoral actions as being moral (Tsang 2002) in order to maintain support for an immoral actor. The mechanics of moral rationalization is embedded in the thinking that affirms to self that immoral actions are consistent with societal norms. It arises as an internal quest to prove to self that it is moral. This is better explained by motivated reasoning which stipulates that preference for a particular action biases judgment of what is right and wrong in the direction of self-preference (Kunda 1990).

In the same line, moral disengagement essentially focuses more specifically on what directly interests this attempt toward an intellectual conversation. The moral self is enshrined in a socio-cognitive self-theory that encompasses self-organizing, proactive mechanisms as opposed to reactive, self-reflective, and self-regulatory mechanisms and these are platforms for explaining the self-theory (Bandura 1999). We find in the aforementioned research that people self-create moral standards that serve as a guideline for evaluating and regulating their conduct in order to prevent self-condemnation. People pay the price for the harm done on them by others irrespective of how the perpetrators justify their deeds but understanding the reasoning behind this possible justification may serve as a road to preventing or dealing with such thought processes. In contrast, this self-criticism may not be as common amongst consumers who tend to admonish a transgression. This is because the previously explained concept accounts for the reasoning of the transgressor and not the perception of the consumer or the brand community. Moral rationalization, therefore, is as a result of conflict of motivations and a craving to see the self as being morally upright (Tsang 2002).

Moral Decoupling and Moral Coupling

As opposed to moral rationalization where a consumer justifies an immorality, thereby reducing self-moral evaluation, moral decoupling, a recently studied phenomenon, is a moral reasoning process that allows consumers who are motivated to admire a brand for its performance and concurrently chide its moral wrong (Bhattacharjee, Berman, and Reed II 2013). It has been shown that moral decoupling applies to instances where the consumer is motivated to particularly admire and support a transgressor. It does not explain the moral reasoning in instances where the consumer is geared to rebuke a transgressed brand. Bhattacharjee, Berman, and Reed (2013) theorized on admiring offended brands but did not describe the moral reasoning behind the converse case where the opposing Republicans were inspired to admonish Clinton. Years after the Bill Clinton scandal ravaged the American presidency, there were questions as to the connection between the morality of President Clinton and his performance as president. It is surprising as 80 percent of those asked mentioned that they believe the president was lying, yet another piece of research showed that about the same percentage of respondents tipped their hat in approval of how he went about his job as president (Miller 1996).

While many Democrats were motivated to support Clinton, they argued along the lines of the question raised by Shogan (1999) but reported by Bhattacharjee, Berman, and Reed (2013) that moral judgment and performance judgment are two separate issues. This is similar to the more recent case of Luiz Suarez as mentioned in the introduction of this chapter. Luis Suarez was the highest European Premiership League (EPL) goal scorer with 31 balls in the net, but bit Giorgio Chiellini in the ear during the 2014 FIFA World Cup in Brazil. Besides receiving universal criticism for such a show of a lack of sportsmanship, he was banned for four months from the pitch and fined but months after the incident, his name was left out of the Ballon d'Or shortlist. His former manager at Liverpool, Brendan Rodgers, argued that Suarez's performance should have been rewarded with a place on the list of the top five contenders for the Footballer of the Year award and that he couldn't see any reason why he was not on the list football-wise (Whittell 2014). To further reiterate his moral reasoning in this case, he argued that Suarez should be judged on his performance on the football pitch which is the criterion for the Golden Boot. A Nigerian football analyst puts it more succinctly, "Luiz Suarez should be judged as a footballer, not as a priest."

Our argument here is that consumers are not only motivated to support, but can also be motivated to oppose. Again, we argue that consumers who are motivated to oppose a brand that has transgressed are most likely to adopt a different reasoning strategy to resolve the tension between desired outcomes and moral standards. We therefore emphasize that this reasoning process is fed more by the self-relevance a consumer derives from such a brand even much more than the relevance of the transgression.

What may be more interesting to know is if there would be a difference in the reaction of consumers if a transgression were perceived as being deliberate (an outright act of deceit that could be imagined as a stab-in-the-back) as opposed to wrongdoing due to a need for survival. A premeditated act of transgression is likely to evoke revenge than any other act of situational transgression. In the same manner that cold-blooded murder is viewed and treated differently from a kill due to self-defense, one would suspect that consumers would embrace a reasoning process very different from moral (de)coupling or moral rationalization.

Also, of interest for further research may be an investigation into why consumers who have had brands transgress against them would pardon or reprimand the transgressor post apology. In a bid to return to status quo, would it be sufficient to publicly apologize, to deliberately engage in honest efforts to right one's wrong, or to frantically attempt to undo the benefits of wrong doings or even a combination of some/all of these? These and many more conversations around unethical actions of brands could help reiterate the message to brand promoters that what is not ethical is not sustainable.

Conclusions

In this chapter, we have discussed how the relevance of transgression to a transgressor is not the only prerequisite for a consumer to be motivated to oppose a brand before engaging in the psychological process of moral coupling, but also the self-relevance of the transgression to the consumer. This, therefore, should sound a note of warning to brands that do not intend to become transgressors but may transgress someday (however careful such brands could be) to understand the self-relevance of their activities to their consumers and be able to project to what extent this could instigate their consumers to combine judgment of performance and morality as an argument to act against them.

Summary

Researchers and practitioners alike pay more attention to strengthening consumer–brand relationship. Trying not to be pessimistic, these groups of people hope nothing harmful happens to such a bond. Precedence has shown that most relationships do not enjoy perpetual bliss but experience friction that threatens their continuity at some point. Previous discussions show that aggrieved consumers react in different ways that do not benefit targeted brands. Therefore, the ability of brands to predict the reasoning process of such consumers better positions them to resolve any impending trouble.

To predict that aggrieved consumers would engage in moral coupling, a psychological moral reasoning process that combines judgment of morality and judgment of performance as a justification to oppose a brand, transgressed brands must realize that transgression relevance may not be strong predictor like consumer self-relevance. A consumer is more concerned about the shame his association with a transgressed brand would bring to him than the direct relevance of the wrong doing to the core function of the brand.

It is hoped that academics and practitioners will invest more resources in understanding how to manage a breach of rules, be they implied or explicit, that defines relationship performance and evaluation in a consumer–brand relationship. As consumers personalize their affair with a brand, it would not be surprising that they also personalize the evaluation of their brand's transgression.

Discussion Questions

1. What qualifies a transgression that makes it significant enough for consumer reactions?
2. What may be different in terms of outcome if the transgression by a brand is conceived as being deliberate as opposed to a careless unintended action or inaction?
3. How easy would it be for a consumer who has chided a brand for its transgression in the past to turn around in the future and support the same brand?

References

Aaker, J., and S. Fournier. 1995. "A Brand as a Character, a Partner and a Person: Three Perspectives on the Question of Brand Personality." *NA-Advances in Consumer Research Volume 22.*

Aaker, J. 1999. "The Malleable Self: The Role of Self-expression in Persuasion." *Available at SSRN 945453*.

Aaker, J., S. Fournier, and S.A. Brasel. 2004. "When Good Brands Do Bad." *Journal of Consumer Research* 31, no. 1, pp. 1–16.

Aaker, J.L., 1997. "Dimensions of Brand Personality." *Journal of Marketing Research*, pp. 347–56.

Aaker, J.L., V. Benet-Martinez, and J. Garolera. 2001. "Consumption Symbols as Carriers of Culture: A study of Japanese and Spanish Brand Personality Constructs." *Journal of Personality and Social Psychology* 81, no. 3, p. 492.

Arnould, E.J., and M. Wallendorf. 1994. "Market-Oriented Ethnography: Interpretation Building and Marketing Strategy Formulation." *Journal of Marketing Research*, pp. 484–504.

Azoulay, A., and J.N. Kapferer. 2003. "Do Brand Personality Scales Really Measure Brand Personality?" *Journal of Brand Management* 11, no. 2, pp. 143–55.

Bandura, A. 1999. "Social Cognitive Theory of Personality." *Handbook of Personality: Theory and Research*, pp. 154–96.

Baumeister, R.F., and L.S. Newman. 1994. "Self-Regulation of Cognitive Inference and Decision Processes." *Personality and Social Psychology Bulletin* 20, no. 1, pp. 3–19.

Belk, R.W. 1988. "Possessions and the Extended Self." *Journal of Consumer Research* 15, no. 2, pp. 139–68.

Berscheid, E., and L.A. Peplau. 1983. "The Emerging Science of Relationships." In *Close Relationships*, eds. H.H. Kelley, E. Berscheid, A. Christensen, J.H. Harvey, T.L. Huston, G. Levinger, E. McClintock, L.A. Peplau, and D.R. Petterson, 1–19. New York: W.H. Freeman.

Bhattacharjee, A., J.Z. Berman, and A. Reed. 2013. "Tip of the Hat, Wag of the Finger: How Moral Decoupling Enables Consumers to Admire and Admonish." *Journal of Consumer Research* 39, no. 6, pp. 1167–84.

Bhattacharya, C.B., and S. Sen. 2003. "Consumer-Company Identification: A Framework for Understanding Consumers' Relationships with Companies." *Journal of Marketing* 67, no. 2, pp. 76–88.

Buss, D.M., and K.H. Craik. 1983. "The Act Frequency Approach to Personality." *Psychological Review* 90, no. 2, p. 105.

Buunk, B. 1982. "Anticipated Sexual Jealousy Its Relationship to Self-Esteem, Dependency, and Reciprocity." *Personality and Social Psychology Bulletin* 8, no. 2, pp. 310–16.

Buysse, A., A. De Clercq, L. Verhofstadt, E. Heene, H. Roeyers, and P. Van Oost. 2000. "Dealing with Relational Conflict: A Picture in Milliseconds." *Journal of Social and Personal Relationships* 17, nos. 4–5, pp. 574–97.

Caprara, G.V., C. Barbaranelli, and G. Guido. 2001. "Brand Personality: How to Make the Metaphor Fit?" *Journal of Economic Psychology* 22, no. 3, pp. 377–95.

Chelminski, P., and R.A. Coulter. 2011. "An Examination of Consumer Advocacy and Complaining Behavior in the Context of Service Failure." *Journal of Services Marketing* 25, no. 5, pp. 361–70.

Cobb-Walgren, C.J., C.A. Ruble, and N. Donthu. 1995. "Brand Equity, Brand Preference, and Purchase Intent." *Journal of Advertising* 24, no. 3, pp. 25–40.

Craig-Lees, M., S. Joy, and B. Browne. 1995. *Consumer Behaviour.* Brisbane: John Wiley and Sons.

Day, G.S., and C. Van den Bulte. 2002. *Superiority in Customer Relationship Management: Consequences for Competitive Advantage and Performance.* Marketing Science Institute.

Dick, A.S., and B. Kunal. 1994. "Customer Loyalty: Toward an Integrated Conceptual Framework." *Journal of the Academy of Marketing Science* 22, no. 2, pp. 99–113.

Ditto, P.H., D.A. Pizarro, and D. Tannenbaum. 2009. "Motivated Moral Reasoning." *Psychology of Learning and Motivation* 50, pp. 307–38.

Dvorak, B.G. 2008. "Dynamic Human Relationships with Wilderness: Developing a Relationship Model." *Theses, Dissertations, Professional Papers. Paper 342.* Retrieved at http://scholarworks.umt.edu/cgi/viewcontent. cgi?article=1361and context=etd

Dutta, S., and C. Pullig. 2011. "Effectiveness of Corporate Responses to Brand Crises: The Role of Crisis Type and Response Strategies." *Journal of Business Research* 64, no. 12, pp. 1281–87.

Elangovan, A.R., and D.L. Shapiro. 1998. "Betrayal of Trust in Organizations." *Academy of Management Review* 23, no. 3, pp. 547–66.

Elegido, J.M. 1994. *Jurisprudence,* 128. Ibadan: Spectrum Books Limited.

Epstein, S. 1977. "Traits Are Alive and Well." *Personality at the Crossroads: Current Issues in Interactional Psychology,* pp. 83–98.

Erdelyi, M.H. 1974. "A New Look at the New Look: Perceptual Defense and Vigilance." *Psychological Review* 81, no. 1, p. 1.

Festinger, L. (1962) 1957. *A Theory of Cognitive Dissonance.* Evanston, IL: Row Peterson. Introduction and Passim.

Fincham, F.D., and T.N. Bradbury. 1987. "The Impact of Attributions in Marriage: A Longitudinal Analysis." *Journal of Personality and Social Psychology* 53, no. 3, p. 510.

Fiske, S.T. 1980. "Attention and Weight in Person Perception: The Impact of Negative and Extreme Behavior." *Journal of Personality and Social Psychology* 38, no. 6, p. 889.

Fletcher, G.J.O., J.A. Simpson, and G. Thomas. 2000. "Ideals, Perceptions, and Evaluations in Early Relationship Development." *Journal of Personality and Social Psychology* 79, no. 6, p. 933.

Fournier, S. 1998. "Consumers and Their Brands: Developing Relationship Theory in Consumer Research." *Journal of Consumer Research* 24, no. 4, pp. 343–53.

Fournier, S., and J.L. Yao. 1997. "Reviving Brand Loyalty: A Reconceptualization within the Framework of Consumer-brand Relationships." *International Journal of Research in Marketing* 14, no. 5, pp. 451–72.

George, S.D., and C. Van den Bulte. 2002. "Superiority in Customer Relationship Management: Consequences for Competitive Advantage and Performance." Report No. 02-123. Cambridge, MA: Marketing Science Institute.

Giacalone, R.A., K. Paul, and C.L. Jurkiewicz. 2005. "A Preliminary Investigation into the Role of Positive Psychology in Consumer Sensitivity to Corporate Social Performance." *Journal of Business Ethics* 58, no. 4, pp. 295–305.

Gilmore, G.W. 1919. *Animism: Or, Thought Currents of Primitive Peoples.* Marshall Jones Company, Boston, MA.

Grayson, K., and T. Ambler. 1999. "The Dark Side of Long-Term Relationships in Marketing Services." *Journal of Marketing Research*, pp. 132–41.

Grégoire, Y., T.M. Tripp, and R. Legoux. 2009. "When Customer Love Turns into Lasting Hate: The Effects of Relationship Strength and Time on Customer Revenge and Avoidance." *Journal of Marketing* 73, no. 6, pp. 18–32.

Gummesson, E. 2002. "Relationship Marketing in the New Economy." *Journal of Relationship Marketing* 1, no. 1, pp. 37–57.

Haidt, J. 2001. "The Emotional Dog and Its Rational Tail: A Social Intuitionist Approach to Moral Judgment." *Psychological Review* 108, no. 4, p. 814.

He, H., Y. Li, and L. Harris. 2012. "Social Identity Perspective on Brand Loyalty." *Journal of Business Research* 65, no. 5, pp. 648–57.

Heider, F. 2013. *The Psychology of Interpersonal Relations.* Routledge: Psychology Press.

Houston, M.B., and B.A. Walker. 1996. "Self-relevance and Purchase Goals: Mapping a Consumer Decision." *Journal of the Academy of Marketing Science* 24, no. 3, pp. 232–45.

Jacoby, J., and D.B. Kyner. 1973. "Brand Loyalty vs. Repeat Purchasing Behavior." *Journal of Marketing Research*, pp. 1–9.

Johar, G.V., J. Sengupta, and J.L. Aaker. 2005. "Two Roads to Updating Brand Personality Impressions: Trait Versus Evaluative Inferencing." *Journal of Marketing Research* 42, no. 4, pp. 458–69.

Johar, G.V., M.M. Birk, and S.A. Einwiller. 2010. "How to Save Your Brand in the Face of Crisis." *MIT Sloan Management Review* 51, no. 4, p. 57.

Johnson, A.R., M. Matear, and M. Thomson. 2011. "A Coal in the Heart: Self-Relevance as a Post-Exit Predictor of Consumer Anti-Brand Actions." *Journal of Consumer Research* 38, no. 1, pp. 108–25.

Kapferer, J.N. 1992. "Strategic Brand Management: New Approaches to Creating and Evaluating Brand Equity." Kogan Page, London, U.K.

Keaveney, S.M. 1995. "Customer Switching Behavior in Service Industries: An Exploratory Study." *The Journal of Marketing*, pp. 71–82.

Keller, K.L. 1993. Conceptualizing, Measuring, and Managing Customer-Based Brand Equity. *The Journal of Marketing*, pp. 1–22.

Keller, K.L. 2001. "Building Customer-Based Brand Equity: A Blueprint for Creating Strong Brands." Working Paper 01-107. pp. 3–38.

Kleine, R.E., S.S. Kleine, and J.B. Kernan. 1993. "Mundane Consumption and the Self: A Social-Identity Perspective." *Journal of Consumer Psychology* 2, no. 3, pp. 209–35.

Koehler, J.J., and A.D. Gershoff. 2003. "Betrayal Aversion: When Agents of Protection Become Agents of Harm." *Organizational Behavior and Human Decision Processes* 90, no. 2, pp. 244–61.

Kopalle, P.K., and J. Lindsey-Mullikin. 2003. "The Impact of External Reference Price on Consumer Price Expectations." *Journal of Retailing* 79, no. 4, pp. 225–36.

Kunda, Z. 1990. "The Case for Motivated Reasoning." *Psychological Bulletin* 108, no. 3, p. 480.

Malhotra, N.K. 1988. "Self Concept and Product Choice: An Integrated Perspective." *Journal of Economic Psychology* 9, no. 1, pp. 1–28.

Mazar, N., O. Amir, and D. Ariely. 2008. "The Dishonesty of Honest People: A Theory of Self-Concept Maintenance." *Journal of Marketing Research* 45, no. 6, pp. 633–44.

Metts, S. 1994. "Relational Transgressions." In *The Dark Side of Interpersonal Communications*, eds. W.R. Cupach, and B. Spitzberg, 217–39. Hillsdale, NJ: Lawrence Erlbaum.

Miller, A.H. 1999. "Sex, Politics, and Public Opinion: What Political Scientists Really Learned from the Clinton-Lewinsky Scandal." *PS: Political Science and Politics* 32, no. 4, pp. 721–29.

Morrison, E.W., and S.L. Robinson. 1997. "When Employees Feel Betrayed: A Model of How Psychological Contract Violation Develops." *Academy of Management Review* 22, no. 1, pp. 226–56.

Olsen, S.O. 2002. "Comparative Evaluation and the Relationship Between Quality, Satisfaction, and Repurchase Loyalty." *Journal of the Academy of Marketing Science* 30, no. 3, pp. 240–49.

Paharia, N., and R. Deshpandé. 2009. *Sweatshop Labor Is Wrong Unless the Jeans Are Cute: Motivated Moral Disengagement*. Boston: Harvard Business School.

Park, C.W., B.J. Jaworski, and D.J. MacInnis. 1986. "Strategic Brand Concept-Image Management." *The Journal of Marketing*, pp. 135–45.

Park, C.W., D.J. MacInnis, and J.R. Priester. 2006. "Beyond Attitudes: Attachment and Consumer Behavior." *Seoul National Journal* 12, no. 2, pp. 3–36.

Parker, B.T. 2009. "A Comparison of Brand Personality and Brand User-Imagery Congruence." *Journal of Consumer Marketing* 26, no. 3, pp. 175–84.

Petty, R.E., and J.T. Cacioppo. 1986. *The Elaboration Likelihood Model of Persuasion*. New York: Springer.

Price, L.L., E.J. Arnould, and F. Bardhi. 2002. "After Commercial Betrayal." *Adv. Cons. Res.* 29.

Price, L.L., E.J. Arnould, and F. Bardhi. 2004. "'Service Providers' Road to 'Hell': Service Betrayal, Its Consequences and Recovery Attempts." *Advances in Consumer Research* 31, pp. 339–42.

Reis, H.T., and C.R. Knee. 1996. "What We Know, What We Don't Know, and What We Need to Know about Relationship Knowledge Structures." *Knowledge Structures in Close Relationships*, pp. 169–91.

Richins, M.L. 1983. "Negative Word-of-Mouth by Dissatisfied Consumers: A Pilot Study." *The Journal of Marketing*, pp. 68–78.

Rook, D.W. 1985. "The Ritual Dimension of Consumer Behavior." *Journal of Consumer Research*, pp. 251–64.

Rusbult, CE., J. Verette, G.A. Whitney, L.F. Slovik, and I. Lipkus. 1991. "Accommodation Processes in Close Relationships: Theory and Preliminary Empirical Evidence." *Journal of Personality and Social Psychology* 60, no. 1, p. 53.

Shocker, A.D., R.K. Srivastava, and R.W. Ruekert. 1994. "Challenges and Opportunities Facing Brand Management: An Introduction to the Special Issue." *Journal of Marketing Research*, pp. 149–58.

Shogan, D.A. 1999. *The Making of High-Performance Athletes: Discipline, Diversity, and Ethics*. Toronto: University of Toronto Press.

Shu, L.L., F. Gino, and M.H. Bazerman. 2011. "Dishonest Deed, Clear Conscience: When Cheating Leads to Moral Disengagement and Motivated Forgetting." *Personality and Social Psychology Bulletin* 37, no. 3, pp. 330–49.

Sirgy, M.J. 1982. "Self-Concept in Consumer Behavior: A Critical Review." *Journal of Consumer Research*, pp. 287–300.

Sirgy, M.J. 1985. "Using Self-Congruity and Ideal Congruity to Predict Purchase Motivation." *Journal of Business Research* 13, no. 3, pp. 195–206.

Smith, A.K., R.N. Bolton, and J. Wagner. 1999. "A Model of Customer Satisfaction with Service Encounters Involving Failure and Recovery." *Journal of Marketing Research,* pp. 356–72.

Sung, Y., and S.F. Tinkham. 2005. "Brand personality Structures in the United States and Korea: Common and Culture-Specific Factors." *Journal of Consumer Psychology* 15, no. 4, pp. 334–50.

Swaminathan, V., K.M. Stilley, and R. Ahluwalia. 2009. "When Brand Personality Matters: The Moderating Role of Attachment Styles." *Journal of Consumer Research* 35, no. 6, pp. 985–1002.

Tsang, J.-A. 2002. "Moral Rationalization and the Integration of Situational Factors and Psychological Processes in Immoral Behavior." *Review of General Psychology* 6, no. 1, p. 25.

Wernerfelt, B. 1991. "Brand Loyalty and Market Equilibrium." *Marketing Science* 10, no. 3, pp. 229–45.

Wharton School. 2013. *BizTalks 2013: Americus Reed on "When Buying Is Being"* [video] Available at: https://www.youtube.com/watch?v=xM7wxNgfODo [Accessed April 20, 2014].

Whittell, I. 2014. *"Luis Suarez should have been in the Ballon d'Or shortlist, says Liverpool manager Brendan Rodgers."* [online] The Telegraph. Available at: http://www.telegraph.co.uk/sport/football/players/luis-suarez/11203661/Luis-Suarez-should-have-been-in-the-Ballon-dOr-shortlist-says-Liverpool-manager-Brendan-Rodgers.html [Accessed February 6, 2015].

Xie, Yi., and P. Siqing. 2009. "How to Repair Customer Trust after Negative Publicity: The Roles of Competence, Integrity, Benevolence, and Forgiveness." *Psychology and Marketing* 26, no. 7, pp. 572–89.

CHAPTER 11

HR Policy for Responsibility

Arjya Chakravarty

All across the globe today, businesses are overstretched to meet profits, as well as manage responsibly. There is heightened awareness in organizations to mindfully advance relationships with all stakeholders, inclusive of our planet Earth. Organizations have to balance the myriad demands of various stakeholder groups such as primary stakeholders (owners, employees, customers, and suppliers); secondary stakeholders (nongovernmental organizations [NGOs], activists, communities, and governments); social needs; and institutional forces (Freeman and McVea 2001; Harrison and Freeman 1999; Von Kimakowitz et al. 2011; Waddock, Bodwell, and Graves 2002). Innovative business practices and management frameworks are enablers of driving positive change on a sustainable basis, in this world.

Employees need to be engaged and passionate about their work, for organizations to create competitive advantage in an ever-changing, complex business environment. Organizations in turn should be able to lead in a responsible manner. The agenda of the human resource (HR) function is to create and implement robust policies and processes that can inspire employees to work toward the strategic goals of the company. Organizations should be able to leverage human potential and enhance the business performance. Policies and processes should therefore, not just motivate but these need to inspire (inspiration being at a higher level than motivation). The employees should feel a sense of ownership and—voluntarily and willingly with his or her heart, mind, and soul—be able to align themselves with the larger purpose of vision, mission, and strategy of the organization.

The defining characteristic of an employee or a manager is that he or she must make decisions to cater for unforeseen circumstances or under constrained resources (Prendergast 1995). So as per this definition, a manager needs to exercise discretion. Whether a manager is going to use this discretion in an efficient manner, can lead us to understand the concept of "Managing for Responsibility." In this chapter, we hope to contribute to a better understanding of HR function in the role of responsible decision making to aid sustainable organizational performance.

Organization, Teams, and Individuals

The organization today has basically evolved to organize itself around three entities:

1. The organization as a whole
2. The teams or groups in the organization
3. Each individual employee or stakeholder

Each of these entities has separate needs, goals, or achievable targets and these in turn are linked to processes or achieving organizational objectives and boosting productivity (Watkins and Marsick 1993). In this chapter we will discuss the HR policies, purposes and their outcomes, with this framework as a background.

The Organization as a Whole

The HR requirements are to act as a facilitator and enabler for creating direction and purpose, facilitate communication channels, and good governance (Chalofsky 1992).

Teams

The HR requirements are to act as a facilitator and process owner to create teamwork, team goals, and cross-functional understanding, in alignment with the organizational objectives.

Individual Employee

The HR requirements are to act as a process owner and create the maximum impact. HR needs to create performance management, behavior counseling, employee satisfaction, and robust recruitment processes.

The organizational HR function has to operate at all the three levels and have a departmental structure to support each level. The need is to reach out at all the levels and customize programs to create responsible HR. In an organization, in general, the policies that enjoy the respect of employees are the one in which:

- Each employee feels that the treatment meted out is just and equitable.
- The same yardstick is used across all organizational levels.
- An employee's complete and authentic well-being is appreciated.

Alignment Across the Three Entities

The need is to go beyond the statutory compliance agenda and craft a more enabling agenda, that is, actionable, profitable, and mutually rewarding. HR function should create processes which ensure alignment with the organizational vision, mission, and strategy. Once the objectives for HR interventions at all the levels are decided, HR has to design innovative interventions (Harris and Harris 1983) which capture the interest of the employees and create employee engagement or high productivity (refer to Figure 11.1). To facilitate the role of HR in the organization's productivity, the top management has to take the crucial decision of the level of involvement required and create budget to justify these needs. Organizations are dynamic and constantly evolving in the nature of their business and HR policies too must evolve and change with the changing business scenarios. The purpose of all human resource policies has to be the welfare and moral of the employee and aligned to the requirement of the business.

Examples to illustrate this case are:

- In case the unit wants to specifically drive in speed and agility, HR should create the team related interventions that will incentivize such behaviors. The team level interventions can be off-site trainings, with the specific objectives like cross-functional camaraderie, high strung team spirit, or a sense of well-being.

Conceptual framework for responsible HR processes and policies

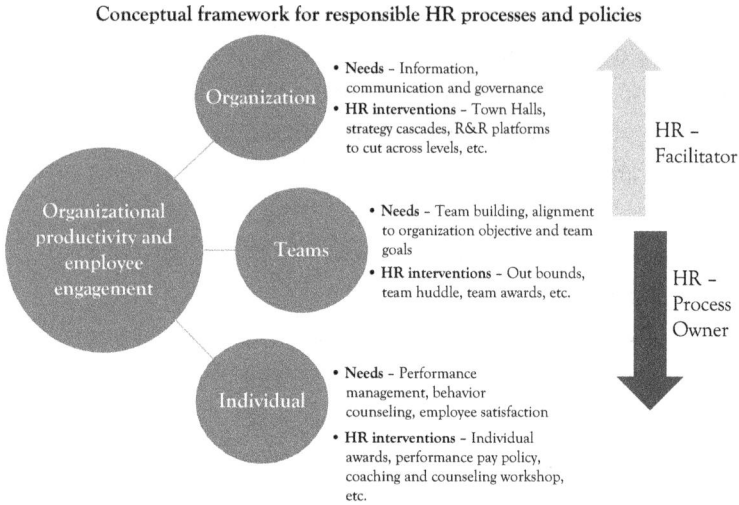

(This framework is based on literature survey and case studies).

Figure 11.1 A conceptual framework for responsible HR processes and policies

- The role of HR does not stop at identifying the high performers through a performance appraisal process. At an individual level, aspirations of high potential performers (Hi-Pots) need to be managed. To make this process powerful, the organization may sponsor leadership trainings at reputed academic institutions or universities as a reward and recognition process (R&R).
- Some organizations differentiate their "A" listers by allocating employee stock options (ESOPs). This has been practised by start-up businesses very successfully.

Challenges

Drucker said that only two things matter in an organization's success—innovation and marketing. The rest is fiction. The point to be mulled over is that both require the right talents. This means that attracting, retaining, and developing the right human talent is perhaps the most important work in any organization. This is a huge challenge. The HR function can help make the process of doing so a lot more productive, effective, and reduce risk by developing relevant policies. Where this usually falls short, is in alignment across the three entities. If policies and processes lose alignment, they become burdensome and counterproductive, that is when employees and other stakeholders become disengaged.

An organization's motive should be to best understand its customers' need and find unique and sustainable ways to fulfil those needs. HR policies should help employees in the organization align themselves to this motive.

Policies that treat employees like responsible citizens and are responsive to the business environment are universally respected. Policies that waste people's energy are those that unnecessarily discriminate or micromanage and create disengaged employees.

When policies treat employees like responsible, trustworthy adults, it automatically leads to more self-service, more awareness of ethical behavior, less to and fro for special approvals which means more time for work and a display of organization citizenship behavior (Rampersad and Hussain 2014).

The challenges for HR function are therefore manifold.

1. HR policies need to be communicated across all levels in a transparent and respectful manner. Instead of a threatening and warning language or tone, it should spread a sense of well-being. Communication to all employees should be an active propagation instead of a reactive mechanism. Each communication whether oral or written, formal or informal, needs to reinforce trust, confidence, and enhance the psychological contract (Robinson 1996).

2. Risks of unethical behavior have multiplied. Organizations motivate employees by attractive salary increments and perks, and insist on cut-throat competition for being a market leader. They have to also ensure that employees remain within the bounds of ethical behavior and conduct. Therefore finding the right balance is a real challenge.

3. Reward mechanisms are created to ensure that employees have greater interest in ensuring profits for the organization (for example,

stock options). This can also encourage excessive risk taking at the expense of stability (or even survival) (Bear Stearns[1] and Lehman Brothers[2] are prime examples).

4. An organization's growth patterns (mergers, acquisitions, alliances, contracts, networks) create a complex entity and yet the organization needs to focus on the stated vision, mission, and goals. This requires policies and processes to eliminate the inherent conflicts of interest.

5. HR policies have to be competitive, so the need is to constantly match up with peers. Yet, there is a deep sense of conflict between HR ownership (principal) and beneficiaries or employees (agents), given that HR is ultimately a cost center where costs or benefits are not immediate but long-term outcomes.

6. Productivity enhancing policies, R&R programs and ESOPs, have to strike a very sensitive balance between short-term and long-term rewards and well-being of the organization.

7. Benefits (medical facilities, education support, etc.) are often linked to seniority, rising proportionately, yet, their need is the highest at the lowest echelons as disposable incomes are the least in that segment. Though the challenge from an overall organizational cost perspective is that junior employees are usually far more in number, and will raise the costs for such organizations. Innovative thinking is required to make employees happy, yet keep the costs manageable. Organizations can offer flexible benefit plans for employees to choose.

8. Evaluation of HR manager's performance is an underfocused area and could be designed such that there is enough incentive for HR managers to strike the right balance between competitiveness (attract or retain talent), organizational sustainability (costs, productivity), and organizational values.

---

[1] www.investopedia.com/articles/07/bear-stearns-collapse.asp

[2] www.investopedia.com/articles/economics/09/lehman-brothers-collapse.asp

Caring @ Coke

During the Gulf War of 2003, Coca-Cola[3] relocated its employees from Bahrain (regional head office) to Dubai and took care of their entire boarding and lodging at Dubai. When the war was over and it was considered safe to return to Bahrain, the company arranged for their resettlement. Although thousands of companies operated in Bahrain, it was only a tiny handful number of companies—Coke included—that took care of their employees.

Organizations like Coke insist on using up the entire annual leave without any exceptions. Seldom do you find organizations insisting on employees to avail their leaves. This organization is also known for its generous stock offers to the employees.

A Culture of Trust at Chevron Corporation

Chevron Corporation[4] creates a compliance culture by spelling out clear guidelines for behavior, while at employment. Once a year they have online training modules which cover issues like harassment, travel, and other global policies. Their global policies are inclusive of the local policies and regulations, in each location. They have taken into consideration the Foreign Corrupt Practices Act (FCPA),[5] while creating their policies.

---

[3] *Coca-Cola is a global multinational company which manufactures and sells carbonated soft drink to the world. Coke, as this drink is termed, is a registered trademark of The Coca-Cola Company in the United States since March 27, 1944 and is one of the world's most valuable brand. http://www.coca-colacompany.com/our-company/*
[4] *Chevron Corporation is a multinational energy corporation, headquartered at the United States in San Ramon, California, and has a presence in more than 180 countries. Chevron is one of the world's largest oil companies and is engaged in every aspect of the oil, gas, and geothermal energy industries including exploration and production; refining, marketing and transport; chemicals manufacturing and sales; and power generation. https://www.chevron.com/*
[5] *The Foreign Corrupt Practices Act of 1977 (FCPA) is a law known for its two main provisions—addressing accounting transparency requirements under the Securities Exchange Act of 1934 and concerning bribery of foreign officials. https://www.justice. gov/criminal-fraud/foreign-corrupt-practices-act*

To ease off workload, Chevron's travel policy does not require their employees to submit documentation up to $50 a day. For expatriates traveling back home each year, they are not required to submit travel tickets and bills. The organization has taken some standard Airline ticket prices and sanctioned a ball park figure to each employee. This creates a sense of trust and well-being for the employees instead of feeling scrutinized and eases monotonous workload from internal compliance or accounts division. There are online programs on the company's intranet to understand performance appraisal issues, to get trained on a good appraisal process and templates for good recruitments. Their employees claim that policies are transparent and there are no blue-eyed employees.

Recent Developments

Unilever India has a process that necessitates long periods of job rotation during the initial first two or three years of a newly hired employee (management trainee or any other apprentice). The employee moves from one location to another location, working and contributing with various teams, verticals, units, or divisions. This process ensures multidimensional thinking process in these employees and broadens their perspective about the business at Unilever. These employees become empowered to use their discretion for organizational decisions. This intervention, facilitated by HR, is very strategic as it comes at the beginning of the career, when the employee enjoys this kind of work and has less bindings and learns immensely during the process. In contrast, the employees of many public sector units (PSUs), who are compulsory asked to relocate during the process of job rotation, feel victimized and burdened.

Some organizations are able to create a "start-up" organization culture, which retains the spirit of ownership and innovation. In the Future Group's[6] head office in Mumbai, the décor is an Indian theme and the reception has the picture of a golden colored bird flying with the engraved words in Hindi (Udna hai, Aaj, Abhi) which translate to "we are ready to fly, right now." The organization claims to be a local player and proclaims

---

[6] *Future Group is a private Indian retail company , with popular supermarket chains like Big Bazaar and Food Bazaar, lifestyle stores like Brand Factory, Central, etc. http://www.futuregroup.in*

that aligning their business practices to the Indian ethos and culture has catapulted them to leverage India's consumption-led growth story.

Moving out of a boxed mentality, diversity in the organizational teams brings about fresh thought process and creates appreciation for better organizational ownership. Wipro[7] has a concept of "Well-Done" cards. These cards can be printed from the organization's intranet and is used by the employees to appreciate the efforts of seniors or peers. These credits get accredited in the R&R programs. Employees can use these credits to buy goods from the organizations designated online shop.

Summary

The core purpose of the HR function is to create and implement policies and processes that can inspire employees to work toward the larger common goals of the company. The defining characteristic of an employee or a manager is to make decisions which cater for unforeseen circumstances. A manager needs to exercise discretion in a responsible manner. The organization today has basically evolved to organize itself around three entities—the organization as a whole, the teams or groups in the organization, and each individual employee or stakeholder. Each of these entities has separate needs, goals, and achievable targets and these in turn are linked to HR processes for achieving organizational objectives and enhancing productivity.

Organizations are dynamic and constantly evolving in the nature of their business and HR policies too must evolve and change with the changing business scenarios. The purpose of all HR policies has to be the holistic welfare of the employee and align this to the requirement of the business. The challenges of HR function today are therefore manifold in order to achieve this right balance. Organizations that excel in both managed better and managed different have been able to create policies to this effect.

---

[7] *India's largest publicly traded companies and seventh largest IT services firm in the world, Western India Products Limited (Wipro) is a global multinational IT consulting and system integration services company. Wipro has 154,297 employees servicing over 900 of the Fortune 1000 corporations with a presence in 61 countries. http://www.wipro.com/services/*

Discussion Questions

1. How can organizations create competitive advantage in today's complex business environment?
2. What is the core purpose of HR and how does this purpose manifest itself in the organization (around the three main entities)?
3. From your own experience or search, list at least three policies that treat employees like responsible citizens.
4. According to you what are the main challenges that the HR function will have to face to implement responsibility in decision-making process in an organization?

References

Chalofsky, N. 1992. "A Unifying Definition for the Human Resource Development Profession." *Human Resource Development Quarterly* 3, no. 2, pp. 175–82.

Freeman, R.E., and J. McVea. 2001. "A Stakeholder Approach to Strategic Management." Darden Business School Working Paper No. 01-02. SSRN: http://ssrn.com/abstract=263511 orhttp://dx.doi.org/10.2139/ssrn.263511

Harrison, J.S., and R.E. Freeman. 1999. "Stakeholders, Social Responsibility, and Performance: Empirical Evidence and Theoretical Perspectives." *Academy of Management Journal* 42, no. 5, pp. 479–85.

Harris, P.R., and D.L. Harris. 1983. "Twelve Trends You and Your CEO Should be Monitoring." *Training & Development Journal.*

Prendergast, C.J. 1995. "A Theory of Responsibility in Organizations." *Journal of Labor Economics*, pp. 387–400.

Rampersad, H., and S. Hussain. 2014. "Alignment with Your Organization." In *Authentic Governance*, 131–42. New York: Springer International Publishing.

Robinson, S.L. 1996. "Trust and Breach of the Psychological Contract." *Administrative Science Quarterly*, pp. 574–99.

Von Kimakowitz, E., M. Pirson, H. Spitzeck, C. Dierksmeier, W. Amann, eds. 2011. *Humanistic Management in Practice.* Basingstoke: Palgrave Macmillan.

Waddock, S.A., C. Bodwell, and S.B. Graves. 2002. "Responsibility: The New Business Imperative." *The Academy of Management Executive* 16, no. 2, pp. 132–48.

Watkins, K.E., and V.J. Marsick. 1993. *Sculpting the Learning Organization: Lessons in the Art and Science of Systemic Change.* San Francisco: Jossey-Bass Inc., 350, CA 94104-1310.

Additional Readings

Björkman, I., and J.E. Lervik. 2007. "Transferring HR Practices within Multinational Corporations." *Human Resource Management Journal* 17, no. 4, pp. 320–35.

Guest, D.E., and N. Conway. 2002. "Communicating the Psychological Contract: An Employer Perspective." *Human Resource Management Journal* 12, no. 2, pp. 22–38.

Nishii, L.H., D.P. Lepak, and B. Schneider. 2008. "Employee Attributions of the 'Why' of HR Practices: Their Effects on Employee Attitudes and Behaviours, and Customer Satisfaction." *Personnel Psychology* 61, no. 3, pp. 503–45.

CHAPTER 12

Managing Conflicts Responsibly—Listening from the Heart

Pramod Pathak and Saumya Singh

Introduction

The Concise Oxford Dictionary defines conflict as a serious disagreement or argument, a prolonged armed struggle, an incompatibility between opinions principles, and so on. Extant literature on conflict says conflict exists whenever two or more people disagree. These notwithstanding conflicts are an inevitable aspect of life. Dictionaries can define conflicts. Literature can describe them and dwell upon their nature and concept. But only human beings can understand them. And in this understanding lies the answer to the issue of managing conflicts with responsibility. True, management thinkers have come a long way as far as decoding the concept and nature of conflict is concerned. But there is still a long way to go when it comes to managing conflicts. One reason probably may be our approach to understanding conflict. Conflicts are not good or bad, they are just there waiting to happen. We usually try to address conflict as a cause-and-effect issue. Naturally, the logical assumption is that if the cause is gone, the effect, that is the conflict, will also go. So far so good. But, the problem is that it does not go far enough. Conflicts reappear in some other guise because we have been barking up the wrong tree. Conflicts usually are not out there in the situation. They are in there, in the minds. The reasons that appear to be creating conflicts are only the tip of the iceberg—nine-tenths being not visible. There is a need to go deeper. And if you go deep into any conflict, you will find cognitions. Recognition of the issues does not matter much. This cognition, however, is difficult to comprehend. One reason being the assumption of the authorities responsible for managing conflict. Since the processes that comprise cognition involve perception, reasoning, judging, and so on, which are all individual specific, it is difficult to draw the right inferences. Though generalizations based on situational analysis are resorted to, they may or may not be helpful in penning the right prescription. Results thus, usually are that the symptoms gets addressed, the aetiology or the cause of it remaining still unattended. Not that the authorities responsible for managing conflict are always unmindful of this fact. But, aware or not, the difficulty is that of limitations of time and resources in hand. More so, in present times, a growing tendency toward conflict has become a significant trend. Conflicts are becoming more frequent because the parties to the conflicts are impatient and the resolution is not effective because the authorities too are not able to address conflict patiently. Conflicts, thus, keep on arising. Just like that. There is need to give relook at conflict.

Conflict—A Relook

The new-age understanding that conflicts are on the rise is based on certain assumptions and we need to examine these in order to understand conflict. Rather comprehend it more elaborately. Yes, conflicts are on the rise and the changing mores of the society are one of the reasons for this.

The increasing awareness and rising aspirations are natural concomitants of the present-day society fashionably referred to as post-modern society or the information age. And for those who believe in this, the society is a technopolis which is shaped by personal experiences, self-interest, and mass media. The religious and moral institutions of the yore which shaped the society are losing relevance.

In fact this is the age of contradictions. Excessive use of technology that was supposed to facilitate human performance is dividing them into the technomanic and the technophobic. Organizations are struggling to contend with this. Then the generational divide. Companies are struggling to manage the intergenerational workforce. The young employees consider the older ones as deadwood. The older ones think that the young are novices. And then there is the gender divide. The number of female employees is rising in the workplace and the idea of equal opportunity is creating a new ground for conflict. The traditional organizations are fast approaching extinction. In the new organization, there is more diversity. All these inconsistencies are increasing conflict vulnerability. Conflicts are also arising due to race, class, caste diversities as apprehensions and threat perceptions are on the rise. Conflict absorption threshold is getting lowered as aggressive tendencies are rising. Psychologists are looking for reasons that range from ambition to hatred, self interest to envy. With changing need patterns, wants, desires, and demands, there may be a growing tendency toward conflicts. Why this is so may not have easy answers. But one reason may be that the Zone of Indifference as conceptualized by Chester Bernard is expanding. So people are not very keen to obey commands. There is, thus, need to move from autocratic, power-driven leadership to servant leadership.

We have to dissect reasons for conflict more finely to manage them more effectively. Let us look back in the past to understand conflict better.

Conflict—The Genesis

Conflicts have been an integral part of human life. Wherever there are people, there are conflicts. From the smallest organizations of the society that is the family to the largest that is the government, conflicts have been there. There is no such thing like a model organization. Nor will there be one. If we refer to the Old Testament, it may be recalled that the first organization that emerged on this world was the family of Adam and Eve with their two children Cane and Abel. Ironically, the first conflict that arose in this world was sibling rivalry leading to the conflict between the two brothers Cane and Abel in which Cane killed Abel. Moreover, there was no big reason. It was just out of envy. The moral of the story—the conflicts are a natural human phenomenon and the reasons are more psychological than real. Social scientists are wont to attribute conflict to the problem of sharing of the resources. But, the two brothers Cane and Abel had the whole world at their disposal. Conflicts are thus inevitable and thinking of avoiding them is just wishful thinking.

The solution lies in managing conflicts. There have been many con-ventional approaches which are being used for managing conflicts. How-ever, the big question is that can there be a better approach to manage conflict different from the already existing ones. Putting it simply can there be an alternate paradigm? Well it is not going to be easy but our hitherto conflict management approaches have proved less effective. Not that efforts have not been made. In fact, evolution of conflict manage-ment approaches suggests that people have been serious in the endeavor to resolve conflict. In the beginning the accepted mode was cordoning off conflict by trying to create situations where the reasons leading to conflicts did not arise. Needless to say, this did not work because people found reason for conflict rather than reasons finding people to come to conflict. Then came the approach of avoiding or glossing over. This proved worse as it created a lose-lose paradigm. Subsequently attempts were made to force conflict resolution. This resulted in either a lose-lose or win-lose paradigm. An improvement on this was the supposedly win-win paradigm called the collaborative approach. But here too we find that it mostly gives a reprieve, some sort of a palliative that temporarily suppress conflicts, wily-nily. From global to local, this has been a case. Despite all these approaches conflicts are on the rise and there is need for a new paradigm.

Needed a New Deal

The previous approaches have been largely focusing on conflict. There is need to shift focus: from methodologies of managing conflict to mind-sets leading to conflicts. With rising diversities within the organizations, new classes have emerged offering more reasons for interpersonal or inter-group conflicts. The one commonality, however, is that all these groups comprise humans whose cognitive processes have remained fairly stable over time and there have been approaches and individuals in the past that have proved how this understanding of human nature can be helpful in managing conflict responsibly. In an article, "Satisfaction in Work" published in Occupational Psychology in July 1947, Nigel Balchin had given fair enough indications of what was to be done for managing con-flict responsibly. These can be summed up in two words "Enlightened

Management." This was the principle that was tested and recommended centuries ago and their impact is eternal, universal. Be it the Indian mythological text Ramayana where the principle "look after your men well" was advocated, or even the practices adopted by Robert Owen as early as 18th century. The Japanese, too have been talking about this when they mention *Omoiyari* and *Sunao mind*.

Even Peter Drucker, a modern management thinker, in one of his contributions "Management Challenges for 21st century," says that employees have to be managed as partners who are to be treated as equals. The relationship is like the conductor of an orchestra and the instrumentalist. To elicit good performance, you need to go beyond the prescribed relationship. Proact rather than react. The Hazelton Story is a case in point.

The Hazelton Story

Hazelton is a place in Penn state that was known for highly unionized coal mines all around. A group of students pursuing their Personnel Management and Industrial Relations program at International Management Development department, college of Business Administration, Syracuse University, New York, United States, were taken to Hazelton for a study tour. The visit was to a factory with some 1,500 workers, manufacturing aircraft spare parts.

The reason for this visit was that although the entire area was surrounded by highly unionized coal mines where the united mines workers of America (UMWA) holds sway, this plant had no union. When the study team members asked the general manager of the plant what was the secret of this scenario, the general manager replied that he did two things regularly. First, he had made it a point to meet every worker at least once a fortnight and ask about his well-being, how is he doing, how is his family, and so on. The second thing which he did was that he would find out the going rate and pay his employees slightly higher than that. That was 1961. Over to 21st century–people want the same concern.

Human beings are human beings who all crave for love and care. They certainly work in companies but they in fact work for people.

Summary

Conflicts have to be managed responsively. Conflict management theories have evolved over time but despite a large number of theories ranging from serious scientific, and rigorously developed ones to intuitive approaches based on observation or armchair philosophising, there is hardly any consensus as to the one best approach. There is a plethora of packaged solutions to tackle organizational issues, many with fancy names and catchy jargons. But these have only confounded the confusion. Thoroughly atomistic and mechanistic approaches that do not account for psychological motives or sociological factors do not work. Managers need to touch the heart. One way to touch the heart is the SouthWest Airlines management philosophy that is based on trust and where employees come first. Rather than using industrial relations (IR) to manage human relations, there is need to use human relations to manage IR like they do in a Kolkata (India)-based Aditya Birla Group company.

Case of an Indian Mining Company

Tony, the Mine Manager of XYZ Mining Company Ltd. had called Raj, head of the excavation department and Vikas, personnel manager, to discuss with them a problem concerning Ravi, a machinist in the excavation department.

XYZ was a newly started open cast mine engaged in mining of coal in South India. The mine manager was in-charge of all mining operations and reported directly to the managing director. The excavation department performed actual monitoring of heavy earth moving machineries (HEMM). The excavation department also looked after the repairs and maintenance of machinery. Personnel department was in-charge of personnel selection, training and evaluation, salary and wage administration, employee welfare, union affairs, and social security schemes. It formulated policies and ensured proper administration of them through line supervisors. It checked all papers processed by the supervisors in other departments and passed the necessary orders to the accounts department for payment. It also kept leave records of the employees. Whenever an employee went on leave, the supervisor concerned informed the personnel department which, after checking his entitlements authorized the accounts department for payment of the wage due to him.

The mine worked in three shifts as per the following schedule:

First shift	-	6 a.m. to 2 p.m.
Second shift	-	2 p.m. to 10 p.m.
Third shift	-	10 p.m. to 6 a.m.

Employees, if required, could be asked to work beyond their normal shift hours and were paid overtime at double the normal rate for extra time worked. Overtime working was not common except in the excavation department where some employees had to work overtime frequently. As per the company's policy, an employee who worked on his scheduled day of weekly off was to be given a day off as compensation (DOC) and reported accordingly to the personnel department. In addition to normal weekly off, employees were entitled to 10 days' casual leave (CL) with pay and if no casual leave was due, the employee could apply for leave without pay (LWP).

One day a particular heavy earth moving machine breaks down and Raj who was in-charge of the excavation department asked Ravi, a machinist who was working on the first shift, to work overtime to bring the machine back into operation as soon as possible. Ravi continues working up to 1 a.m. the next day. Thus, in addition to his normal 8 hours of work, he puts in 11 hours of overtime work which resulted in his working 19 hours at a stretch. Since there was a gap of only 5 hours between finishing his work and the start of his next shift that day, it was not considered desirable and practical to let him work on his normal shift. Raj, therefore, permitted Ravi not to work on his regular shift on that day and reports his absence as DOC granted to him. Raj also mentioned in the report that DOC had been granted to Ravi in view of the overtime worked by him. On receipt of this report the personnel department found an obvious error in reporting. They knew from the report that the off had been granted in view of the overtime worked and not for having worked on a scheduled weekly day of rest. Since Ravi had enough casual leave to his credit, the personnel department changed the leave from DOC to CL. Although the personnel department in the past had followed a procedure of referring back to the department concerned the irregularity of the reports for necessary correction, in this particular case, they themselves corrected the error as they considered it as an obvious error.

On receiving the pay slip at the end of the month, Ravi found that the off granted to him had been charged against his casual leave. He reported the matter to Raj and pleads that the treatment accorded to him was not fair as he worked overtime at the request of the company. Raj took up the matter with the mine manager. He said that the granting of leave was a prerogative of the immediate supervisor and not of the personnel department. He had no intention of giving Ravi casual leave for that day and thus penalizing him for the overtime worked at the company's request. He further argues that the personnel department was strictly a staff department and played an advisory role only. Even if the papers were not in order, they should have been brought them to his notice as done in the past for his advice and comments. He mentioned that even if the reports were referred back to him in this particular case, he would not inclined to penalize Ravi by charging the DOC to his CL for the services rendered to the company.

Vikas, in turn told the mine manager that the policy of granting DOC was very clear. Since it was an obvious error in reporting and as they were ensuring the proper administration of the policy, they did not want to waste time and increase paper work in referring the report back to Raj.

Summary

Conflicts are facts of life, more so, organizational life where people from diverse cultures and intellectual ability have to work together and at the same time compete with one another. Reconciling this collaboration with competition is a ticklish issue and not easy to resolve. But they must be resolved because organizational performance is an outcome of joint efforts of different individuals collectively. Herein, comes the role of managing conflicts effectively that is responsibly and responsively. Being responsive leads to identifying the right problem and being responsible leads to the right solution. It involves application of that all important human faculty wisdom which involves combining intellectual ability, emotional maturity, and ethical orientation that gives sensitivity to decision makers. Responsiveness is an attribute of this sensitivity. The problem is that in this information-driven age sensitivity have taken a back seat and responsiveness has been lost in a welter of rules and regulation. The best course is to realize that rules and regulations are general guidelines to action and not actions in themselves. Best actions come from a combination of head and heart that gives responsiveness.

Discussion Questions

1. Why conflicts are supposed to be essential attribute of organizational life and what purpose do they serve, if any?
2. "Conflicts are more perceived than real." How far do you agree with this statement? Discuss to highlight the essential nature of conflict.
3. How best can conflicts be resolved given the fact there is always an event of psychology involved. Discuss.

References

Brown, J.A.C. 1974. *The Social Psychology of Industr,* 276. London: English Language Book Society and Penguin Books.

Cappelli, P., and B. Novelli. 2010. *Managing the Older Worker,* 4. Massachusetts: HBR Press.

Evans, C. 1978. *Psychology: A Dictionary of Mind, Brain and Behaviour,* 63. London: Arrow Books Limited.

Freiberg, K., and J. Freiberg. 1996. *Nuts–South West Airlines Crazy Recipe for Business and Personal Success.* Austin, TX: Bard Press.

Kidz, Om. 2015. Cain and Abel, 365 Bible Stories. New Delhi: Om Books International, p. 16.

Luthans, F. 2002. *Organisational Behaviour,* 10. Boston: McGrawHill Asia.

Pathak, P. April 2001. "Management, Does It Really Matter?" *Indian Management* 40, no. 4, pp. 23–25.

Pathak, P., and S. Singh. January–March 2010. "Benchmark Human Relations (HR) Practices–A Case Study of a World Class Manufacturing Unit." *Growth* 37, no. 4, pp. 48–53.

Pathak, P., and S. Singh. 2012. "Creating High Performance Organisations–The Critical Factors." *Growth* 40, no. 1, pp. 47–53.

Pearsell, J. ed. 1999. "Oxford Concise Dictionary." New Delhi: Oxford University Press.

Rao, N.J. 2006. "Servant Leadership–Influence Not Force Matters." *Effective Executive* 8, no. 2, pp. 49–50.

Sekaran, U. 2005. *Organisational Behaviour.* New Delhi: Mc Graw Hill.

Weiten, W., and M.A. Lloyd. 2007. Psychology Applied to Modern Life, 221. Wadsworth Publishing.

CHAPTER 13

Negotiation

The Role of Cultural Sensitivity

Uche Attoh and Chantal Epie

Managing groups effectively requires the capacity to obtain people's willing collaboration and, in our global world, this calls for cultural sensitivity. The process of obtaining another person's agreement is essentially one of negotiation (Epie 2005). We are therefore going to focus our reflections on negotiation skills to put into use when managing groups.

Let us consider two scenarios: one involving an out-group and another involving an in-group. The first episode was selected as a graphic illustration of the impact of culture on the way people seek to manage conflict with a hostile or exploitative out-group. Negotiation tactics may be very different in the case of conflicts with an in-group, but will still derive from the cultural mindset of the negotiator.

Scenario 1: Negotiating with an Out-Group

As Mrs. B was leaving her office at 5:30 p.m., the managing director called from Murtala Mohammed international airport. He wanted the file at the British Airways check-in counter at the airport's departure lounge. Mrs. B got the file, called Monday, her official driver, and quickly left for the airport.

As she arrived at the airport, she told Monday that, as she did not intend to take long, there would be no need for him to use the airport car park which was rather far away. "Just drive 'round' a couple of times; by that time I will be back and ready to go."

Monday drove "round" once and, unwilling to go on, stopped the car where he hoped Madam would soon appear. He kept the engine on and waited for the imminent appearance of Mrs. B. However, within a few seconds, an official airport towing vehicle had chained the car for illegal parking. Monday had not noticed what was happening as no warning had been given.

On the point of leaving the departure lounge, Mrs. B saw the situation and realized she would have to engage in a difficult negotiation. She knew that the airport police was not interested in reporting infractions but would insist on the immediate payment of a heavy "fine" for which there would be no receipt. Ignoring a wailing Monday, she politely greeted the officer-in-charge (OC) and asked him, not only to impound the car, but to jail the driver as this was the straw that broke the camel's back and it was time Monday should be dismissed.

At these words, Monday prostrated himself on the floor, wailing. Mrs. B walked away with all her personal belongings, making ostensibly a loud phone call to the Human Resource Manager to report "useless Monday" and asking him to send her another car.

At this, the OC and his staff all ran after Mrs. B, imploring her to forgive Monday and telling her she could recover her car and go. She eventually consented to do so.

Once out of the reach of the airport security staff, Monday looked exclaimed "well done, Madam."

For residents in Nigeria, the above scenario is not only familiar but regularly re-enacted, in one form or the other, in virtually all transactions where two or more parties have to "resolve" or "settle" an "issue." In nearly all African societies, there is a preference for a "settlement" of all "conflicts" or "issues" in a way that will be "acceptable" to the community (Best 2006). These "acceptable" means of settling conflict are in most cases different from the officially prescribed means, whether in organizational or civil life. However, these methods produce satisfactory outcomes because they lead to mutually acceptable and therefore long-lasting solutions to conflicts, so that former adversaries can now develop positive relationships (Acemoglu and Robinson 2013). There are a number of reasons why the method adopted in the above scenario is a generally accepted one in Nigeria.

The first reason is that conflicts are often unduly blown-up by one of the parties so as to increase the stakes and create an opportunity for a one-sided negotiation (extortion). An uninitiated person may completely misjudge the situation. Bribery is the action of someone who pays to obtain something to which he or she has no right and it is clearly unethical. Extortion is the action of a person who extracts money from someone unjustly; this also is clearly unethical. What should a person do when faced with an attempt at extortion? From a developing country perspective, it has been argued that if traffic policemen in the community almost never impose official fines but prefer to collect money from offenders to enrich themselves, it will actually be unjust for them to impose a fine on one particular person and not on others (Elegido 2004). The second reason is that all parties to conflicts in the African context are very wary of officially designated institutions for settlement. This is because these institutions are still weak and therefore very susceptible to manipulation (Utomi 2006). In western societies, conflicts such as arise from infractions of rules are routinely settled through the instrumentality of the judiciary. In Nigeria, the law enforcement agents will often like someone to break the law so as to create an opportunity for private settlement rather than resort to official channels, the outcome of which is uncertain.

The third reason is that the psychological make-up of the Nigerian appears to predispose him to "see" "negotiation" opportunities in every situation. Rather than accept "no" for an answer, the Nigerian will look for any window of opportunity for a negotiated settlement, and this window is created through the adoption of a culturally appropriate negotiation strategy, tactics, and emotional intelligence.

In the above case of perceived aggression by a hostile out-group, Mrs. B used the surprise attack tactic. She expressed agreement with the OC and asked for greater punishments for her driver. Not prepared for such a reaction, the OC and his staff fell into her trap. To save Monday (who was very much like "one of us"), they helped him out of this situation.

Far from being a victim, Mrs. B fought her attackers. Not interested in a long-term relationship, she chose a win-lose strategy and won the game.

The effectiveness of this negotiation with a hostile out-group is based on four elements:

- **Negotiation tactics**: Mrs. B used the **Red Herring** trick. She got the security staff to forget about the wrong parking and instead focus their attention on dismissal from work.
- **Negotiation strategy**: Mrs. B **escalated** the issue. She transformed her problem into Mondays' problem.
- **Nigerian culture**: Empathy is deeply ingrained in the Nigerian culture. The OC did not want to cause a worker's dismissal.
- **Body language**: Mrs. B made a show of anger at her driver and Monday made his own show of desperation in perfect synchrony.

The strategy was successful because, although it was *objectively* a win-lose game (with Mrs. B obtaining all she wanted and the OC getting nothing), it ended in a *subjective* win-win situation (for Mrs. B because she neither had her vehicle impounded nor did she have to pay a bribe, for the OC because he felt happy to save Monday's job).

Many are likely to frown at the entire drama as being a lie and hence unethical. They will argue that one would have expected any law-abiding citizen to obey the law, which in this case is to park cars at designated areas, or perhaps that she should have negotiated a less-severe penalty using official channels. In addition, the approach by Mrs. B tended more toward deception than negotiation.

On the other hand others will ask: Was the society negatively affected by her actions? Within the socio-cultural context of Nigeria, what constitutes an offence and the fine rates are determined by the law enforcement agents more than by the law itself, and to protect oneself from abuse is not detrimental to society. There is no real crime committed in picking up or dropping a passenger. Even where parking is not allowed, waiting a short while with one's engine on can be tolerated. No warning was issued that Monday had overstayed at the drop-off place where he was waiting for Mrs. B. It was the law enforcement agent who was going beyond the law and trying to take advantage of the situation for personal gain.

Anyone living in Nigeria or other similar cultural environment is likely to encounter this type of situation and must carefully evaluate their options. Lies and deception cannot lightly be deemed harmless to society. However, there are rituals attached to negotiation situations that should not be interpreted as lies because people should know what to expect. Take for example, the bargaining ritual common in Africa and the Middle East. A seller begins by extolling his goods and demanding an outrageous price, to which the prospective buyer responds by denigrating the goods and making a ridiculously low offer; then each one lowers a little his demand and the whole process is repeated until a fair price is reached. This sequence of "false" statements is a ritual normally well understood by both parties and cannot be considered unethical.

It is however true that there are other options that may be effective when dealing with exploitative law enforcement agents. One of the authors often extricated herself from such situations through skillful use of relevant cultural factors: friendliness, smiling at the threatening policeman and greeting him in his own language, appealing to the respect owed to elders ("I could be your mother! Please do not harass an old woman!"), to pride in one's power and higher status ("Officer, I beg you, please forgive me for this once…"). As a nation, Nigerians are essentially friendly and generous, respect older people, and are happy to do a favor to someone who politely asks for it.

Let us now consider another scenario concerning negotiation with an in-group.

Scenario 2: Negotiating with an In-Group

Mr. A was concerned by the lack of initiative of his senior managers and the high staff turnover among his key employees. He thought of ways to get his team more involved and more committed. He could not afford to raise salaries substantially at that time. Knowing the importance of status symbols in Nigeria, he obtained good second-hand four-wheel-drive vehicles for them at a reasonable price and ensured that their offices in the new headquarters he was building would be quite large and equipped with good quality furniture. He appointed a management team and transferred to his senior managers some of the powers he had hitherto reserved for himself, after having a conversation with each one to clarify expectations. He gave his newly promoted general manager (GM) authority to make spending decisions on his own up to a certain amount beyond which the GM was asked to consult him (not to ask permission) before making his own decision. In management meetings, he had just one vote just like the other team members, so that decisions were reached with everyone's participation. Staff turnover soon dropped sharply and the senior managers became zealous and responsible in running the affairs of the company (Epie 2014).

In this situation, a long-term relationship was involved and Mr. A adopted a win-win approach. There was dialogue. There was an exchange of benefits. He gave due consideration to the interests of the staff while promoting his own interest as a business owner. He gave them good cars, spacious offices, and authority, all of which are indicators of high status. Nigeria is a high power distance culture and senior managers appreciated the higher level of authority and autonomy they were given. At the same time Mr. A obtained what he wanted: a high commitment on the part of his team.

Mr. A, steeped as he was in his own culture, instinctively realized that his staff would value a show of material possessions as much as a salary raise. He also understood his senior managers' desire to be perceived as people with high authority. He wanted them to feel good about their work and their status and sought to provoke positive emotions in them. He did not seek to manipulate them but truly gave them value. He willingly relinquished some of his own power to empower his managers, thus creating a win-win situation as the managers responded with greater dedication and responsibility in their work. Mr. A behaved very ethically, respectful of the needs and legitimate aspirations of his staff.

Conclusion

How Did Culture Influence Mrs. B's and Mr. A's Way of Negotiating?

Let us review some cultural factors (see Table 13.1) and examine their impact on Nigerians' negotiation (Epie 2002).

Depending on the objective of a negotiation, different cultural factors can help to achieve the desired result.

Table 13.1 Cultural factors and their impact on negotiation

Cultural factor	Negotiation impact
Negotiation intent	Get both contract and relationship
Attitude (preferred strategy)	Collaborative (win-win)
Level of formality	Formal and respectful
Communication style	Indirect, proverbs
Sensitivity to time	Of little importance
Team organization	Consensual
Orderliness	Discipline
Agreement Form	Specifics
Emotions	High

Source: Derived from Salacuse (1998).

It should also be noted that Mrs. B's negotiation scenario was not planned well in advance, was really informal although it had an appearance of formality, and it had to be won quickly to avoid being lost. By contrast, Mr. A's negotiation scenario was planned to ensure that each party would win; it was carried out formally within the framework of company regulations, and required some time to achieve desired results. Our analysis is presented in Tables 13.2 and 13.3.

Summary

In this chapter we looked at two negotiation scenarios in the context of Nigeria: one involving a hostile out-group and the other an in-group. We examined various cultural factors that influence the methods used by negotiators and their effectiveness. With regard to the first scenario, we discussed the distinction to be made between a situation of bribery (actively seeking to corrupt someone) and one of extortion (when a corrupt person seeks to take unjust advantage of another). We looked at ways in which a cultural lens can affect the ethical evaluation of certain techniques and suggested alternative tactics to extricate oneself from difficult situations through the use of relevant cultural factors. The second scenario showed the importance of culture in identifying benefits that will be really attractive to the negotiating parties and lead to an agreement. Finally we reviewed various cultural factors and how they impact negotiation with Nigerians.

Table 13.2 Mrs. B's negotiation

Factor	Discussion	Goal-high importance	Goal-low importance
Goal of negotiation	The goal of Mrs. B was **getting a particular result** rather than building a relationship. The chance of their meeting again on the negotiation table was slim, so it was important to make the most of the current situation.	Getting a particular result	Building a relationship
Attitude (strategy)	The situation demanded an aggressive approach because if Mrs. B failed to deliver her message to the police, the police would have executed their threat toward her. So she had to put in her best performance and come out as a winner. Fortunately for her, her driver was quick to understand her strategy and supported her by playing his part in the charade. It was more of a win-lose than a win-win strategy, but it had to be implemented without letting the other party realize it. The emotion factor was well matched to the strategy as is shown below.	Win-lose	Win-win
Personal style	Mrs. B was indeed formal and respectful personal style. She showed her respect to the uniform when requesting that the police should go ahead with the impounding of the vehicle and the arrest of the driver, thus letting the police know that she recognized their authority.	Formal and respectful	Informal or humility
Communication pattern	In order to carry out her strategy, Mrs. B made it very clear to the police that this was her best opportunity to get rid of Monday. She furthered her cause by calling up the HR, asking for a new car. Her communication pattern was very clear, though her real agenda was concealed.	Direct and open	Indirect (proverbs) and vague
Sensitivity to time	Mrs. B knew that the whole act might take some time and she did not try to hurry up the situation.	Of no importance	Vigorous, quick action

	Rather, by taking out her belongings from the car and calling for another car, she made it clear that she was willing to wait and had all the time in the world to discuss the current situation, thus putting the police under pressure.		
Team organization	Mrs. B might not have actually won the negotiation if Monday had not participated in her charade. Since he had to perform his task as a wronged man, he did so effectively by wailing and other acts. They worked as a team.	High individuality	Consensual
Orderliness	There was only one point of discussion: the wrongly waiting car. Instead of discussing who was at fault and why, Mrs. B came directly to the point by blaming it completely on Monday and announcing she would make sure he was fired. There was no other discussion on her part.	To the point	Discuss horses
Agreement form	The only agreement form here was that Mrs. B told the police to execute their threat, which they did not really want to do. Monday knew he had to give his best performance. And he did!	Specific	General or detailed
Emotions	This was the biggest factor that Mrs. B played on, and she succeeded.	High, impulsive	Neutral

Table 13.3 Mr. A's negotiation

Factor	Discussion	Goal-high importance	Goal-low importance
Goal of negotiation	The goal of Mr. A was **building a relationship**. He and his team had to work together over time.	Building a relationship	An immediate particular result
Attitude (strategy)	The situation demanded an empathetic, collaborative approach as it involved a permanent working relationship. It required a win-win strategy.	Win-win	Win-lose

(Continued)

Table 13.3 Mr. A's negotiation   (Continued)

Factor	Discussion	Goal-high importance	Goal-low importance
Personal style	Mr. A's personal style was indeed formal and respectful. He showed respect for his employees by not just pretending to give them additional value, but by truly enhancing their situation even at the cost of personal sacrifice.	Formal and respectful	Informal or humility
Communication pattern	Mr. A communicated both by his actions and by his words that he valued his team and relied upon their competence and sense of responsibility.	Open and sincere	Indirect and vague
Sensitivity to time	Once he had understood the problem, Mr. A took steps to change the situation. Although he hoped for quick results, he was willing to wait before he would see the results of his efforts.	Of no importance	Vigorous, quick action
Team organization	Mr. A did everything he could to enlist the willing collaboration of his managers in achieving high performance and got them involved in decision making.	Consensual	High individuality
Orderliness	Mr. A took one step at a time, always keeping in mind his objective.	To the point	Attention to side issues
Agreement form	Mr. A obtained the tacit agreement of his managers to devote themselves to their work in a responsible manner.	General	Detailed
Emotions	Mr. A did his best to provoke positive emotions in his employees. He did that by providing them with highly coveted status symbols and giving them a level of real authority.	Positive	Neutral

Discussion Questions

1. Identify two or three significant cultural differences between Nigeria and your own country. How would these differences affect negotiations in each country?

2. Is it ethical to submit to extortion? Suppose you urgently need a visa to travel and solve a serious family problem but the embassy officer at the gate will not let you pass unless you pay him a certain amount of money. What will you do and why?

3. What do you think of Mr A's way of negotiating higher commitment from his staff? Would it be equally successful in every culture?

4. What ethical means do you think Mrs. B should have used to recover her car?

References

Acemoglu, D., and J. Robinson. 2013. *Why Nations Fail*. New York: Crown Publishing.

Best, S.G. 2006. *Introduction to Peace and Conflict Studies in West Africa: A Reader*. Ibadan: Spectrum Books.

Elegido, J. 2004. *Fundamentals of Business Ethics–A Developing Country Perspective*. 3rd ed. Ibadan: Spectrum.

Epie, C. 2002. "Nigerian Business Negotiators: Cultural Characteristics." *Journal of African Business* 3, no. 2, pp. 105–26.

Epie, C. 2005. "Negotiation: A Problem-Solving Approach to Conflict." In *Conflict Resolution Techniques*, ed. V. Subbulakshmi's. Hyderabad: ICFAI University Press.

Epie, C. 2014. "Improving Talent Retention in a Nigerian SME–Reflections on a Case Study." *International Journal of Employment Studies* 22, no. 1, pp. 60–76.

Salacuse, J.W. 1998. "Ten Ways That Culture Affects Negotiating Style: Some Survey Results." *Negotiation Journal* 14, no. 3, pp. 221–40.

Utomi, P. 2006. *Why Nations Are Poor*. Lagos: Business Day Books.

CHAPTER 14

Sustainable Management Practices

Sustainability or CSR?

Christian Katholnigg

Sustainability and sustainable development have been defined in many ways, but the most frequently quoted definition is from "Our Common Future," better known as the Brundtland Report (WCED 1987)

> Sustainable development is development that meets the needs of the present without compromising the ability of future genera-tions to meet their own needs. It contains within it two key con-cepts: • the concept of needs, in particular the essential needs of the world's poor, to which overriding priority should be given; and • the idea of limitations imposed by the state of technology and social organization on the environment's ability to meet present and future needs. (p. 43)

The CSR Concept in the Anglo-American Region

The beginning of the debate on Corporate Social Responsibility (CSR) in the United States dates back to the article "Social Responsibilities of the Businessman" by Bowen. He added that social responsibility of corporates needs to be orientated on societal expectations and values. In the last decade mainly the four levels of Carroll (1991) model of cor-porate responsibility namely economic, legal, ethical, and philanthropic responsibility were linked with the CSR approach; thus, leading to fostering the philanthropic aspects.

It changed when in 2006 Porter and Kramer (2006) developed the term "strategic CSR"—leading them to the model of "Shared Value." Caroll also draw the connection following that "CSR is involving into the core business function, central to the firms overall strategy and vital to its success" (Caroll 2011, 2).

The European Way—CSR Obligations by the EU Commission

In 2001 the EU commission published a communication concerning

> Corporate Social Responsibility: A business contribution to Sustainable Development. In this communication CSR is defined as: a concept whereby companies integrate social and environmental concerns in their business operations and in their interaction with their stakeholders on a voluntary basis. (COM [2002] 347 final, p. 5)

It states further on that in this context, an increasing number of firms have embraced a culture of CSR. Despite the wide spectrum of approaches to CSR, there is large consensus on its main features:

- CSR is behavior by businesses over and above legal requirements, voluntarily adopted because businesses deem it to be in their long-term interest;
- CSR is intrinsically linked to the concept of sustainable development: businesses need to integrate the economic, social and environmental impact in their operations;
- CSR is not an optional "add-on" to business core activities—but about the way in which businesses are managed. (p. 5)

Sustainability is the goal that organizations try to achieve—whereas corporate social responsibility provides these organizations with the tools to reach this aim.

CSR? A Concept or a Business Case?

But How to Implement and Measure CSR in This Context?

The EU commission suggests management systems such as Total Quality Management systems, which "could allow enterprises to have a clear picture of their social and environmental impacts, help them to target the significant ones and manage them well" (COM[2002], p.5). In addition the paper mentions also the Eco-Management and Audit Scheme (EMAS), allowing voluntary participation in an environmental management scheme.

> It is a scheme for companies and other organizations that are willing to commit themselves to evaluate, manage and improve their environmental and economic performance. In addition, active employee involvement is a driving force for EMAS and a contribution to the social management of organizations. (COM [2002], p. 5)

The economic crisis and its social consequences in 2008 lead to a damage in consumer confidence and levels of trust in organizations. As shown in the yearly published Edelman Trust barometer, in 2009 nearly 2 in 3 informed publics—62 percent of 25-to-64-year-olds surveyed in 20 countries—claimed they trust corporations less now, than they did a year ago. When it came to being distrusted, business was not alone. The survey also pointed out that globally, trust in business, media, and government was half-empty; and trust in government scores even lower than trust in business (Edelman 2009). To regain trust Edelman states that companies "will need to adopt a strategy of public engagement, by means of a shift in policy and communications" (Edelman 2009, p. 8). The public engagement as described consists of four pillars, one of which is:

> Mutual social responsibility: Companies must realign their business practices so they deliver dual objectives: benefit society and the bottom line. (...) Companies must integrate into their products and services approaches to societal problems such as climate change, health care, and energy independence. Immediate

stakeholders like employees and customers must be invited to participate in a company's social responsibility decisions and actions—and the public at large must be kept informed about the progress the company is making toward those goals. (Edelman 2009, p. 8)

Public attention on the social and ethical performance has risen as consequences to the crises. In the year 2011 a new communication was published by the EU commission titled "A renewed EU strategy 2011–14 for Corporate Social Responsibility" (COM [2011] 681 final), containing a new definition of CSR as "the responsibility of enterprises for their impacts on society" (COM [2011] 681 final, p. 6).

To show that, responsibility organizations need to respect applicable legislation, and strain for collective agreements between social partners. "To fully meet their corporate social responsibility, enterprises should have in place a process to integrate social, environmental, ethical, human rights, and consumer concerns into their business operations and core strategy in close collaboration with their stakeholders, with the aim of:

- Maximizing the creation of shared value for their owners or shareholders and for their other stakeholders and society at large;
- Identifying, preventing, and mitigating their possible adverse impacts." (COM [2011] 681 final, p. 6)

As part of the EU strategy on CSR, the EU Commission launched a proposal to enhance the transparency of certain large companies on social and environmental matters in April 2013. The Directive amended the 2013 Accounting Directive on the preparation of annual and consolidated financial statements. The objective of the Directive was to increase the transparency and improve the performance of large European companies on environmental and social matters, thereby contributing to long-term economic growth and employment. Specifically, it aims at increasing the quantity of reporters and the quality of the information disclosed, and at enhancing diversity in companies' boardrooms. Approximately 6,000 companies in the EU will fall under its scope.

According to the new measures, large (more than 500 employees) public interest enterprises will have to report on environmental, social and employee-related, respect for human rights, anticorruption, and bribery matters. The statement also has to include a description of the policies, outcomes and the risks related to those topics. To leave some flexibility to companies, they will have to explain why, if they do not pursue policies ("report or explain").

Although the Directive does not introduce a requirement on the reporting framework that should be used to report, companies should rely on one of the internationally recognized instruments. As there are the Global Reporting Initiative (GRI) Framework, the UNGC Principles, the UN Guiding Principles on Business and Human Rights, the OECD Guidelines for Multinational Enterprises, ISO 26000, the ILO Tripartite Declaration of principles concerning multinational enterprises and social policy, and European Eco-Management and Audit Scheme (EMAS).

How to Fulfill These Obligations?

Sustainability Operating System by Blackburn

Most of the enterprises have a management system already in place—may it be ISO 9001 in behalf of quality management, the ISO14000 family in the field of environmental management systems or the SA 8000 in the field of social accountability. Regarding these standards, Blackburn defines in his book the advantages of management system standards in implementing sustainability into a company.

Following the structure of a management system standard he proposes 10 steps to implement a so-called sustainability operating system (SOS) standard.

1. Define the scope and purpose—organization wide level or/and business units.
2. Set up definitions for the terms used in this management system.
3. Develop a sustainability policy and describe the management process.
4. Planning process: Identify and evaluate requirements, prioritize issues or topics, set objectives, a strategic and tactical plan.

5. Implementation and operation: Seek management commitment, implement structure and responsibilities, trainings, provide human, technical, and additional resources, set up a change-management process, set up plans and processes for emergency or crisis response, set up documentation, foster ongoing management support.

6. Monitoring and corrective and preventive actions, in the field of corporate governance, setting up reports and data, investigate incidents, develop, record, and track preventive and corrective actions.

7. Analysis and reporting, internally by reports on sustainability risks, performance business benefits, effectiveness of this SOS, an external reporting, following for example the GRI guideline.

8. Recognition and accountability, by measuring individual and group performance against sustainability objectives and goals.

9. Management and stakeholder feedback, by involving stakeholders on a regular basis.

10. And finally, continuation of process cycle to close the gaps (Blackburn 2007).

Strategic CSR and the Evolution to the Shared Value Model by Porter or Kramer

In their article in the Harvard Business Review from December 2006, Michael Porter and Mike Kramer developed the idea of "strategic CSR."

Strategic CSR moves beyond good corporate citizenship and mitigating harmful value chain impacts to mount a small number of initiatives whose social and business benefits are large and distinctive. Strategic CSR involves both inside-out and outside-in dimensions working in tandem. It is here that the opportunities for Shared Value truly lie (Porter and Kramer 2006).

CSR to their point of view should no longer be responsive, but has to be integrated into the core business of the company.

Between 2006 and 2011, Porter and Kramer developed their concept further on in a way, that companies gain economic value in a manner which generates value for the society. They define Shared Value as:

"Corporate policies and practices that enhance competitiveness of the company while simultaneously advancing social and economic conditions in the communities in which it sells and operates" (Porter and Kramer 2012).

Between 2007 and 2008 this concept has been implemented in several enterprises especially in the Small Medium Enterprises (SME) sector in Austria by a project funded by the Austrian Chamber of Commerce. The outcomes of this project amongst others were that the Shared Value Concept:

- Has a high connectivity to Managers.
- Can be used for "beginners" and for "advanced."
- Has a pragmatic, market-oriented approach.

The next step was to find a model to measure Shared Value. A Measuring Shared Value process affects key areas of action of the company, such as communication, value, and market strategy, with the result that entrepreneurs may discover new potentials for the development of social engagement. Future strategy steps are based on quantitative and qualitative key figures or indicators (Shared Value Outcomes) making visible and supporting corporate management and organizational development tasks. Three workshops are conducted to deliver the results.

Workshop #1: Definition of stakeholders and analysis of their concerns in relation to the business.—Q: Which are the company's stakeholder groups and how other concerns addressed in context to the operational activities of the company?

Workshop #2: Assignment of performance indicators (output indicators) of the Company (e.g., from the profit and loss account, value added statement) to the identified Stakeholder groups.—Q: Which output indicators correlate with the formulated stakeholder groups and concerns?

Workshop #3: Measuring effectiveness through the development of Shared Value outcome figures showing the real impact of sustainability or Shared Value Initiatives represent the business environment and its stakeholders.—Q: Which output indicators to measure Shared Value can be established (Moore and Jasch 2014)?

According to the Impact-Output-Outcome-Impact (IOOI) method (Bertelsmann Stiftung 2010), the outcome defines the immediate results of output. Developed by Bertelsmann Stiftung in cooperation with Price Waterhouse Coopers and various other companies, the IOOI method deals with impact assessment of corporate social commitment.

- Input includes all means and resources that are invested by the company to implement a planned CSR activity; that is human, financial, and material resources.
- Output refers to services that can be achieved with the available input.
- Outcome covers the effects, which are achieved for a target group by the CSR activities.
- Impact refers to effects that can be achieved for society in the long term (Bertelsmann Stiftung 2010).

The object of this project was to develop a Measuring Shared Value Strategy with four selected companies. This strategy had to include metrics related to business and society. The figures, which are different for every company, should support the professional management and the development of the Shared Value Strategy.

The participating companies were:

- Austria Glas Recycling GmbH
- Löffler GmbH, Sportswear
- MAM Baby Products GmbH
- VBV pension fund AG

In the project, the participating companies analyzed their CSR or sustainability commitment by the Porter model. They identified the Shared Value factors, evaluated and supported the factors with figures. The companies associated their value added statement with the stakeholder concerns and evaluated their business model and certain individual projects on their social impacts. In addition ideas for strategic anchoring and professional management of CSR or sustainability strategy were developed as well as benchmarks for future evaluation strategy had been elaborated in the project.

The ISO 26000 as a Management Tool?

The ISO 26000:2010 provides guidance to all types of organizations, regardless of their size or location, on:

- Concepts, terms, and definitions related to social responsibility
- The background, trends, and characteristics of social responsibility
- Principles and practices relating to social responsibility
- The core subjects and issues of social responsibility
- Integrating, implementing, and promoting socially responsible behavior throughout the organization and, through its policies and practices, within its sphere of influence
- Identifying and engaging with stakeholders
- Communicating commitments, performance and other information related to social responsibility (ISO 26000 2010)

It defines the responsibility of an organization for the impacts of its decision and activities on society and the environment, through transparency and ethical behavior that:

- Contribute to sustainable development, including health and welfare of society
- Takes into account the expectation of stakeholders
- Is in compliance with applicable law and consistent with international norms of behavior
- Is integrated throughout the organization and practices in its relationship (ISO 26000 2010)

By applying the standard the organizations are encouraged to go beyond legal compliance, recognizing that compliance with law is a fundamental duty of any organization and an essential part of their social responsibility. It is intended to promote common understanding in the field of social responsibility, and to complement other instruments and initiatives for social responsibility, not to replace them (ISO 26000 2010).

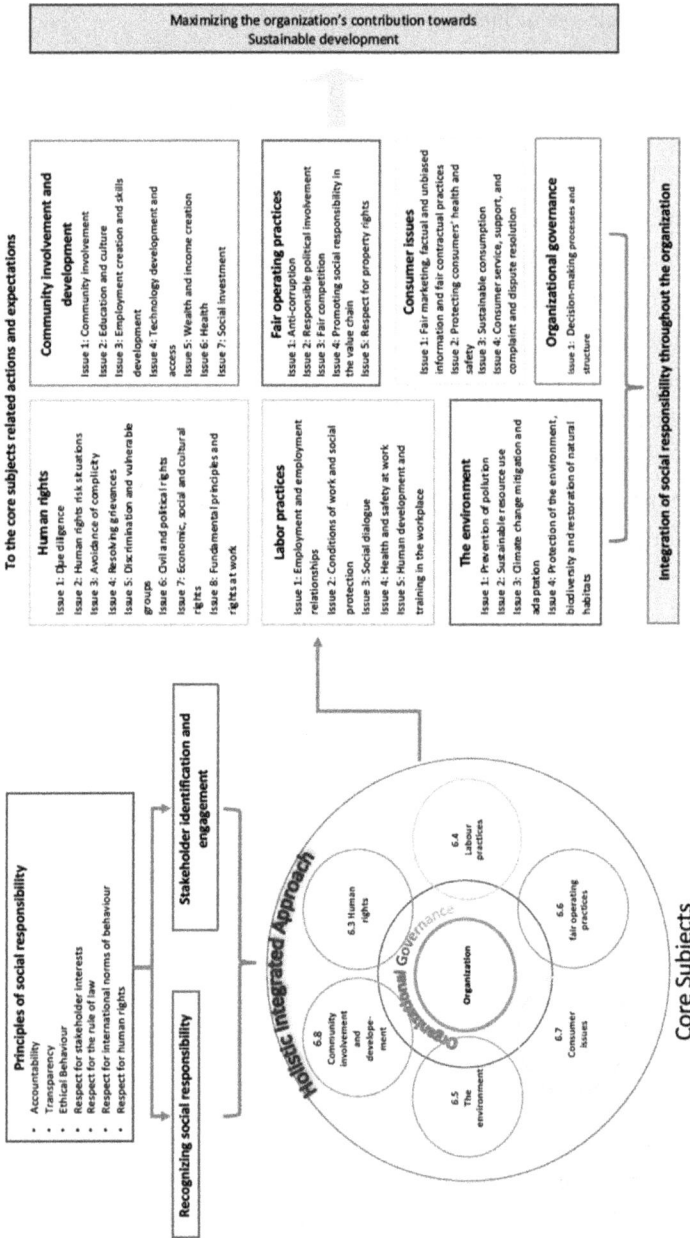

Figure 14.1 Schematic overview on ISO 26000 following ISO

Source: ISO, adopted by the author.

When applying ISO 26000:2010, it is advisable that an organization has to take into consideration societal, environmental, legal, cultural, political, and organizational diversity, as well as differences in economic conditions, while being consistent with international norms of behavior.

The ISO 26000 was never intended to be certified. But as the market demanded a certifiable standard some standardization bodies in Europe developed standards which can be third party certified. Amongst them the Austrian Rule (ONR) "The ONR 192500 [...] describes not only the terms of a management system process of integration and ongoing development of social responsibility in the company, but also defines content requirements and recommendations to be used for a self-declaration or evidence by an independent third party (certification organization)" (Austrian Standards 2011).

Spain, Denmark, the Netherlands, and Slovakia already have or are developing national standards that enable certification.

Conclusion

CSR may be considered as a tool and way of doing business toward sustainable development. Porter and Kramer's model of Shared Value or the ISO 26000 and the certifiable national standards are some of these tools which help organizations to walk into a sustainable future.

Summary

Sustainability and sustainable development have taken a different development in Europe and in the United States. While in the United States the term CSR was originally used in a philanthropic approach, this approach has been further developed by Porter and Kramer become a strategic CSR approach. This was offset by the model of the reputable businessman in Europe. In 2001, a communiqué was published by the EU Commission which defined CSR as a concept for companies' social and environmental concerns in their interactions with their stakeholders on a voluntary basis.

How can CSR be introduced and implemented? The EU Commission is proposing in this regard, management systems, which should enable the company to gain a clear picture of their social and environmental impacts. This led in 2011 to a new communication from the Commission entitled "A renewed EU strategy 2011 to 2014 for Corporate Social Responsibility."

To meet these requirements, there are a number of management system standards such as the sustainability Operating System from Blackburn, the Shared Value Model of Porter and Kramer, the IOOI, a model of the Bertelsmann Stiftung to be mentioned. In addition to the aforementioned models also the ISO 26000 and their country-specific certifiable standards have proven to be effective tools, to meet the requirements of the EU Commission.

Discussion Questions

1. What are the differences between the Anglo-American and the European approach to CSR?
2. Describe the differences between the Porter and Kramer model from 2006 and that of 2011.
3. DIN ISO 26000 is a so-called Guidance Standard. What are the reasons that this standard has not been adopted as a certifiable standard?
4. Discuss the schematic approach of ISO 26000 and the main core subjects for their implementation in the company.

References

A renewed EU strategy 2011–14 for Corporate Social Responsibility. n.d. "Parliament, the Council, the European Economic and Social Committee and the Committee of the Regions." http://eur-lex.europa.eu/LexUriServ/LexUriServ.do?uri=COM:2011:0681:FIN:EN:PDF

Austrian Standards Institute. 2011. "ONR 192500—Gesellschaftliche Verantwortung von Organisationen–CSR." https://shop.austrian-standards.at/Preview.action;jsessionid=AF146C6A2B69DEA37769263BD234EC65?preview=&dokkey=392068&selectedLocale=de

Bertelsmann Stiftung. 2010. "iooi method (Input–Output–Outcome–Impact)." www.sustainicum.at/en/tmethods/view/12.iooi-Methode-Input-Output-Outcome-Impact-der-Bertelsmann-Stiftung

Blackburn, W.R. 2007. *The Sustainability Handbook*, 169–76. Earthscan NY: London.

Caroll, A.B. 1991. "The Pyramid of Corporate Social Responsibility: Toward the Moral Management of Organizational Stakeholders." *Business Horizons* 34, no. 4, pp. 39–48.

Directive 2013/34/EU of the European Parliament and of the Council. June 26, 2013. "On the Annual Financial Statements, Consolidated Financial Statements and Related Reports of Certain Types of Undertakings." http://eur-lex.europa.eu/LexUriServ/LexUriServ.do?uri=OJ:L:2013:182:0019:0076:EN:PDF

EuropäischeKommission. 2011. Eineneue EU-Strategie (2011–14) für die sozialeVerantwortung der Unternehmen (CSR), Mitteilung der Kommission an das EuropäischeParlament, den Rat, den eüröpäischenWirtschafts- und Sozialausschuss und den Ausschuss der Regionen, KOM(2011) 681, Brüssel. (Download)

European Commission. 2013. "Proposal for a Directive of the European Parliament and of the Council." http://eur-lex.europa.eu/LexUriServ/LexUriServ.do?uri=COM:2013:0207:FIN:EN:PDF

GRI (Global Reporting Initiative). 2016. "Sustainability Reporting Framework." www.globalreporting.org/information/about-gri/what-is-GRI/Pages/default.aspx (page visited on 25.11.2016).

ISO (International Organization for Standardization). 2010. "International Standard for Social Responsibility (ISO 26000)." www.iso.org/iso/home/standards/iso26000.htm (page visited on 25.11.2016).

Moore, C., and C. Jasch. 2014. *Measuring Shared-Value*. Österreich: Wirtschaftskammer.

OECD (Organisation for Economic Co-operation and Development). 2011. "Guidelines for Multinational Enterprises." www.oecd.org/daf/inv/mne/oecdguidelinesformultinationalenterprises.htm

Porter, M.E., and M.R. Kramer. 2006. *Strategy and Society: The Link Between Competitive Advantage and Corporate Social Responsibility*. Boston: Harvard Business Review.

Porter, M.E., and M.R. Kramer. 2011. *Creating Shared Value—How to Reinvent Capital Is Mandunleash a Wave of Innovation and Growth*. Boston: Harvard Business Review.

Porter, M.E., and M.R. Kramer. 2012. "Shared Value. Die Brücke von Corporate Social Responsibility zu Corporate Strategy." In *Corporate Social Responsibility. VerantwortungsvolleUnternehmensführung in Theorie und Praxis*, eds. A. Schneider, and R. Schmidpeter, 138–54. Berlin, Heidelberg: Springer.

UNGC 10 Principles. 2004. "The Ten Principles of the UN Global Compact." www.unglobalcompact.org/AboutTheGC/TheTenPrinciples/index.html (page visited on 25.11.2016).

United Nations. 2011. "Guiding Principles on Business and Human Rights" Implementing the United Nations "Protect, Respect and Remedy." Framework www.ohchr.org/Documents/Publications/GuidingPrinciplesBusinessHR_ EN.pdf

WCED (World Commission on Environment and Development). 1987. *Our Common Future*. Oxford: Oxford University Press.

CHAPTER 15

Responsible Organizational Change in the Information Age

Jyoti Bachani

In 2015, the largest taxi service in the world does not own a single car and the largest hotel company in the world does not own a single room, for Uber and Airbnb (bnb being shorthand for bed and breakfast), are the information-age companies with radically new business models that use the power of technology and information. Uber allows anyone with a car and some time to spare to sign up and become a contracted taxi for their customers. Uber's customers are told that ordering a Uber taxi is just like asking a friend to give them a ride, with the exception that this friend will be willing to accept a payment for offering the ride, albeit a comparatively modest payment compared to a traditional taxi service. In order to make this really seem like a friend offering a ride, all payments are handled electronically with the customer paying Uber online when they order their taxi, and Uber paying their contracted drivers electronically too, so there is no money related exchange between the driver and the customer.

Similarly, for Airbnb, anyone with a room to spare in their home can upload the photos of it to attract any visitors to their area who might prefer to stay there for less money or a different experience than using a standard hotel room. It takes Airbnb a mere couple of weeks to add 10,000 new rooms by offering incentives for new hosts to join. In contrast, a hotel chain, such as Marriott, would need upto three years of aggressive building to add that same number of rooms. Technology-mediated information exchanges are enabling these trades that were not possible in the industrial era economy that flourished in the late 20th century.

The shift from the industrial age to the information age has led to organizational changes that are so fundamental that new ways of conceptualizing organizations are needed. If in the industrial era it was appropriate to consider organizations to be driven by their strategy, structure and systems, the information age organizations need to radically rethink that. Toward the end of 20th century, forward-thinking organizational scholars (Ghoshal and Bartlett 1999) had written about organizations being more than mere economic entities. They argued to bring the sociological aspects of organizations into the theories of organizing, postulating that it is essential to consider the purpose, process, and people aspects of organizing beyond the strategy, structure, and systems. When an organization is driven by a clear purpose, it is able to attract the people who believe in that cause, and with the alignment between the individual and organizational purpose and values, one can realize the full benefit of organizing using the right processes.

Other research has claimed that the end of capitalism is near and offered fresh alternatives, such as conscious capitalism or benefit corporations. There are even earlier concepts that have been adopted by businesses, such as the triple bottom line, where social, environmental, and financial goals were incorporated to guide organizational priorities. The cumulative impacts of external changes in social, environmental, economic, and technological changes are leading to organizations having to reinvent themselves. Organizational change is no longer a matter of the change models that have dominated the past debates, such as incremental or radical changes, top-down or bottom-up changes, and punctuated equilibrium models of evolutionary changes. Organizational change is a redesign of the fundamentals of organizational activity. The strategy-structure-systems models need to be supplemented with purpose-process-people considerations. The redesigned organizations challenge the simplistic descriptions of being global or local, centralized or decentralized, for-profit or not-for-profit, competitive or charitable, small or large, and many other ways that they have been characterized traditionally.

Rather than describe this organizational change at a conceptual level, let us understand it with an example of a 21st-century firm. This exemplar case-study illustrates one of the ways of organizing in a manner appropriate for the information age, and will be a basis to explain the organizational changes that are needed today. This company is called Thrive Solar (Thrive henceforth). The case-study describes what the company does and how it was formed and organized. Thrive is a good example of a sustainable and responsible business that is quietly changing lives around the world. Thrive is organized in a manner that redefines and challenges many of the theoretical distinctions that are used to describe industrial-age firms. Using the theoretical ideas from traditional management theories developed in the 20th century to understand this case study yields the contrasts that are the crucial changes that firms need to make to adapt for the 21st century information age world. The firms need to change in ways appropriate for their context as a way to prepare for thriving in the information age. By making these changes, the organizations are more likely to become a sustainable and a responsible business model. Contrasting Thrive and its practices against the commonly held beliefs about the organizations from the dominant theories of organizational change will help existing organizations to review their ways and adopt the practices that are appropriate in their context to make the needed changes.

Thrive Solar: An Exemplar Case Study of An Information Age Company

Thrive Solar is a rapidly growing company that provides essential lighting products to impoverished people in developing countries with a focus on sustainability through reliable, durable, and affordable products of high quality. Three million people across 15 countries in Asia, Africa, and Latin America have bought and used Thrive products. Occasionally, these efforts were made possible with support from aid organizations such as the World Bank, Oxfam, Care, Save the Children, the Government of India, and several microfinance organizations such as the National Institute of Rural Development and external aid projects for Africa.

Thrive's major product line is based on low-cost, super-efficient solar lights that use durable LED bulbs. The lights are customized for children, mothers, workers, farmers, and artisans, and are suitable for use outdoors, in the home, and at work for a variety of income-generating activities.

These are cleaner and cheaper to own and operate than the kerosene lamps that they replace. The basic product is very affordable at a price of under $5. It is custom-built with an emphasis on design for rugged use, ease of manufacture, long life with easy maintenance, and recycling of consumable parts with proprietary off-grid lighting technology.

Although working with the most destitute populations in remote parts of the underdeveloped world, Thrive is not a charitable organization. Thrive leadership believes that charity creates dependence and is best used in occasional dire situations. It has provided portable solar lights for disaster victims in Haiti and Nepal after earthquakes and other emergency situations. However, these acts of charitable giving are not core to its mission. Thrive considers itself to be a compassionate business that is committed to being financially profitable. It is also empowering local people by sharing Thrive's technology and products to help them also set up their own financially viable operations for assembly and maintenance of these lights.

Thrive has a global reach with a product development center in California (United States) and manufacturing units in Hyderabad (India) and Kenya. It has approximately 300 employees, mostly women from low-income families. The company was formed by Dr. Ranganayakulu Bodvala (Dr. Ranga), an MBA, PhD and a post-doctoral Takemi fellow of Harvard School of Public Health. Dr. Ranga had accumulated years of experience leading several global public health initiatives with the United Nations organizations. Sohrab Kakalia, an engineering graduate from the Indian Institute of Technology at Bombay with 30 years of experience in management consulting and technology design, including as the Vice President at Infosys, where he lead the Global Technology Consulting practice in Silicon Valley, joined Thrive while it was in its infancy. He saw the potential to change the world using Thrive's products and wanted to help scale it up. He established smart design, strategic business development, and sustainable supply chains with an emphasis on recyclable and reusable local components. In recent years leading up to 2015, Thrive has been doubling its business every year on a variety of metrics. Sohrab believes that it can grow even faster with the right distribution and marketing partners.

Sohrab and Dr. Ranga believe that in this digital age, the poor should not have to rely on kerosene lamps with repeated expenses on fuel and poor quality lighting that comes with health risks from polluting the air and potential burn risks. Thrive offers a sustainable, responsible, alternative source of light that charges from the sunlight during the day, provides better light, giving over eight hours of it on a single charge, with no recurring expense, no risk of burn, no air pollution, and no related health risks for the users. Thrive's vision is to provide basic lighting to two billion people around the globe who do not have it yet. This is estimated to be a $60–100 billion market. Thrive intends to do this in partnership with development and relief agencies and with local partners who are willing to invest to build phased local operations in the various countries.

Comparative Analysis of Thrive

This section provides a diagnostic for the readers on how to change their own organizations and create a change agenda applicable for their organization. The comparative analysis here uses Thrive as an example, but the reader can use whatever company they are intimately familiar with instead to develop their own diagnostic and change agenda. The intention of this comparative analysis is to explicate the organizational changes implemented by Thrive, and recommended for others. Each organization has to tailor their changes to suit their own organization's context even as Thrive provides an example to do so.

While traditional organizational theories recommend that organizations ought to have a primary goal that is to deliver profit or shareholder wealth maximization, the vision that Thrive offers is different. Its main emphasis is on delivering value to the customer and being a sustainable and responsible organization. Financial well-being is a goal too but it is not the first or the only goal. Thrive leadership has set the intention of generating financial well-being for all those affiliated with it, including founders, management, employees, suppliers, partners, and customers. The conventional wisdom that business ought to only be about making money is to be supplanted with what value does your business create and add, and how does it deliver that.

At Thrive, producing a high-quality product is not in conflict with keeping it affordable. Costs are continuously being driven down even as quality is being improved. The leaders at Thrive simply refuse to buy into the mindset that quality and cost are a dichotomous trade-off. Managers need to see quality and cost as a coexisting duality. When Sohrab thinks of his product in the hands of a customer, he wants to not just provide a solar LED light that is cheaper and better than the kerosene lamp, but he wants to provide one that is rugged, durable, long-lasting, and that has locally replaceable and recyclable components. The responsible organizations must focus on creating genuine customer value.

Sohrab invests time and resources in product development with multiple iterations. He makes frequent field trips to the most remote and rural areas in the underdeveloped parts of the world to see how customers might use these so that the reality of the local conditions informs what parts are used and what kind of handle, panel, or light quality will be best. For example, LED bulbs tend to give focused light with an intense central illumination and poor diffusion. To overcome this, there was a special cover designed for the lights that spreads the light evenly to provide a diffused illumination that would be more helpful for the users. Traditional management thinking may consider iterations and field trips as inefficient or even wasteful. The organizations' role ended with product launch. The idea of going to remote places to gather customer input by seeing how the product is actually used in its many iterations would be frowned upon. In a conventional organization, such ideas of iterative processes of product development might be seen as wasteful or unnecessary. This needs to change as organizations move into the information age. As the information age customers voluntarily share so much information about their needs, multiple iterations and version would be needed to reach all customers, perhaps with flexible product design.

For Thrive, the product design improvements are made by the research and development team located in California, while the actual manufacturing and production happens in Hyderabad. This makes Thrive both a local and a global company that is neither centralized nor decentralized. There are centers of excellence, with product and business development based in the United States, product manufacturing in India, and other countries for local production, and coordination on an as-needed basis.

When the local problem requires a technical solution, then the California team builds the proposal and prototype to address it before transferring responsibility for manufacturing to India or the local country. They grow by establishing local partners and markets in the customer's country and even give away their manufacturing advice if there are local partners willing to build the lights in the home country. There are also examples where the entire customer relationship is handled from Thrive's Indian office, and the same product that is used in India is simply exported to the new country where it might not need to be modified for any local conditions. Thus, other organizations wanting to adopt a sustainable and responsible approach can also be similarly flexible in how decision making is flexible and best located in one country or another, depending on the best way to meet the customer needs.

Another way that Thrive maintains a highly flexible approach to their product development is by not automating their operations. This intentional choice reflects the values of the founders. When each light is hand assembled by workers, it generates employment, mostly for women. Thrive management may not agree if someone tries to convince them that automation will lower their product costs and be more efficient for a fast-growing business. They would argue that by staying with manual production of lights, they make Thrive more flexible. They can easily change product design with multiple iterations without incurring the costs of having to re-tool every time. With the new technologies becoming available in solar and LED lights, they have redesigned the product several times in the spirit of continuous improvement. The manual production process also allows for customization for different uses, countries, and conditions. With automated runs, they would be locked into a limited set of parameters for most effective batch-sizes for each run, whereas their flexible manufacturing allows them to keep the customer needs at the center of each batch. With customers spread all over the globe, they can consider the needs of island dwellers in the Philippines to the mountain dwellers of Nepal in the customization of the product. Organizations wanting to move forward into the information age might consider how to change to attain scale with flexibility, and efficiency without the rigidity imposed by expensive automation. Information availability through digital mediums already has led to customer involvement in design of products but only a flexible organization can use that input to iterate through multiple product designs for mass customization. These ought to be on the agenda for manufacturing companies wanting to embrace organizational change to become more responsible and sustainable.

Thrive products primarily serve the populations at the so-called the bottom of the pyramid (BOP). Management guru C.K. Prahalad popularized the term BOP. His theory was that organizations can be a source of good while doing business, i.e., selling their products and services to those at the BOP. The organizations responded by offering their products in smaller packages at lower price points to make the popular branded consumer products accessible to those aspiring to the lifestyle they had only seen in advertisements before. Products such as Tide laundry detergent and or branded shampoos were made available in single-sachet sizes for one-time use for those who were so poor that they could not afford a box of laundry detergent or a bottle of shampoo. These consumers could now buy the single-use packet of Tide to use just for their best clothes or a single use shampoo to use for a special occasion like a birthday or wedding.

While this seemed to be a good way for businesses to grow by reaching new customers that they could not serve earlier, this did not turn out to be the way for businesses to change the world for the better. It may be possible to argue that you have made several people happier by allowing them to wash their best clothes in better laundry detergent or to wash their hair in fragrant shampoo to feel good on their special days, it fell short of its promise to bring development to the BOP. Although large parts of the world have vast majority of people living in this economic category, even with their sheer numbers, they could not offer enough profits to bring substantial growth to the businesses either. Driven by advertising, there was some aspirational demand for these goods, but it did not meet the more pressing basic needs for this population. The environment suffered with single-use packaging proliferating and creating waste. The idea that had been received with a lot of excitement and promise had essentially failed to deliver the promise of improving the lives of the people or the environment, and it did not bring windfall profits to the organizations either.

The very terminology used for the poor as being at the BOP had a bias built-in which implied that poverty puts people at the bottom. It does, but only if money is the dominant measure for everything. A more accurate description would have been to qualify that this is purely an economic perspective. The people may be at the bottom of the economic pyramid, but there is more to the world than economics alone. If we were to consider pyramids of creativity or sustainability, then the poor people may well be the ones at the top of these pyramids, as they manage to sustain themselves using a small fraction of the resources that the more affluent may consume. Thus, the poor may actually be considered to be at the top of the sustainability pyramid.

In contrast, let us consider Thrive's approach. There is an inherent respect for the consumer even if they are poor. The value proposition offered by the Thrive solar-powered light is one that works within the parameters of the consumer patterns of using kerosene-based lamps that will be replaced. The lights are designed to be affordable so that any consumer who uses kerosene lamp and incurs the recurring expense of buying fuel for the lamp, can use the same resources to buy the Thrive light that costs about what a month's worth of fuel may cost to keep the kerosene lamp burning. By investing a month's worth of cost of lighting, the consumer is moving to a source of light that is better in being free of recurring expense, plus free of pollution. That is a genuine value offered to the consumer. In contrast to the goods offered with sachet-packages sold with heavy duty marketing to promote the affordability for the consumer by companies that were trying to find the fortune at the BOP, this product sells itself as the people experience it and come to rely on it. It radically improves their experiences of a basic commodity utility product, light, making it affordable and sustainable. Thus, in conclusion, the prime directive for organizational change is to create value that puts people before profits, be it the consumer, the managers, the employees, suppliers or the distributors. Enlightened corporate leaders are cognizant of this and are making these changes. The CEO of Unilever, Paul Polman, was quoted in Washington Post (www.washingtonpost.com/blogs/on-leader-ship/wp/2015/05/21/the-tao-of-paul-polman/) (Cunningham 2015):

"It's not just about making money, especially for the millennial generation. They want to make a difference in life, so they look for companies that have a strong purpose."

He goes on to add that:

Less than 30 percent of people are happy at work nowadays, which is a frightening statistic given the time that we spend there. And often that is because the values that you permeate at home with your family are not the same as the ones at work. That's sad, because it means you either have to wear a mask or you have to be a good actor, and that's going to catch up with you at one point in time. People disengage from corporations, big corporations especially.

Sustainable organizations have clarity of purpose that energizes their people. Such organizations go beyond the financial and economic considerations to include social and environmental goals as part of how they measure the value they deliver to their stakeholders.

Summary

Organizations need to change to adapt to the changing world environment as the world shifts from the industrial age to information age. Using an exemplar case-study of Thrive Solar, the organizational changes needed to become a sustainable and responsible business are described. Organizations need to change their purpose to focus on creating genuine value. The processes need not be automated but must be highly flexible for cost-efficient flexibility in design and iterative product development that caters to diverse customer needs. High quality and costs are dualities and creative ways to strike the right balance requires engaged people. Founders, management, employees, suppliers, partners, and customers must all find value in what the organization enables. Organizations need to change to go beyond the financial and economic considerations, to refocus on the social and environmental goals.

Discussion Questions

1. How has the information age changed the context of your business?
2. How have your competitors and customers changed in the digital era?
3. How has your organization adapted to these external changes?

4. How does your organization deliver value to the customer?
5. How can you learn from the Thrive Solar example to adapt your organization?

References

Cunningham, L. 2015. "On Leadership: The Tao of Paul Polman." *The Washing Post*, May 21. www.washingtonpost.com/blogs/on-leadership/wp/2015/05/21/the-tao-of-paul-polman/

Ghoshal, S., and C.A. Bartlett. 1999. *The Individualized Corporation: A Fundamentally New Approach to Management*. New York: Harper Collins.

Thrive Solar's Products. 2014. http://thrivesolarenergy.com/

CHAPTER 16

Creating Value for Society—The Role of Social Entrepreneurship

Andreas Pinkwart

Introduction

In the wake of the introduction and global dissemination of entrepreneurship as a scientific subdiscipline, the term of social entrepreneurship has, in the last three decades, quickly spread to all parts of the world. Since the early contributions (Dees 1998; Drayton 2002; Bornstein 2004; Mair and Martí 2006), many papers on the definition and differentiation of the term and the systematic analysis and structuring of the various manifestations thereof have been published (Certo and Miller 2008; Zahra et al. 2009; Huybrechts and Nicholls 2012). Obviously, such developments emerge as clearly identifiable socio-technological changes, as is evident through the important examples of social entrepreneurship from the early years of the industrial revolution.

In order to ensure a better understanding of the needs for and the limitations of social entrepreneurship, several basic considerations will be provided at the start of this chapter, which regard the importance of the civil society sector and the challenges associated with it. Both the recourse from the early works of Adam Smith on the subject of philosophical economics and more recent sociological papers serve toward this purpose. Prior to this foil, the range of social entrepreneurship possibilities that are presented in current literature will be outlined, and significant drivers of the current social entrepreneurship hype will be examined, from the aspects of both supply and demand. Based on the example of crowdsourcing, new directions for social entrepreneurship in the 21st century will be demonstrated. The chapter will close with a critical reflection on the degree of novelty and the myth of social entrepreneurship.

What Adam Smith Taught Us About Creating Value for Societies

Contrary to the impression generated by the frequently cited invisible hand, Smith (1991) did not only dedicate his great work, *The Wealth of Nations*, to the specific way in which markets function and the considerable impact that can be assumed due to the effects of economic freedom of the individual on the wealth of the nations. Likewise, contrary to the frequently presented abbreviated versions, his work is not limited to a contrast between an unlimited market and a night-watchman state that has been reduced to a few core tasks. Closer examination of his philosophically schooled view of basic economic interdependencies within collaboratively organized national economies reveals that he has extended the scope of assessment to embrace two additional dimensions.[1]

First of all, he substantiates the need for a type of intermediate level between private economic entities that strive toward maximizing profit on the one hand, and, on the other hand, the state, which is strictly limited due to its unproductive efforts in terms of the welfare interests of the people (Smith 1991). Secondly, in The Theory of Moral Sentiments, Smith (2006) deals with the phenomenon that he observed, whereby, in order to maintain and increase their own feelings of happiness, individuals who have become exceptionally wealthy due to the powers of the free market voluntarily strive toward helping poorer and weaker people improve their living conditions. Smith thereby provides some interesting evidence that the inclination of successful people to support the needy is heavily influenced by the fact that this support should be provided as efficiently and effectively as possible. This corresponds to justified misgivings in terms of the efficiency of public performance at a central level (Smith 2006). This lack of efficiency in the public sector is compounded

---

[1] I thank my daughter Kerstin Pinkwart for important suggestions on this approach.

by imperfections in the market, which only appear in the area of free trade in terms of goods and services.

On the intermediate level between the market and the state, Smith gives more consideration—admittedly somewhat vaguely—to local offers from schools and the regional infrastructure (Smith 1991). However, in his arguments in favor of the advantages thereof, he also allows for other forms of efficient service provision that are useful to society. Local and associative self-management in terms of subsidiary fulfillment of social tasks and also voluntary, autonomous social engagement, as perceived by individuals, can also be seen as civil society in the broader sense. It forms the basis for a liberal, lively society between the market and the state (Dahrendorf 1999). In the welfare states and emerging markets of today, this intermediate level has developed into an extremely complex and very strong third sector.

In the process, Smith also realized at an early stage that all three sectors tended toward the concentration of power due to formation of cartels and associations and, thereby, to growing inherent inefficiency. The resultant unfavorable developments can often be seen in highly developed state welfare organizations (Dahrendorf 1980; Hettlage 1983). Therefore, Biedenkopf (2009) is justified in warning that, besides economic power, a social power also exists that is responsible for similar individual problems of limitations to freedom, such as economic power, without being curbed by the relevant regulatory policies in terms of justified forms of power and control. Transparency, competition, and autonomy therefore represent decisive prerequisites for the functional capacity of all three sectors. The more functional the markets are the less need will be there for social support by civil society and the state. And the more autonomous, transparent, and competitive the operation within civil society, the better the third sector will be able to perceive its function of stabilization and supplementation. In other words, as a modification of Ludwig Erhard's mission statement (1957): The freer the economy and the society are, the more social they will be.

One could, thereby, also describe the private household as a society-supporting form of organization, or, to put it something pathetically, the mother of all social entrepreneurship. As opposed to subsistence economies, private households within collaborative economies are usually able to resort to their own agricultural cultivation areas in times of shortage, but, with the absence of the prerequisites required for the self-organization of the dignified survival of family members. They can only succeed if they possess other resources that are in demand within the various markets, which they can then convert into money in order to be in a position to purchase the goods necessary to meet their daily requirements and a minimal quantity of merit goods, including those required for safeguarding them against health risks. In the case of collaborative economies, it is the task of the state to ensure, as efficiently as possible, that every household receives the crucial minimum income required in order to ensure the minimum requirements for existence (Werner 2007).

Furthermore, it is the duty of the state to create the conditions required in order to do so through the implementation of a functional regulatory framework to enable the economic entities to optimally bring the national economy to its full potential in terms of development and growth potential through the development of their innovative, performance, and competitive skills, and thereby increasing the welfare of their country as a whole. Deficiencies in the national regulations and controls, particularly in terms of competitive and cartel rights and dynamics resulting from technical advances and open national economies, lead to the economic entities succeeding in making considerable profits in various ways, though sometimes only on a temporary basis, while other economic entities must expect negative effects on their income and assets.

The resultant national and global spreading of the income and wealth distribution, employment, social security, health care provision and environmental protection raise the need for political action on the one hand, while, on the other hand, increasing the leeway for (de)regulation, innovation, and globalization leaders in terms of raising their involvement in civil society, thereby countering upheavals on the regional, national, and international levels. Thereby, they either help themselves to the resources offered by the many nonstate, federal, or communal organizations, or they become active themselves, facing the social challenges head-on through the development of their own social entrepreneurial initiatives. To express it in the words of Dahrendorf (1980):

People document the attitude that constitutes the prerequisite for the market society in the same measure to which they take matters into their own hands—as parents, as residents of a street or a quarter, as advocates, and so on—because the counterparts of the entrepreneurial personalities of the former capitalistic market economy are the participating personalities of the market economy. Both need initiative, self-confidence and the willingness to take over responsibility without the protective "umbrella" of the state.

Definition, Types, and Dimensions of Social Entrepreneurship

The multitude of contributions that serve toward the conceptual clarification of this branch of research, which is still young when compared to entrepreneurship, make it clear that the definition of the term "social entrepreneurship" proves to be at least as difficult as entrepreneurship itself. The complexity of the term is determined both by the multitude of dimensions that are included and the consideration of the various characteristics of these factors.

For the systematization of the different types of social entrepreneurship discussed in literature, various dimensions and their individual characteristics can be utilized. Thereby, contributions that focus on the social entrepreneur and his different characteristics are differentiated. Alongside these, there are contributions that are concerned with social enterprise and the nonhuman assets, goals and specific resources and stakeholders, and, finally, contributions that focus on explaining social entrepreneurship as an innovative process. A cursory view of the various approaches is presented by the simple overview of the definitions provided in Table 16.1.

According to this, social entrepreneurship is brought to a place where, in conjunction with existing organizations in the sense of an entrepreneurial management approach, it is able to achieve effective solutions in terms of civil-societal problems. On the other hand, this is realized in the form of new ventures in which social challenges should be overcome more effectively by the founding of new companies. This resulted in the following definition by Volkmann, Tokarski, and Ernst (2012): "Social

Table 16.1 Overview on selected definitions of social entrepreneurs, social enterprises, and social entrepreneurship

Author	Year	Definition
Social entrepreneur		
• Drayton	2002	"A major change agent, one whose core values center on identifying, addressing and solving societal problems."
• Alford, Brown, and Letts	2004	"Creates innovative solutions to immediate social problems and mobilizes the ideas, capacities, resources and social arrangements required for social transformations."
• Harding	2004	"Entrepreneurs motivated by social objectives to instigate some form of new activity or venture."
Social enterprises		
• Shaw	2004 2008	"The work of community, voluntary and public organizations as well as private firms working for social rather than only profit objectives."
• Certo and Miller	2015	"… a new social venture requires identifying funding sources that are primarily interested in creating social—as opposed to economic—value."
• Engelke et al.		"… we understand social enterprises as businesses with social objectives, whereby profits are reinvested in the business or other initiatives to further support social purposes. Social enterprises focus primarily on generating social value instead of maximizing profit for shareholders and other stakeholders."
Social entrepreneurship		
• Mort, Weerawardena, and Carnegie	2002	"A multidimensional construct involving the expression of entrepreneurially virtuous behavior to achieve the social mission … the ability to recognize social value creating opportunities and key decision-making characteristics of innovation, pro-activeness and risk-taking."
• Seelosa and Mairb	2005	"Creating new business models to serve the poor directly to basic human needs that remain unsatisfied by current economic or social institutions."
• Austin, Stevenson, and Wei-Skillem	2006	"We define social entrepreneurship as innovative, social value creating activity that can occur within or across the nonprofit, business, or government sectors."
• Zahra et al.	2009	"Social entrepreneurship encompasses the activities and processes undertaken to discover, define, and exploit opportunities in order to enhance social wealth by creating new ventures or managing existing organizations in an innovative manner."

entrepreneurs can be recognized as driving forces of social and economic change in several contexts. They recognize or discover and exploit new opportunities; they enter a process of innovation, adaptation and learning. They generate social and economic wealth."

According to the typology of Zahra et al. (2009), in the case of the establishment of a start-up, in essence, the following three types can be distinguished: While the so-called Hayek Type of social enterprise aims at the closing of geographically close gaps in supply by means of targeted (ab) use of regional advantages, the Kirzner Type involves a start-up with a scalable, inter-regional business model, which aims to detect generally accessible business opportunities, which have not (as yet) been recognized or exploited by others. Ultimately, the so-called Schumpeter Type is important in terms of the development and assertion of inventions in the social sector, which—as the name suggests—is theoretically based on Schumpeter's Theory of Creative Destruction. The radicalness of this approach is often expressed by the fact that the social entrepreneur is only able to put his new business model into practice when he succeeds in either developing the pre-existing set of rules within the framework of an experimental clause or developing them beyond the existing set of rules. Otherwise, he must work toward a change in the legal framework conditions in order to realize his business model. This could involve a new legal form and financing option, a new type of sourcing form, a recombination of resources for the creation of new products or processes, and new marketing or company forms.

The question of the main objective function of the company poses a particular challenge in terms of the differentiation of social entrepreneurship. Social enterprises, in the true sense of the word, can be perceived as a continuum of anything from traditional, nonprofit oriented organizations to purely profit-oriented companies (Alter 2007; Berntsen, Gamnes, and Widding 2012; Volkmann, Tokarski, and Ernst 2012). In a broader sense, social entrepreneurship can also be attributed to organizations when these institutions are involved in welfare activities that have their own income at their disposal, such as profit-oriented companies, which pursue charitable activities as secondary objectives or which undertake social projects within the framework of corporate social responsibility on a regular basis. In Figure 16.1, both extremes of the continuum constitute the interface to the state sector or the market.

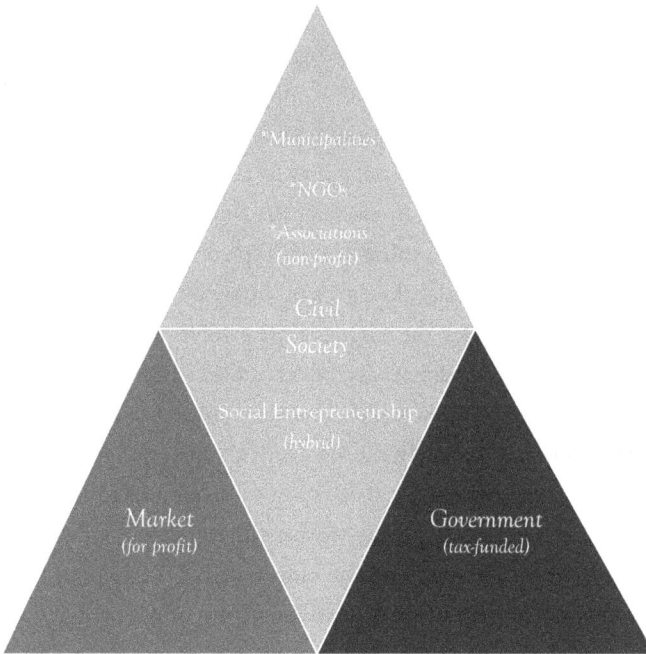

Figure 16.1 Social Entrepreneurship as a dynamic field of civil society (own illustration)

Drivers of Social Entrepreneurship

General Push- and Pull-Factors

Even in the years after the financial crisis, analysis of income and asset development in the Organisation for Economic Co-operation and Development (OECD) states shows a further increase in the imbalance between a growing number of high-income and wealthy people and people with high qualifications on the one hand and a growing number of people with low income, limited qualifications, and poor employment perspectives on the other (OECD 2014). Exacerbated by the financial crisis, the financial capacity of public authorities is decreasing at the same time in terms of them being in a position to cope with the growing prosperity gap both nationally and globally by means of state programs. This increases both the need for action and the scope of possibilities as the particularly high-powered economic entities have, in some cases, significantly increased financial resources with which to promote social initiatives. Added to this, there are often individuals who have pronounced personal creative drive and entrepreneurial skills by which they are willing to take advice in terms of eliminating the social shortcomings—which they recognize for themselves—through their own entrepreneurial initiatives, rather than trusting in charitable organizations or the state.

Added to this is the increasing willingness of individuals to tackle social challenges themselves. This can also be explained with the help of the classical Maslow Pyramid (Maslow 1943). The larger the number of people who, due to their education and income, are able to (more than) fulfill all the basic social requirements, the more people will be there who will strive toward social recognition and personal self-realization. Both favor social entrepreneurship.

The (at least subjectively) perceived inefficiency and, in part, the bureaucratic paralysis of state-run and semi-state-run organizations and NGOs constitute a significant pull factor for social entrepreneurial initiatives. In detail, the identifiable push and pull factors of social entrepreneurship (see also Alter 2007; Huybrechts and Nicholls 2012) can be illustrated as follows (Figure 16.2):

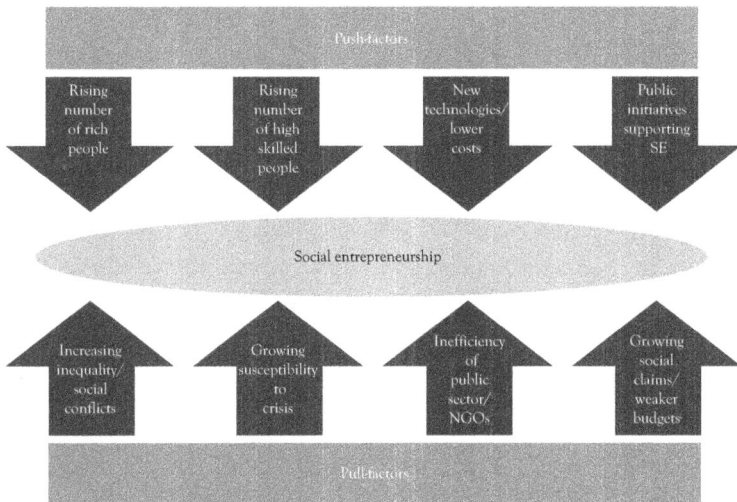

Figure 16.2 Push- and pull-factors of social entrepreneurship (own illustration)

Protagonists of Social Entrepreneurship

The entrepreneurial personalities themselves, who support the ideas and drive them forward powerfully, are significant drivers of social entrepreneurship. In view of the numerous different forms of social entrepreneurship, a few protagonists have emerged in literature over time, each of which exerted very specific influences on social entrepreneurship in their heyday. This applies in view of more recent times to almost all contributions regarding the cases of social entrepreneurship described by Drayton (2002) und Yunus (2003) and of the Raiffeisen, Schulze-Delitzsch and Haas for the time of Industrial Revolution. Interestingly, in all three cases, it involves entrepreneurial initiatives that work toward improving the financing conditions for people, private households, and traders in order to bring positive change to the social living conditions of people, directly or indirectly. At the same time, they represent a large number of social entrepreneurship initiatives from Asia, Europe, the United States, and worldwide. The instrument of crowdsourcing, which will be examined more closely in Section 5 and which is currently enjoying more and more popularity, fits seamlessly into this line-up.

The Troika Raiffeisen, Schulze-Delitzsch and Haas and
the Cooperative

In order to reduce the growing need that developed during the course of industrialization, Raiffeisen initially developed the idea of a charitable institution through which the wealthy citizens would make cheap credit available to less wealthy smallholders, initially "in good faith" (Wikipedia 2015a). The focus was on charity in order to help the genuinely needy without any pursuit of profit. However, only when combined with the importance of the joint liability of all the members, as recognized by Hermann Schulze-Delitzsch, which he established through the mandatory purchase of company shares by the debtors, did the needy become partners instead of mere beggars. This marked the birth of the cooperative business model, which aims toward meeting the interests of the members in the best way possible under the secondary condition of economic sustainability. Haas' gain was the quick spread of the new business model in various federal states in Germany, and their fusion into inter-regional umbrella organizations. The first inter-regional universal co-ops, which traded with both money and goods, followed. The co-op idea closed a gap that, at the time, was not covered by the as yet undeveloped social state. In those times of an excessively bureaucratic, overextended social state, when the term social entrepreneurship had not yet been coined, consideration was already given to a renaissance of the cooperative system (Hettlage 1983).

Drayton with Ashoka

The transformation of King Ashoka of the Maurya Dynasty (273BC-232BC) from a bloodthirsty monarch to a "benevolent" king more than two-and-a-half thousand years ago and his resultant exemplary behavior still command great respect today, particularly in India. It is therefore no wonder that William (Bill) Drayton (2002) named the social enterprise that he founded in Arlington, Virginia (United States), two-and-a-half decades ago after this famous king (www.ashoka.org). The organization focuses on the financial and other miscellaneous advancements of as many social entrepreneurs as possible worldwide (Sen 2007).

Ashoka makes venture capital available to entrepreneurs who found purchase-oriented companies that, with small investments, enable the achievement of large leverage effects in terms of the sustainable improvement of social conditions in the various countries. This social venture organization works toward this goal in cooperation with thousands of nominators worldwide in order to identify particularly promising social innovators to support them in a targeted manner and to invest small sums of money in them.

Yunus' Grameen Bank

The goal of the Grameen Bank, which was founded in Bangladesh by Muhammad Yunus, was to fight poverty in rural areas (www.grameen-info.org). Yunus, who went on to win the Nobel Peace Prize later, recognized that many poor Bangladeshi women would be in a position to improve their situation if they had access to microloans, with which they could establish small businesses. Up till then, building up their own existence had usually failed due to the lack of collateral. In order to solve this structural problem, Yunus developed the idea of so-called credit-rings. These function in such a way that the loans are not taken out by individuals, but rather by a group of debtors.

Because the debtors see themselves as a group and control one another mutually, the social network takes the place of financial collateral (Yunus 2003). Yunus' innovation thereby solves the problem of credit rationing by means of the recombination of financial resources, which are offered by the banking market in the form of loans, with social resources that are created by poor women in the rural areas by the formation of small working groups.

Crowdsourcing—New Opportunities for Social Venturing

Subject to the following chapter are the different forms and cases of crowdsourcing-based instruments, which can be used as platforms as well as business models for social enterprises. Referring to the working-paper presented by Hagedorn and Pinkwart (2013), the different concepts will be briefly explained and discussed. The chapter starts with the umbrella term "crowdsourcing" and continues with the term "crowdfunding." In the second part of this section, the theoretical framework will be explained by briefly presenting and discussing the case of Wikipedia, one of the most successful examples of modern social entrepreneurship.

General Explanation and Current Developments

Crowdsourcing

The term "crowdsourcing" itself was first used by Jeff Howe in 2006, in an article in *Wired*, an American high-tech magazine. He defined it very specifically as: "[…] the act of a company or institution taking a function once performed by employees and outsourcing it to an undefined (and generally large) network of people in the form of an open call." (Howe 2006). The application of modern information technologies can be seen as a prerequisite to the development of crowdsourcing-based venture instruments (Brabham 2008). The infrastructure of the web-technology is perceived as mandatory in order for any ordering party to be able to reach networks of consumers quickly and easily. It promises various creative ways to get in touch with a large number of people in order to solve a problem or get ideas, reduces communication costs, and offers manifold ways to get the people to express themselves.

Crowdsourcing is a neologism of the words "crowd" and "outsourcing." The terms "crowdfunding" and "crowdinvesting" were created analogically. "Crowdsourcing" in general means the outsourcing of a special problem to a large, unspecified, and anonymous group of individuals (the "crowd") with the intention of solving the problem by drawing on their assets, resources, knowledge, or expertise (Kleemann, Voß, and Rieder 2008).

Crowdsourcing can be used as an open innovation tool in the field of micro-financing or as a strategy of outsourcing of knowledge production and problem-solving to external agents, through a public call to a group of people. Some authors did research on the motivation for the people who participate, mostly as a kind of "unpaid workforce." Reichwald and Piller (2005) identified three main categories of motivation: extrinsic motivation, intrinsic motivation, and social motivation. While intrinsic motivation occurs in accordance with the expectation of the pleasure or fun of doing the task (Schwienbacher and Larralde 2010), extrinsic motivation relates to the (positive) circumstances or implications that results from doing a particular task. This can be an external reward, for instance money and goods, career benefits, learning, recognition or it can even stem from dissatisfaction with current products.

Social motivation occurs if the actions are influenced by others or have an influence on others. For example, if the actions of individuals are made known to others, a number of socio-psychological factors trigger human actions. Hereby, the advantage of the Internet is a means of fostering social interaction and densities (community building) at a lower cost. Reichwald and Piller (2005) mention the possibility of an increasing willingness to innovate due to the creation of a common sense (the so called "social momentum," Reichwald and Piller 2005, 13).

Howe (2006) argues that crowds can be more efficient than individuals or small teams. According to Brabham (2008), this efficiency of crowds in terms of problem solving is analogous to the theory of successful teams. It is related to its composition, while diversity and efficiency are positively correlated. The advantage of the crowd is their ability to accumulate wisdom. This "wisdom of the crowd" is due to the aggregation of solutions and further development by participants, who then finally come up with better overall solutions (Surowiecki 2004).

Crowdfunding

Although the idea of using the financial resources of a group of people to implement projects is not a new one, modern communication technologies play a vital role in the rise in popularity and systematic use of the instrument (Hagedorn and Pinkwart 2013). Schwien-bacher and Larralde (2010) describe crowdfunding as follows: "Crowdfunding involves an open call, essentially through the Internet, for the provision of financial resources, either in form of donations or in exchange for some form of reward and/or voting rights, in order to support initiatives for specific purposes."

Crowdfunding has three acting parties: the crowd, which contributes money to the project or venture and the intermediary, for instance a website with the character of a social network. It consists of an undefined and anonymous group of individual supporters, which can be members or followers of an Internet platform. So the success of a project not only correlates to the way an offer is designed, but also to how well-known the crowdfunding website is and how capable the platform provider is in terms of managing it. It aims to activate an undefined group of people (a crowd for financing an idea or project instead of professional parties (Hemer 2011). Therefore, it helps to realize artistic, social, or commercial projects.

According to our studies, crowdfunding for social reasons is mostly done through donations or sponsoring. Hemer distinguishes between the donor-model, where donations are made, and the reward-model in which the supporter receives an incentive for providing funds. In crowdfunding for economic reasons (crowdinvesting), the capital is provided in the form of various types of stock shares, silent partnerships or (subordinated) participating profit loans (Kortleben and Vollmar 2012).

Wikipedia—The Worlds' Largest Crowdsourcing Platform

In an era of exponential knowledge propagation and accelerated devaluation of existing knowledge, there is an increased demand for the availability of generally accepted overviews of current knowledge, which are accessible to as many people as possible. This has resulted in the traditional business model of publishers establishing commercially run lexicons with the support of experts becoming obsolete. In its place, Jimmy Donal Wales founded the online encyclopedia, Wikipedia, which survives on the concept of crowdsourcing, thanks to a large number of registered online authors, who, without remuneration, make suggestions for new topics and terms and are also responsible for updating existing contributions. These contributions are often verified by sources and require careful research and precise formulation (Stegbauer 2009; Wikipedia 2015b).

While the knowledge capital is mainly provided by the crowd, the processes of internal quality assurance and the technical requirements need to be financed. Because Wikipedia forgoes advertising revenue in the interest of keeping the platform neutral, whilst also striving toward giving all people free access to the knowledge base, the crowdsourcing platform is dependent on financial support from the crowd. To this purpose, fundraising campaigns are often implemented on the Wikipedia website, whereby the social enterprise dually serves as a crowdfunding platform. Through new methods of collective knowledge capturing and updating and the voluntary financial support of the system, which is spread among many individuals within the crowd, the social enterprise of Wikipedia closes a substantial gap in this era of information and knowledge. The idea behind this has such a large effect on people that they see themselves as intrinsically, extrinsically, and socially motivated to ensure the continued existence of this great project.

Final Remarks

Even the protagonists of social entrepreneurship doubt whether it really is a new phenomenon but rather a new term for activities that have already been practiced by mankind for a long time (Volkmann, Tokarski, and

Ernst 2012). Moreover, there are critical contributions that do not expect any better solutions from this approach, but rather call it a myth. Such as the famous entrepreneur Peter Thiel who writes in his current book: "Social entrepreneurship aim to combine the best of both worlds and 'do well by doing good.' Usually they end up doing neither." (Thiel 2014, 165)

Certainly, examples could be given from almost all periods of human history, in which homo sapiens made an effort to contribute toward solving social problems with entrepreneurial initiatives in order to close supply gaps. Nevertheless, the author finds it important to also examine the basic issues of human coexistence in collaborative economies that lie behind social entrepreneurship, such as the importance of market control not only for the private sector but also for the third sector. Recent examples indicate the great potential that social entrepreneurship can have due to the rapid scalability that is made possible by new media.

Digitalization facilitates the access to and the realization of social projects because many small donations and other support via social networks and platforms can quickly accumulate to become substantial sums which can quickly be transferred to the place where they can be best used, with low transaction costs and limited social interaction. Particularly in view of the focus on social issues and areas with a limited level of development, those requiring assistance can evolve from being the ones affected to being part of the solution, thanks to social media. This promises a high degree of leverage effects and success rates due to social entrepreneurship, thereby drawing in particularly innovative individuals and those who are interested in the best outcomes possible.

At the same time, the new media, and in some cases also the commitment of individuals to civil society, bring changes to the basic motive structures. Thereby, the previous sociological findings in terms of reasons for human cooperation are being questioned due to the new communication relationships on the basis of so-called "social software." Thereby, social entrepreneurship is assigned particular emphasis in current research on the influences that digitalization has on the economy.

Summary

This chapter gives a cursory overview of the different types, dimensions, and drivers of social entrepreneurship. In order to show that social entrepreneurship may be a relative new term and research field, but isn't a real new phenomenon, short cases are presented from the current time of digital revolution as well as from the time of the First Industrial Revolution. To ensure a better understanding of the needs for and the limitations of social entrepreneurship, several basic considerations are provided, which regard the importance of the civil society sector and the challenges associated with it. Therefore the early works of Adam Smith on the subject of philosophical economics and more recent sociological papers are specifically included in the analysis. Prior to this foil, the range of social entrepreneurship possibilities and significant drivers of the current social entrepreneurship hype are examined. Based on the example of crowdsourcing, new directions for social entrepreneurship in the 21st century are presented and discussed.

Discussion Questions

1. Why can social entrepreneurship be so important for free-market economies?
2. What are the current drivers of social entrepreneurship?
3. Are there in general special needs for social entrepreneurship in times of fundamental change?
4. Which new opportunities and limitations unfold the new technologies for the design and success of social entrepreneurship?

References

Alford, S.H., L.D. Brown, and C.W. Letts. 2004. "Social Entrepreneurship: Leadership That Facilitates Societal Transformation." Working Paper, Center for Public Leadership, John F. Kennedy School of Government.

Alter, S.K. 2007. "Social Enterprise Typology. VirtueVentures." www.4lenses.org/setypology/print (March 13, 2015).

Austin, J., H. Stevenson, and J. Wei-Skillern. January 2006. "Social and Commercial Entrepreneurship: Same, Different, or Both?" *Entrepreneurship Theory and Practice* 30, no. 1, pp. 1–22.

Berntsen, G., B. Gamnes, and L.Ø. Widding. December 2012. "Are All Ventures Social Ventures? A Method for Evaluating a Venture's Social Efforts and Social Effects." *EnergyProcedia* 20, no. 12, pp. 334–45.

Biedenkopf, K. 2009. "Innovationen in Der Sozialen Ordnung." In *Finden und Erfinden. Die Entstehung des Neuen*, ed. J. Mittelstrass. Berlin: Berlin University Press.

Bornstein, D. 2004. *How to Change the World: Social Entrepreneurship and the Power of Ideas*. Oxford: Oxford University Press.

Brabham, D.C. 2008. "Crowdsourcing as a Model for Problem Solving: An Introduction and Cases." *Convergence: The International Journal of Research into New Media Technologies* 14, no. 1, pp. 75–90.

Certo, S.T., T. Miller. July–August 2008. "Social Entrepreneurship: Key Issues and Concepts." *Business Horizons* 51, no. 4, pp. 267–71.

Dahrendorf, R. 1980. "Der Markt als Kraft des Fortschritts." www.zeit. de/1980/43/der-markt-als-kraft-des-fortschritts (March 30, 2015).

Dahrendorf, R. 1999. "Impulse für die Bürgergesellschaft. Die Kraft des Dritten Sektors." In *Reflexion und Initiative*, 10–15. Hamburg: Körber-Stiftung Hamburg.

Dees, J.G. 1998. "Enterprising Nonprofits." *Harvard Business Review* 76, no. 1, pp. 55–66.

Drayton, B. 2002. "The Citizen Sector: Becoming as Entrepreneurial and Competitive as Business." *California Management Review* 44, no. 3, pp. 120–32.

Erhard, L. 1957. *Wohlstand für alle*. Düsseldorf: Econ-Verlag.

Engelke, H., S. Mauksch, I.L. Darkow, and H.A. von der Gracht. January 2015. "Opportunities for Social Enterprise in Germany—Evidence from an Expert Survey." *Technological Forecasting and Social Change* 90, pp. 635–46.

Hagedorn, A., and A. Pinkwart. 2013. "Crowdinvesting as a Financing Instrument for Startups in Germany. A Critical Platform Analysis." HHL Working Paper 120.

Harding, R. 2004. "Social Enterprise: The New Economic Engine?" *Business and Strategy Review* 15, no. 4, pp. 39–43.

Hemer, J. 2011. "A Snapshot on Crowdfunding." Fraunhaufer ISI Working Papers Firms and Region No. R2/2011.

Hettlage, R. 1983. "Genossenschaftsmodelle als Alternative." In *Chancen und Grenzen des Sozialstaats*, eds. P. Koslowski et al. Tübingen: Mohr/Siebeck.

Howe, J. 2006. "The Rise of Crowdsourcing." www.wired.com/2006/06/crowds (March 30, 2015).

Huybrechts, B., and A. Nicholls. 2012. "Social Entrepreneurship: Definitions, Drivers and Challenges." In *Social Entrepreneurship and Social Business*, eds. C.K. Volkmann, K.O. Tokarski, and K. Ernst, 31–48. Wiesbaden: Gabler Verlag.

Kleemann, F., G.G. Voß, and K. Rieder. 2008. "Un(der) Paid Innovators: The Commercial Utilization of Consumer Work Through Crowdsourcing." *Science, Technology & Innovation Studies* 4, no. 1, pp. 5–26.

Kortleben, H., and B.H. Vollmar. 2012. "Crowdinvesting: Eine Alternative in der Gründungsfinanzierung?" PFH Research-Papers No. 2012/6. Göttingen.

Mair, J., and I. Martí. February 2006. "Social Entrepreneurship Research: A Source of Explanation, Prediction, and Delight." *Journal of World Business* 41, no. 1, pp. 36–44.

Mort, G., J. Weerawardena, and K. Carnegie. 2002. "Social Entrepreneurship: Towards Conceptualization and Measurement." *American Marketing Association Conference Proceedings* 13, no. 5.

Maslow, A.H. 1943. "A Theory of Human Motivation." *Psychological Review* 50, no. 4, pp. 370–96.

OECD (Organisation for Economic Co-operation and Development). June 2014. "Income Inequality Update: Rising Inequality." Insights from the OECD Income Distribution Database. www.oecd.org/els/soc/OECD2014-Income-Inequality-Update.pdf (March 30, 2015).

Reichwald, R., and F. Piller. 2005. "Open Innovation: Kunden als Partner im Innovationsprozess." www.researchgate.net/profile/Frank_Piller/publication/235700667_Open_Innovation_Kunden_als_Partner_im_Innovationsprozess/links/0deec52c78a7d3b478000000.pdf (March 30, 2015)

Schwienbacher, A., and B. Larralde. 2010. "Crowdfunding of Small Entrepreneurial Ventures." In *The Oxford Handbook of Entrepreneurial Finance*, ed. D. Cummings. Oxford University Press, Oxford.

Seelosa, C., and J. Mairb. May–June, 2005. "Social Entrepreneurship: Creating New Business Models to Serve the Poor." *Business Horizons* 48, no. 3, pp. 241–46.

Sen, P. June 2007. "Ashoka's Big Idea: Transforming the World Through Social Entrepreneurship." *Futures* 39, no. 5, pp. 534–53.

Shaw, E. 2004. "Marketing in the Social Enterprise Context: Is It Entrepreneurial?" *Qualitative Marketing Research: An International Journal* 7, no. 3, pp. 194–205.

Smith, A. (1776) 1991. *The Wealth of Nations*. New York: Random House.

Smith, A. (1759) 2006. *The Theory of Moral Sentiments*. New York: Random House.

Stegbauer, C. 2009. *Wikipedia—Das Rätsel der Kooperation*. Wiesbaden.

Surowiecki, J. 2004. *The Wisdom of Crowds*. Why the Many Are Smarter Than the Few and How Collective Wisdom Shapes Business, Economies, Societies and Nations, Doubleday, London.

Thiel, P. 2014. *Zero to One. Notes on Startups, or How to Build the Future.* New York: Crown Business.

Volkmann, C.K., K.O. Tokarski, and K. Ernst. 2012. "Background, Characteristics and Context of Social Entrepreneurship." In *Social Entrepreneurship and Social Business*, eds. C.K. Volkmann, K.O. Tokarski, K. Oliver, and K. Ernst. Wiesbaden: Springer.

Werner, G.W. 2007. *Einkommen für alle*. Köln: Kiepenheuer and Witsch.

Wikipedia. 2015a. "Friedrich-Wilhelm-Raiffeisen." http://de.wikipedia.org/wiki/Friedrich_Wilhelm_Raiffeisen (March 30, 2015).

Wikipedia. 2015b. "*Wikipedia*." http://de.wikipedia.org/wiki/Wikipedia (March 30, 2015).

Yunus, M. 2003. *Banker to the Poor: Micro-Lending and the Battle Against World Poverty.* New York: Public Affairs.

Zahra, S.A., E. Gedajlovic, D.O. Neubaum, and J.M. Shulman. September 2009. "A Typology of Social Entrepreneurs: Motives, Search Processes and Ethical Challenges." *Journal of Business Venturing* 24, no. 5, pp. 519–32.

Index

This book is a publication in support of the United Nations Principles for Responsible Management Education (PRME), housed in the UN Global Compact Office. The mission of the PRME initiative is to inspire and champion responsible management education, research and thought leadership globally. Please visit www.unprme.org for more information.

The Principles for Responsible Management Education Book Collection is edited through the Center for Responsible Management Education (CRME), a global facilitator for responsible management education and for the individuals and organizations educating responsible managers. Please visit www.responsiblemanagement.net for more information.

—Oliver Laasch, University of Manchester, Collection Editor

- *The Human Side of Virtual Work: Managing Trust, Isolation, and Presence* by Laurence M. Rose
- *Designing Ethical Workplaces: The Moldable Model* by Donald D. Dunn
- *Responsible Governance: International Perspectives For the New Era* by Tom Cockburn, Khosro S. Jahdi, and Edgar Wilson
- *Environmental Policy for Business: A Manager's Guide to Smart Regulation* by Martin Perry
- *Teaching Ethics Across the Management Curriculum: A Handbook for International Faculty* by Kemi Ogunyemi
- *Personal and Organizational Transformation Towards Sustainability: Walking a Twin Path* by Dorothea Ernst
- *Stop Teaching: Principles and Practices for Responsible Management Education* by Isabel Rimanoczy
- *Teaching Ethics Across the Management Curriculum: Principles and Applications, Volume II* by Kemi Ogunyemi
- *Dark Sides of Business and Higher Education Management, Volume I* by Agata Stachowicz-Stanusch and Gianluigi Mangia
- *Dark Sides of Business and Higher Education Management, Volume II* by Agata Stachowicz-Stanusch and Gianluigi Mangia
- *Teaching Ethics Across the Management Curriculum: Contributing to a Global Paradigm Shift, Volume III* by Kemi Ogunyemi

Announcing the Business Expert Press Digital Library

Concise e-books business students need for classroom and research

This book can also be purchased in an e-book collection by your library as

- a one-time purchase,
- that is owned forever,
- allows for simultaneous readers,
- has no restrictions on printing, and
- can be downloaded as PDFs from within the library community.

Our digital library collections are a great solution to beat the rising cost of textbooks. E-books can be loaded into their course management systems or onto students' e-book readers. The **Business Expert Press** digital libraries are very affordable, with no obligation to buy in future years. For more information, please visit **www.businessexpertpress.com/librarians**. To set up a trial in the United States, please email **sales@businessexpertpress.com**.

www.ingramcontent.com/pod-product-compliance
Lightning Source LLC
Chambersburg PA
CBHW060351200326
41519CB00011BA/2111